Retail Strategies

Understanding why we shop

Retail Strategies

Understanding why we shop

Jim Pooler

JAICO PUBLISHING HOUSE

Ahmedabad Bangalore Bhopal Chennai
Delhi Hyderabad Kolkata Lucknow Mumbai

Published by Jaico Publishing House
A-2 Jash Chambers, 7-A Sir Phirozshah Mehta Road
Fort, Mumbai - 400 001
jaicopub@jaicobooks.com
www.jaicobooks.com

Originally published in hardcover by Praeger Publishers,
an imprint of Greenwood Publishing Group, Inc., Westport, CT.
This edition by arrangement with Greenwood Publishing Group, Inc.

RETAIL STRATEGIES
ISBN 978-81-7992-925-4

First Jaico Impression: 2008
Second Jaico Impression: 2010

Printed by
Kaveri Printers Pvt. Ltd.
19, Ansari Road, Daryaganj, New Delhi-2

CONTENTS

Chapter 1

INTRODUCTION

A set of ideas that made sense a century ago shaped the modern perspective on shopping. Some of these old-fashioned ideas are that people shop for dollar value, that shopping decisions make practical sense, or that shopping is mostly about acquiring *needed* goods and services. A new perspective on shopping is now required. It is time to abandon the principles that have shaped our image of shopping for some one hundred years and come to the realization that there is a completely new world of shopping that does not work by the old rules.

There is a new mode of thought in the shopping environment. No longer does it suffice to identify simple consumer demands and try to satisfy them. The new consumer is operating on a fresh plane of needs that is totally different from that used by his predecessors. The new consumer shops for reasons that seem strange and inexplicable from a conventional point of view. Modern shoppers buy things to reward themselves, to satisfy psychological needs, or to make themselves feel good. Modern shoppers buy things *because* they are expensive. They buy things to make a statement, to show off their personality, or to boost their self-esteem. Purchased items have become an affirmation of the psyche. Buying an item because you have a real physical necessity for it, in the way that our parents used to shop, has become the *least* of the modern shopper's concerns.

Why We Shop tries to understand the modern shopper and the complex environment in which he or she shops. It tries to grasp the nature of the modern shopper's emotional needs, and attempts to gain a picture of what that shopper *really* wants when he buys something. It's about understanding what drives and motivates the shopper of the twenty-first century.

The retailer must make an adjustment or become a dinosaur. He or she has to give up those antiquated notions of what shopping and shoppers are all about. No longer does it suffice to see a shopper as a rational creature making rational decisions. No longer is it enough to think that the shopper acts in a way that makes sense from an economic or logical point of view.

Shopping today is complicated. The retailer that hopes a consumer will buy a product simply because it offers good value at a good price is fooling himself. The consumer may be shopping in order to show off his personal success, to achieve a sense of self-respect, or to fulfill deep, inner psychological needs. That audio system, or those designer jeans, may carry an outrageous price tag, but they may also fulfill some profound emotional compulsion that the shopper has. This is shopping today.

EMOTIONAL SHOPPING

Picture it. A middle-aged husband who owns a perfectly good set of golf clubs lusts after a new, state-of-the-art set of titanium clubs worth $2,000. Given the state of their joint checking account, he knows there is no way that he and his wife can afford such a frivolous purchase. Nevertheless, knowing of his desire for the clubs, his wife buys them for him as a gift anyway, out of that same bank account. Is the husband upset with the purchase? Of course not. Not only does he love his new clubs, but also his wife is delighted to have been able to give them to him.

What just happened here? A couple made a purchase they could not afford, for an item they didn't need, yet they were both extremely pleased with the result. Is this a typical outcome for a typical family spending decision? Yes it is. In fact, such an apparently illogical purchasing decision represents the way most people shop most of the time. It is the contention of this book that, just like those golf clubs, about two-thirds of everything that people buy is really unnecessary.

The golf clubs are just one simple example of the unusual manner in which people make purchases. Other such examples are common. Consider the husband who trades in the family van, long before such a trade is warranted, in order to buy a brand-new, stylish, sport-utility vehicle. Consider, similarly, a teenager that relegates to the closet perfectly good clothing in favor of brand-new clothing that is more in style. People buy all kinds of apparently unneeded things and make all kinds of apparently illogical shopping decisions. Yet there is a rationale to it all if we just look beneath the surface to the real reasons why people shop.

Consider the impulse buy. Who among us has not bought something on impulse? Everybody knows the feeling. The rational shopper is out to buy something when all of a sudden she spots an item—often a piece of clothing—that she just has to have. There is no *plan* to buy the object—it may not even fit the budget—but the determined impulse shopper has *got to have it.* What is the emotional justification for such behavior? Why do we all find ourselves buying things on the basis of sudden and unanticipated urges, and regardless of whether we need them or not? The impulse buy is a revealing indicator of modern shopping behavior.

Simple shopping can provide an emotional experience. Who hasn't felt the thrill of walking out of a store having just bought that certain item that was just what they wanted? The shopping experience can sometimes be so stimulating that it produces a rush of adrenaline. The successful shopper can feel like he has just conquered the world through the mere act of buying an item that is pleasing to him. Everyone has experienced the ecstatic thrill of the perfect shopping event, and the feelings of victory that can come from making a successful purchase. There can be an emotional high to shopping that is like no other. This is what the new shopping is all about.

A recent ad for a General Motors automobile epitomizes the ultimate goal of modern shopping. It asks, "When was the last time you felt this good in something?"

SHOPPING DEFINES THE SELF

Shopping is a form of self-expression. People define themselves through their shopping. How they shop, where they shop, and what they buy serves the purpose of letting people express their desires, their needs, and their personalities. Sometimes just driving a new car gives people an enormous feeling of joy. Likewise, a new set of clothing can create feelings of pleasure and self-satisfaction. How is it possible to put an economic value on the feelings that shopping can create? How can we understand the shopper unless we understand these deep emotional aspects of the items we buy?

There is an excellent, everyday example of the intense feelings that shopping creates. Many people, especially teens, will bring home a new item of apparel and *wear it around the house* when they first get it home.

They are so enamored of the purchase that they just cannot wait to wear it. They feel a need to put the new item on immediately, in order to experience the pleasure that it provides. This universal behavior provides one very clear demonstration of the psychological importance of shopping.

Houses, cars, clothing, hairstyles and innumerable other purchased items allow people to express themselves. The products of shopping convey a sense of the self. When teenagers wear the uniform that is in vogue for their generation, they are not just dressing to be in style. Far from it. Rather they are saying something about who they are and where they fit in the world. They define themselves, their friends, and their lifestyle through their clothing. The statement that clothing makes about the self is profound.

Adults wear their own uniforms. By the vehicles they drive, the houses they own, the trips they take, and the entertainment they frequent, they make a statement about who they are and where they see their place in the scheme of things. Adults are just as concerned as being in style as teenagers are; it just isn't so obvious or so fast moving. Adults spend large sums of money to make sure they are in step with their peer group and are just as concerned about appearances as are teens. The route to success at these endeavors is through shopping, and people spend countless hours and countless dollars in the effort to define the self.

THE IMPORTANCE OF SHOPPING

Shopping is important, and it is underestimated. It's one of the most common things we do, and it dominates our lives. Think of the wide range of things we shop for, from groceries to household items, and from designer clothes to new houses. Almost everything in life requires shopping. Whether one works out in an aerobics class or plays golf, some amount of shopping is required. If one works in an office, shopping is required in order to conform to the established dress code. For people going out socially, shopping for appropriate attire is requisite. People shop even when they go on vacation.

When it comes to shopping, everyone can participate. Shopping is the most common shared experience—everyone does it and everyone talks about it. *Everyone thinks they are good at it.* Shopping is not normally considered as a form of recreation or as a hobby but that's exactly what modern shopping has become.

Shopping is about decision-making and we probably all make more shopping decisions than any other kind. Sometimes we agonize over seemingly simple choices. Often, decision making in shopping involves setting one's very priorities in life. Does the family choose to go to Disney World or save extra money for college? Do they elect to buy a bigger house or save for retirement? Do they take that extra cash and spend it on a new boat, or should they be more conservative and put it in the bank? Many of life's fundamental decisions are made in the context of shopping.

Shopping is about the big things in life, like that new house, and shopping is about the small, but significant things in life, like that new baby outfit. Shopping is about the highs and the lows of life. Some of life's happiest moments involve shopping, like buying that first car. Some of life's lowest moments involve shopping, like selling that first car.

People go out to shop even when there is absolutely nothing they wish to purchase. They let the stores make their decisions for them, trusting that they might find something they want as they browse. The stores are accommodating. There are more of them, they are open seven days a week, with longer hours than ever, and they provide more choices than ever. There is an explosion of product choices.

Shopping is culture. It is a solemn rite, a ceremonial act that is an integral part of every person's life. There are unwritten rules of shopping, customs of shopping, and conventions to be followed. There are many interesting things to learn by studying our own day-to-day culture and shopping is one of the primary parts of it. Shopping is an almost invisible element of our daily culture that is central to our lives.

Children are indoctrinated into the shopping culture at an early age. The shopping experience becomes a unique one that is endowed with significance. In shopping for special clothes, for instance, the shopping experience is imbued with a charm and magic. A young boy shopping for sports equipment with his dad celebrates a male bonding experience, while a young girl shopping for party attire with her mom creates a defining moment in mother-daughter relations.

Shopping is sexist. Stores are compartmentalized into sections that are obviously intended for males (automotive, hunting, fishing, tools) as well as those for females (makeup, jewelry, lingerie, kitchen). Regardless of whether these sexual stereotypes are appropriate, they are nevertheless an integral part of store design and a functional part of the shopping experience. What man has not felt the unease of being herded through the women's lingerie section of a department store?

Women do 75 percent of all shopping. That tells us a lot about the nature of retailing and the direction that marketing should take. It also tells us something about the sexes. Do men hate to shop? It could be argued that men—as competitors—are the most intense shoppers of all. When it comes to things they really want, men are among the world's most diligent shoppers.

Shopping gives people a sense of accomplishment. For many, it gives life a sense, a purpose, value, and a function. The successful shopper feels a sensation of satisfaction, execution and fulfillment. The shopper usually sees himself or herself on a mission, and completion of that mission brings a feeling of achievement. For many people shopping provides a feeling of self-worth, independence and respect. There's a lot more to shopping than just buying things.

Irrational expenditures are seen as acceptable when it comes to shopping. While most people would be shocked if a man were to buy his girlfriend a $5,000 birthday present, nobody gives it a second thought if he spends that much on an engagement ring. In fact, it's expected. It doesn't make economic sense, but to most people it makes emotional sense. It's shopping.

Shoppers are of two minds. There is the logical mind and there is the emotional mind. The logical mind evaluates price and quality in a sensible manner and makes a rational decision on the purchase of a product. "That four-door sedan is just what the family needs." The emotional mind looks at purchases from an entirely different point of view. Logic goes out the window as desires and feelings come to the fore. Passion, excitement, and sensation take control of the mind as the shopper contemplates a purchase. "That sports car is just what I've always wanted. And it's red." The two ends of the shopper's mind are poles apart, and often the shopper is caught in an unsolvable quandary between them. Everyone will be intimately familiar with the experience that has just been described, and everyone knows that sometimes shopping decisions can be among the most agonizing ones that we make. No one said that shopping was easy.

OUR LOVE-HATE RELATIONSHIP WITH SHOPPING

People love to shop. It's an excuse to go out. It's fun. There can be lots of interesting things to see, to do, and to look at. It's an opportunity to browse, to speculate, and to imagine. Many shoppers shop as a means of socializing. Alternatively, it also presents the occasion to get out alone and lose oneself in the anonymity of the crowd. A person can spend hours and hours shopping yet never buy anything. It presents the ultimate opportunity to fantasize, to touch and feel, try on, test drive, and dream about owning the things that are beyond one's financial reach. The sights, sounds, and smells of shopping tempt the senses and make for one of the most exciting and engaging experiences imaginable.

People also hate to shop. It's time consuming, exhausting, and demoralizing. Shoppers hate to force their way through crowds only to find that the stores do not have the items they want. There are pushing, shoving, seas of humanity that make the shopper feel like she is part of a herd of cattle. Then there are the inconsiderate or nonexistent sales staffs that are never around when the shopper needs them. Shoppers must stand in endless lines at cash registers, waiting to hand over hard-earned cash for second-rate merchandise that was not really what they wanted in the first place. Meanwhile, other shoppers aimlessly wander the aisles and seem to frustrate the shopper's every move. When it comes to shopping for clothing, the shopper finds small changing rooms where she is not only embarrassed, but also made to feel like a common thief. Then there is the shopper who cannot find anything she likes, and the things she does find are not available in her size. Shopping can be one of the most frustrating, annoying, and tiring experiences of all.

WHY THE NEW SHOPPING?

> It's hard to think of any behavior more unique than the act of shopping; yet we have no "theory of shopping" . . . This is true partly because this behavior isn't well addressed by borrowed theories, but even more so because we haven't adequately described the phenomenon of shopping in the first place.
>
> Marsha Richins, President
> Association for Consumer Research
> September, 1999

The new shopping is unprecedented. Never before has so much emphasis been placed on shopping, and never before has it assumed the central place in our lives that it now does. Shopping for emotional and psychological reasons has become the new mantra of modern society. Why is shopping so important? What are the forces that are driving why we shop?

There was an important psychologist in the 1940s who revolutionized the way we think about our lives. Abraham Maslow invented a new way to look at how people live, how they order their priorities and set their goals in life. Maslow suggested that life consists of five levels. The five levels range from an elementary one where we satisfy the most basic needs, like those for food and shelter, to one where we satisfy our highest psychological needs, like those for inner emotional fulfillment. Maslow suggested that the higher needs can only be fulfilled once the lower needs are met. This book argues that, when it comes to shopping, our lower level needs *have* been met and that we are now shopping on a higher plane, where a higher level of needs is being satisfied. This is a central reason why we shop.

Today we shop to self-actualize—to fulfill the highest level of Maslow's Hierarchy of Needs. The modern shopper can only be understood if he is viewed as a being that is shopping to fulfill emotional needs.

Acquiring basic consumer needs is now a trivial matter for most people. Everyday items are readily available and almost everyone has enough income to take care of the essentials. We are living in an affluent society. As the simple levels of Maslow's set of needs are more easily met, consumers move to a higher stage. We have moved beyond the basic levels into those where emotion and personality come into play. We used to be happy to have a nice house and a clean car. Today our feelings of inner well-being, achievement, and prosperity arise from a more intricate world. Today we feel good when we wear fashionable clothes, drive a sophisticated vehicle, or own the right designer labels. There has been a change in priorities.

Shoppers used to be content to buy a simple cup of coffee. Today they demand a double grande latte from Starbucks. The everyday, simple shopping experience of buying a cup of coffee has been replaced by one where the customer gets an emotional lift and a sensory experience from the event. It's almost a therapeutic experience.

Whether it is for a $2 cup of coffee or a $50,000 vehicle, today's shopper shops for the mind. The shopper who buys an expensive sport-utility vehicle is just like the shopper who buys at Starbucks. He is buying self-confidence, self-esteem, and a boost for his ego. He is buying an emotional lift, he is making himself feel good, and he is probably rewarding himself for the good job he does at work. The purchaser of the sport utility vehicle is buying an image of himself and his lifestyle. It is supposed to say that he is a rugged, off-road type of person who likes the great outdoors and who likes to get away from it all. Today's buyer of a sport-utility vehicle is shopping at a higher level of needs than the shopper of the past. He is not just buying transportation. The purchase is about everything *but* transportation.

Demography plays a central role in the shift that is underway in shopping. The well-known demographic groups are the baby boomers, and the offspring of the boomers, the so-called echo boomers. These two groups are driving the shopping environment with their unprecedented levels of demand for products. The baby boomers, people aged 35 to 54, are a unique group. They grew up in a world where they were indulged by their parents at every opportunity—their parents were anxious that they have a better life than their own—and so they are the first generation to be raised with everything they could possibly want in life. As the boomers have aged, their lifestyle has continued, and when it comes to shopping they are not to be denied. The boomers want *everything,* and they want it *now.* No generation in history has been as indulged as much as the boomers when it comes to shopping. This is another reason why the new shopping has come into existence.

The *echo boomers,* the children of the baby boomers, are another interesting generation. They have been raised by their parents to expect the best of everything in their life, and they thus represent another huge group of shoppers that is just now coming on the scene. As Diane Crispell reports in *Fruit of the Boom,* "Today's cohort of children and youth aged 4 to 21 currently numbers 70 million, compared with 77 million in the original baby boom." This huge group of young shoppers represents a source of demand for shopping that continues the trends originated by their parents, the boomers. As the boomers themselves create unprecedented demand for shopping at the higher levels of need, so too do their children as they enter the age of shopping. Both of these groups of shoppers have been raised to have all of the basic needs and wants in life, and so they are both shopping at the upper levels of Maslow's Hierarchy of Needs. This means that there are *more shoppers* shopping at levels where emotional and psychological reasons for shopping are significant.

Kids are more important than ever when it comes to shopping. Not only are they important in their numbers, but they too are shopping at a different level of need. Marketers and advertisers have done an outstanding job of creating emotion and psychological *needs* for products where none existed before. As Crispell notes, "The most striking difference between the children's market of the 1990s and that of the 1960s is its size—not the number of kids, but the number of products and the sheer volume of the marketing effort directed at the group." This creates demand for products that did not exist previously and creates a generation of kids where emotional expectations are higher than they were before. This is a reason for the new shopping.

Another dimension of the new shopping comes from the fact that there is more wealth now in society than there ever was before. More people are able to afford to shop at a higher level these days and this translates into new levels of demand for products that satisfy higher emotional needs. People have always binge shopped, but traditionally this behavior has been limited to the rich. Nowadays more people than ever, including the baby boomers and their children, have the wherewithal to binge spend on more esoteric products. "Conspicuous consumption" used to be a phrase that applied to the wealthy (when it was first coined) but today it applies across all levels of society and at all ages. In the present era of conspicuous consumption, there is more reason to shop and more reason to do so at a higher emotional level.

Products are becoming ephemeral. In decades past, economy and thrift were the order of the day. Nothing was thrown away no matter how little value it seemed to have. Every purchased product was important and every dollar was worth saving. Today, products are less durable and are meant to be disposed of. Cigarette lighters, contact lenses, and even watches and cameras have become throwaways. Similarly, clothing and accessories are perishables in the sense that once they are out of style their usefulness expires. In regard to the new shopping this means that consumers, young and old, are becoming more used to living in a world where things are disposed of quickly and readily, and new things are bought to replace them. As the pace of life increases steadily there is more demand for more throwaway products. Our emotional attachment to personal products is becoming less over time and that means that there is ever more demand for more products.

People are buying more than they used to. Greater wealth has transformed Americans, for example, into the greatest shoppers in the world. Americans spend now more than they did in the past and they spend it on luxuries. As Todd Thibodeaux, chief economist for the Consumer Electronics Manufacturers Association indicates,

> Indeed, fully 20 million Americans have purchased big-screen TVs costing $2,000 or more. That figure is all the more striking when you contrast it with the sales curve for color TVs three decades ago. In 1961, the average color TV cost about $2,000 in today's dollars, and only 300,000 Americans had one.

What better evidence could there be for the argument that there is a new mode of shopping that exists out there? People are indulging themselves far more than they did in the past for luxury products and this lends credence to the idea that shopping in general has moved to a higher plane of needs.

If people are shopping more than ever and doing so for emotional reasons, they must be paying for the exercise somehow. How is it that consumers can afford to shop so much more freely for the finer things in life? One answer is that there is more wealth in society than there ever has been before. As society advances, the amount of disposable income also increases. As people find it easier to satisfy their basic needs they find themselves shopping for more exotic and emotional products than they ever have before. But another answer is that people are shopping more by going into debt more. This is a stunning revelation because it means that people are so desperate to buy the things they feel they must have that they will even go into debt to do so. Being able to afford something really isn't a problem any more. Today's consumer spending is different than that of any other period and surely this lends credence to the argument that there is a new shopping.

Television is more important than ever, and the shows we watch are accompanied by hours and hours of advertising. This heavy dose of advertising leads to more shopping and especially shopping for those high-end products that are featured. As Ana Marie Cox reports, one study found that "the more time people spend watching television, the more likely they are to believe that other Americans have tennis courts, private planes, convertibles, car telephones, and swimming pools." Sociologist Juliet Schor's own research yields this surprising fact: "I found that every hour of television watched per week raised annual spending by $208 per year." This surprising statistic not only indicates the power of television to influence people's behavior, it also demonstrates that shopping is directly influenced by it as well. The more people watch television—and presumably, use the Internet—the more they will be inclined to try to buy the products and lifestyles that they see. This will only lead to shopping at higher levels. Hollywood is the most watched city in the world because it is featured so much on television. Shoppers will aspire to buy for themselves the glamorous and upscale lifestyles that they see on television.

An important part of the new shopping is buying gifts. Little do people recognize the startling fact that most gifts are purchased for the self. Shoppers buy gifts to reward themselves for their efforts, and high-end gifts are the best way of doing so. As Pam Danziger of Unity Marketing notes, "Gift market is a misnomer, since most consumers buy gift products for personal consumption."

Is there more shopping than there used to be? Do people spend more time at it than they ever have before? The answer is a resounding "yes," because people are indulging *themselves* when they shop more than they ever have in the past. As Danziger goes on to note,

> Our latest survey reveals that the gift market is misnamed. While some product categories that are included in gifts, such as greeting cards and stationery, are primarily purchased to give to others, the majority of products encompassing gifts are self-purchased.

What better way to reward oneself for a hard day at the office than to go out and buy yourself a gift? Particular products are favored when it comes to self-reward and, as Danziger notes,

> The most purchased category in gifts is Personal Care, including special soaps, lotions and skin care products. This category is booming now because it taps into the consumer trend toward buying personal indulgence products that make the consumer feel "special."

Even food has become sexy. Years ago shopping for groceries was considered to be a dull and boring routine where the goal was just to get the job over. Today, with exotic products from all over the world, shopping for groceries has become a much more enjoyable experience in which more people are willing to indulge. The implication is that the shopping itself becomes a desirable experience that is for the emotional reasons of the shopper. From the 1950s to the 1980s food stores remained staid places where American-made products dominated. Today one can travel all over the world just by making a visit to the local grocery store. As Anj Medhurst notes in *Metamute,*

> While supermarkets have a captive market (everybody needs to eat) there is no doubt that their aggressive marketing techniques are encouraging us to purchase increasingly expensive goods.

She also notes, "The weekly amble around aisles filled with produce from exotic holiday destinations presents an opportunity to daydream away an hour or so." This is a new kind of reasoning that is characteristic of the shopping of the 1990s and beyond.

In sum, there are more reasons than ever to believe that a new mode of shopping exists. The rules have changed. The motivations have changed and the very act of shopping has become something far more than an exercise in buying goods and services. There have been enormous changes in shopping in recent decades and this has culminated in the new shopping patterns of the new millennium.

WHO SHOULD READ THIS BOOK

Understanding shopping is important. Everyone is a shopper, yet how often do people stop to actually evaluate their shopping behavior? Why do they buy designer labels? Why is it so important to them that they own that big-screen TV? Why do they want to shop after a bad day at work? Why do they always keep going back to the same stores? How does their mood influence their shopping decisions?

Understanding shopping is important for retailers. Every retailer struggles to satisfy customer demand, yet how many ever step back and give any real thought to the customer or her motivations? Are retailers aware that most things that people buy are bought for personal self-gratification, rather than out of real need? If they are aware of this, does it change their attitude toward the customer? Can retailers come to see shoppers in a new light, where purchases are motivated by social, emotional, or psychological desires, rather than by rational choice? If so, how should they adjust their sales and marketing strategies?

How do advertisers approach the new world of shopping? If the customer has a new set of motivations, how good are old ads that appeal to common sense? Why target a consumer with the practical aspects of a product when research shows that these are the furthest things from his mind? Given the goals and motivations of the modern shopper, the advertising world needs to reinvent itself. It needs to target the new consumer, who is shopping on a level of personal needs that is far removed from the practicalities of everyday life. Surveys show that if you ask owners of the most highly rated cars in the world why they bought them, one of the features that garners the most attention is the cup holders. If this is how consumers evaluate major vehicle purchases, how do they see other items they buy? What's really important about the things we purchase? And which is more important, the features of the item or the emotional state of the customer?

THE CHALLENGES OF SHOPPING

There is more to shopping than the emotional needs and desires of shoppers. The shopping patterns and behavior of people can best be understood as taking place at different *levels of shopping need* that explain's not only why shopping takes place but why shoppers buy the things they do. The argument is that there are several *layers* of shopping needs and desires, each stacked upon the other, and that the behavior of shoppers can best be considered as a process whereby shopping needs are satisfied, in succession, one level at a time.

Demography is a hot topic today. We can tell a lot about people and their shopping through simple demographics, and we can predict their behavior. We know, for instance, that older shoppers have more money available to them, but less time. This gives us valuable clues about how we should market to them. It tells us what they want and how they want it. Similarly, we know that teenage shoppers have less income but more time. This fact provides retailers with important information about these customers and provides them with a guide as to how they should position their sales strategy. Basic facts about the age and sex of shoppers provide key insights into their behavior. Understanding the demographics of shopping is essential to understanding shopping. A good example of the role of demographics in action comes from the auto industry. There is an old truism that says, "You can sell a young man's car to an old man, but you can't sell an old man's car to a young man."

The modern shopper today has another shopping option open to him—the Internet. It is not possible to address the issue of contemporary shopping without considering the significant role that shopping on the Web has come to play. Traditional retailers have entered a new era of shopping competition where they must compete with *invisible* foes that are able to offer products to shoppers in their homes. What are the shopping impacts of the Internet? What is the future of this exciting new mode of shopping? What are the implications for traditional retailers? Can they survive? There are other questions of retail strategy to be considered. For instance, what is the role of store *location* when it comes to retail competition? What is the organization of the retail environment, and how can merchants benefit from being aware of it? What is the role of the shopper's *mental map* when it comes to store choice and selection, and how can the retailer ensure that her place of business establishes its place in the shopper's psychic roadmap?

Part I

HOW SHOPPING HAS CHANGED

Chapter 2

SHOPPING OUTSIDE THE BOX

Want to try a puzzle? Take a look at Figure 2.1. Your task is to take a pencil and see if you can connect all of the dots in the diagram *using no more than four straight lines and without lifting your pencil.*

If you are like most people, you will find that when you try to connect all the dots with four straight lines you always seem to end up with one dot left over. The problem seems impossible to do. The approach to solving the problem that most people follow is illustrated in Figure 2.2. You can see that one dot is left unconnected in this attempt.

The problem of connecting the dots is only doable if you allow yourself to "think outside the box." Consider the solution to the problem that is presented in Figure 2.3. There you will see that four straight lines have

Figure 2.1
Connect the dots puzzle

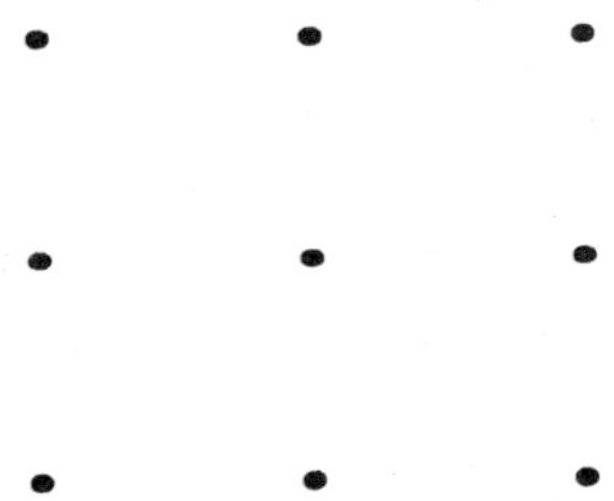

• • •

• • •

• • •

Figure 2.2
Unsuccessful solution to connect the dots puzzle

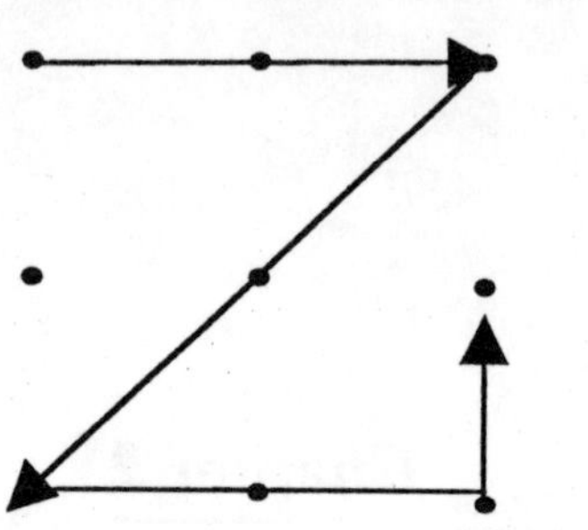

Figure 2.3
Successful solution to connect the dots puzzle

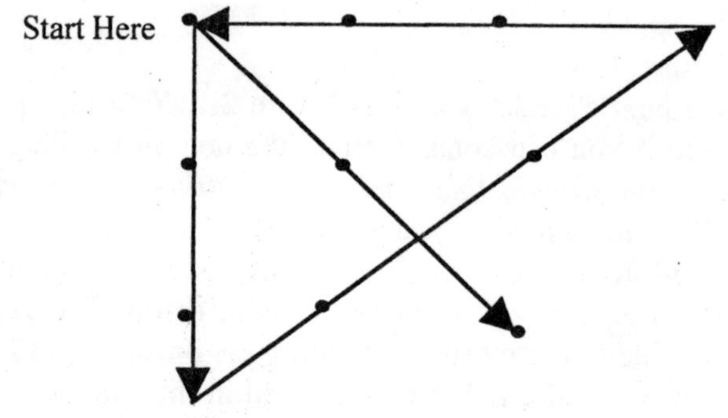

connected all of the dots without any dots being left over. All that was required was that the person solving the problem had to allow the lines to extend outside of the box that is created by the pattern of the dots. This is exactly where the phrase "thinking outside the box" originates. The reason why most people cannot solve the puzzle is that they have a preexisting mindset *to interpret the dots as a square,* and then to try to solve the problem while *staying inside that square.* Interesting, isn't it, that without being told to, we stay inside the square? We've all been conditioned our whole lives to see the problem from this limited, box perspective. But once we are able to see the problem outside of the box, the solution becomes obvious.

This is what thinking outside the box is all about. It's about casting off the limiting perceptions that we have, and instead looking at problems from a new perspective. This is also what shopping outside the box is all about. It is time, in other words, to start looking at shopping from a new point of view. What's good about shopping? What's bad about shopping? What do people like about shopping? What do they dislike? How can we gain a new point of view on one of the oldest of human endeavors?

It is often said that prostitution is the oldest profession, but even it requires some shopping on the part of participants. Shopping is one of the most fundamental and basic of all human activities and pervades just about every part of our lives. Regardless of whether we are considering work or leisure, shopping is usually a part of it. We shop for the clothes we wear to work and we shop for the things we use, and do, when we have spare time. We shop for our houses, our vehicles, and just about everything else in our lives. We even shop just for something to do. Unfortunately, because shopping is so pervasive in our lives we tend to see it from inside the box. We are limited in what we see by the perceptions of the past and the blinders of our upbringing. It takes a new perspective, a view from outside the box, to see shopping in a new light.

As just a small example of what we might call the new, self-indulgent shopping, consider the grocery-shopping housewife. Imagine that this housewife, while shopping on a budget, indulges herself in a bunch of fresh cut flowers at the end of her tedious journey through the aisles. This is an excellent example of the new shopping in action. What is the shopper's reason for purchasing the flowers? Buying them may overspend the food budget and it is clear that they offer no concrete value for the price paid. What do they provide? How can we make sense of the spontaneous purchase of a bunch of cut flowers? And remember, unlike a painting of flowers, or plastic flowers, they will wilt, expire, and die. In spite of their cost, the flowers are perishable. Why buy them? It is clear that they offer some esthetic value, but surely that is not the primary reason to buy them. After all, even a houseplant would offer greater longevity for the dollar. It must be that the cut flowers provide the shopper with something else—something that is important, but not obvious, something that makes them worth the expense, even though they are fleeting. Clearly the flowers provide some sort of indescribable personal pleasure or enjoyment to the shopper.

Grocers do not understand why the housewife buys the cut flowers, all they know is that she does, and they are more than happy to satisfy the demand, whatever its reason or motivation. This is the crux of the new shopping. Identifying and trying to comprehend behavior like this is what understanding the world of shopping is all about.

Ten years ago cut flowers were nonexistent in grocery stores, yet today they are everywhere. We need to ask, What other products are there that retailers can use to woo and indulge their shoppers? Similarly, what are the extra services that retailers could offer? Retailers on the cutting edge are looking to satisfy such fleeting and emotional demands in all kinds of retail environments, including those beyond the grocery store.

Thinking outside the box in shopping is about trying to understand the behaviors and motivations of shoppers in order to get a better grip on the kinds of purchases they are likely to want to make. Purchasing fresh cut flowers in a grocery store is an excellent example of just what is meant by shopping outside the box. Here is a perishable, nonessential, expensive product that is purchased only for the purpose of the shopper's personal pleasure. We cannot even describe in words what is going on with the flowers, but we know it works.

What are the other opportunities that are being missed? What are the other things, like the flowers, that could be offered for sale in a million different stores if someone could just know what the shopper wants? What are the countless missed opportunities for retailers if only they could pinpoint the momentary and private desires of shoppers? How can looking outside the box open our eyes to the new shopper?

NEEDS VERSUS WANTS

A fundamental distinction to make when it comes to understanding shoppers is the difference between needs and wants. The usual approach is to think of needs as those things that are essential, and wants as those things that are superfluous. Thus, in the example of the grocery shopper, the traditional approach would be to think of the basic groceries, such as bread or milk, as *needs,* and the extras, such as flowers, as *wants.* Similarly, one might think that a shopper has a *need* for a new pair of pants but would think that a desire to buy *designer-label* pants is a *want.* As another example, consider the shopper who needs a car—this might be either an inexpensive, no-frills model that satisfies the shopper's basic need, or it might be a costly upscale car, loaded with features, that satisfies the buyers wants. This is the traditional way we usually look at wants and needs when it comes to shopping. Needs are considered those things we *must* have to exist, while wants are considered to be things that are extras, that are needless or at least excessive. The implication is that basically people can do without wants. They've *got* to have basic food and clothing, but cut flowers and designer labels are things they can do without.

Take this idea and turn it around. It can be argued that in our modern economy virtually all purchases, even those that appear to be excessive, reflect real *needs* on the part of shoppers, and that nothing less will satisfy them. Those flowers may be as important to that shopper, if not more so, than the loaf of bread. Those designer-label jeans are so important to that customer that absolutely nothing less will do; she would not be caught out in public in plain, no-name jeans. That upscale car is so meaningful to that shopper that he will spend far beyond what he intended to, just to get what he *needs.* The idea is that shopping has become so important in our society that wants have become real needs. A teenager just doesn't *want* the latest fashion trend. Rather in his mind it is absolutely *essential* that he have clothes or accessories that are in style. An adult does not just *want* that home theater system. Rather, because all of his friends have one, he just *has* to have one. Nothing less will do, even if it requires going into debt to have it. This is the essence of shopping in the modern economy, where virtually everything, no matter how superfluous, is perceived not as a want, but as a need.

In order to understand shopping in this new economy we must look at the consumer as undertaking a form of shopping outside the box. The new consumer is not shopping in the traditional way, where long-established products satisfy basic needs. Today it takes more to satisfy consumers. We need to understand shopping patterns when consumer demand has been turned upside down. We need to see what is happening when a want becomes a need, when a product that should be viewed as a superfluous or excessive want, becomes instead a highly demanded necessity. This is an area of consumer demand that is almost beyond comprehension. It is obscure and puzzling.

The cut flowers are a good example of shopping outside the box, but so is a pair of designer jeans. Consumers demand such products for no *apparent* logical reason. But shopping now takes place in a world where we can say with a straight face things such as "Wearing the right clothes gives a person confidence or self-esteem." It is a world where designer jeans become an extension of the person, and where they give the wearer a sense of emotional joy and self-assurance such that their value is totally inexplicable from a traditional *economic* point of view. Shopping outside the box is the consumer shopping for a $300 pair of designer jeans with the conviction that they are a must-have item.

Retailers need to understand that they are sometimes selling to a higher plane or different level. The consumer who is idly looking at a simple product such as shoes, a watch, or a DVD player may be shopping for nontraditional reasons; shopping where he or she has not a want, but a real *need* for the item in question. The implication is that the consumer's desire for the product may be much higher than expected, given the nature of the product.

Of greater interest is the task of trying to identify those other areas where consumer demand leads outside of the shopping box. Clearly there are many domains where consumers are shopping outside the normal bounds of the genre. One thing is certain: we have not yet even begun to satisfy the limits of nontraditional consumer desires even in places as routine as the everyday grocery store. The challenge to retailers is to find niches of esoteric demand that have not yet been filled, remembering that products as intimate as cut flowers may present a not-yet-foreseen source of consumer interest.

Shopping outside the box is shopping for all the wrong reasons. It's about buying things that one does not really need or at the wrong price. It's about buying things that are ridiculous from a practical point of view. Shopping outside the box is closely related to impulse buying but it is much more than that. It's someone buying an item or a service for a reason that they can't explain. What kinds of purchases are illustrative of this form of shopping?

THE NEW SHOPPING

Anyone who goes to the movies will be familiar with the extent to which moviemakers are aiming to entice audiences. Movies have more extreme special effects, violence, sex, gore, horror, and strong language than ever before. Teen gross-out comedies explore new depths of crude humor, while adult films push the envelope of taste and public acceptability. The goal is to create movies that are at the cutting edge and it is such movies that are representative of shopping outside the box. These are those few movies that create huge demand, where audiences view them as must-see, and where viewers just cannot wait for the second-run theater or the video release. This is not an ordinary, run-of-the-mill movie, but rather a movie event that comes around just once in a while. People feel they just *have* to see it, at virtually any cost. In fact, some people's intensity of demand for the movie is so high that they often go to watch such movies over and over again. This is shopping outside the box personified.

Consider the viewers who essentially *buy* television shows. Yesterday's fare is tame by comparison with today's extreme television. Today we get real police chase scenes, car crashes, wild animals attacking people, on-air confessions of personal indiscretions, television guests in fist fights, and so on, in addition to new extremes of sex, violence, and language. Millions of people watch these shows and the advertising they sell. Watchers shop for the ultimate in thrills and extravagance. Television isn't ordinary anymore. As competition for audiences heats up, television fare gets closer and closer to the edge. Viewers who shop for shows are shopping for new levels of entertainment, and the old standards of the past have fallen as the producers of television strive to attract greater audience share with content that breaks all the rules.

Extreme sports are all the rage today. No longer are consumers satisfied with routine or ordinary sporting events. Whether these are participant events, such as bungee jumping or wind surfing, or observer events, such as bridge swinging or tough-man competitions, they push the limits of human ability. These are events for which demand is huge but again almost inexplicable. Why is it that people want to push themselves to the very limits of personal endurance and are willing to pay for the chance to do so? Why is it that people are also willing to pay to see others challenge the limits of survivability? How do we explain, from a common-sense point of view, that people are literally willing to risk their lives in exchange for the thrill of extreme sports? And how much is this worth in dollars? Clearly this is an environment where traditional needs are not met by traditional products.

Amusement and theme park rides represent another area in which nothing less than the ultimate extremes will do. Rides and coasters in such parks are being designed in more extremist forms than ever before and indeed, there is competition among the various theme parks to see who can produce the most dangerous, scariest, most thrilling ride of them all. Consumers *want* to be pushed to the limits of their tolerance when they ride rides, and the more outrageous the ride is, the better. Gone are the days when routine Ferris wheels and merry-go-rounds would provide a thrill. The old-fashioned rides seem utterly tame by today's new standards. The point is that shoppers for extreme rides are shopping outside the traditional box of consumer demand. Traditional thrills on traditional rides are passé. The new shopper looks for a product that provides him or her with the ultimate in indescribable personal reward and personal pleasure.

Music represents another area of entertainment where it is possible to identify a virtually insatiable demand for a product. When a new hit song and its video hit the charts, demand for them is almost infinite. The radio and television stations cannot play the song enough times a day to satisfy the audience. This is probably especially true of preteen and teen listeners, although even adults can become literally *obsessed* with hit songs. Hot tunes rocket to the top of the charts as people scramble to buy the CD. Never mind that they know only one song on the CD—and likely will never come to know the others—they are willing to pay the price to get that one favorite song. The explanation for such insatiable demand is puzzling. How is it that people are so obsessed by a song that they will spend the price of a new-release CD just to be able to play that single song? The answer is that this is an area of demand where the consumer will spend whatever it takes to acquire what he or she wants. Never mind that the consumer will soon tire of the tune and that it will expire. When the consumer wants the product this badly, the obsessively high level of demand prompts the purchase. And, once again, the reward for buying the product is purely a psychological one.

Most everyone needs a vehicle and most people manage to find something basic that suits their needs. But then there are those exceptional shoppers who buy more extreme vehicles such as sports cars, sport-utility vehicles, and luxury cars. There is no practical reason for most people to own a sport-utility vehicle, a sports car, or a luxury sedan. The sport-utility vehicle is big, impractical, and inefficient. Most of them never leave the pavement and seldom are they used in the rugged way their users envisage them being used. In most cases they are used as simple suburban passenger vehicles and are indistinguishable in use from a basic sedan. Sports cars are also impractical, usually being too small for many uses. In addition, their users never get to drive them at the high speeds they imagine themselves driving. Luxury cars are just that—a luxury; the very name implies that they are needlessly extravagant and excessive. There is really little in a practical sense to distinguish a luxury car from a basic, plain-Jane, vehicle. Are these shoppers guilty of buying things they do not really need or at the wrong price? No, they are not. They have a real psychological *need* for these products. They are shopping outside the box by buying vehicles that are impractical and extreme, yet their need for them is genuine. Sport-utility vehicles, sports cars, and luxury vehicles are in demand as never before. People are so obsessed by them that they are willing to pay outrageous prices. This is a product where people feel that they just *have* to have it, regardless of the cost. It is a product that typifies the idea of shopping where the demand for a product is *intense*—so intense that desire for the product overshadows any semblance of common sense about either the price of the vehicle or its practicality. It's definitely outside the box.

It was indicated above that shopping for designer jeans could be considered a form of the new shopping. More generally it can be said that shopping for most clothing is shopping outside the box. There are few things about which people obsess more than their clothing. Desire for particular clothing, shoes, and accessories can be so extreme as to be beyond the bounds of everyday reason. Consider the teenager looking for new designer jeans, the young woman looking for special shoes, or the young man shopping for a particular jacket. In each case, there can literally be a crisis of confidence unless and until the desired product is found. People get upset if they can't find an elusive product they are looking for. Moreover, when they find that perfect item, they are willing to pay almost any price to get it. This is where the obsession with clothes really comes to the forefront. If people ultimately find that elusive item that they have been so desperately seeking, they are usually so pleased to find it that price is no object.

People are obsessive about clothing and this shows in the extreme levels of demand that they have for it. Shopping for clothing is about being impractical and obstinate. It's about being fussy and particular. It's about being desperate and frantic. It's about going to just one more shoe store or just one more clothing store. It's about driving all the way across the city because there is that one store that just might have exactly what you want. It's about buying things you've searched for endlessly at virtually any price. It's shopping for things you want so badly that you can't even put it into words. Shopping for clothing is an area where needs replace wants. Where that $300 designer jacket is needed as much as the air we breathe. Where the demand for those designer shirts and pants is so high that that the buyer cannot even imagine wearing anything else. Nondesigner, no-name clothing is simply out of question—absolutely, period. This is shopping where there is no visible, practical, or obvious reason for that level of demand. This is demand that is fueled by the mind alone, where the reward for buying the product is solely and exclusively inside the buyer's head and where the payoff is psychological. This is shopping that is way beyond the bounds of the box of traditional supply and demand.

What about the shopper who is obsessive about buying high-end sports paraphernalia, for example, the adult male who is passionate about playing golf or tennis and who shops for products to improve his game. Are there any lengths to which such a shopper will not go in the attempt to improve his performance with better or more expensive equipment? Are there any limits to the time, effort, or money that this shopper will expend to become a better competitor?

There are probably many other examples of shopping outside the box. The point is only to convey the message that there exists a form of shopping that extends beyond the limits of what we usually think of as normal shopping behavior. There are many situations in which shoppers are *driven* to buy products for a variety of personal and/or emotional reasons, situations where the rules of normal shopping are thrown out the window and instead the soul of the shopper takes over. The cut flowers are one good example. The common thread is that shopping outside the box is about shopping for emotional reasons that are beyond normal economic reasoning.

TAKING THE SHOPPER'S TEMPERATURE

Shopping outside the box is not just about the examples given above. It occurs whenever there is a level of demand for a product or service that is extremely high—so high, in fact, that it goes beyond everyday logic. It's demand that is emotional. People may have an excessively high level of demand for a particular pair of designer glasses, a high-end fishing reel, a new kind of kitchen appliance, or even a pair of earrings. It all depends, not on the product, but on the consumer's *level* of demand. Some consumers may be as emotional about a new fishing lure as some are about a new luxury car. Demand is all relative to the shopper's lifestyle and income level. In any case, we can imagine that there are different levels of demand that exist for different products and that shopping outside the box represents one of the highest, if not *the* highest, level. It is convenient to break down consumer demand for goods and services into four levels.

At the first level we can identify the situation in which the consumer has some desire for items but is largely cold or negative about them. Thus the cold shopper may or may not want the items in question and is sensitive to their price. For example, the consumer may be partially attracted to a particular piece of clothing or a CD but is indifferent enough that a high price may be a deterrent to a purchase. The product is seen to have weaknesses or deficiencies and the consumer is diffident. Everyone is familiar with the type of situation in which one's level of interest in a product is so low as to be easily turned off. Everyone is used to seeing the cold shopper. They browse and they browse but they never seem to make a purchase. They are interested enough in a product to look at it, perhaps even intently, but they are rarely interested enough to buy. The shopper who looks and looks but ultimately does not buy anything is a feature of every store. Occasionally such consumers will change their mind and decide to make a purchase, but in most cases their level of demand is so weak it prevents them from opening their wallets.

This shopper, when he does buy, often buys on impulse, where indifference for a product suddenly turns to enthusiasm. This is the exception rather than the rule however. The cold shopper personifies diffidence.

A second level of consumer demand might be identified as being tepid or lukewarm. This consumer is interested enough in products to have a genuine attraction to them. We might imagine the shopper who looks at shoes and is interested enough to try them on and to genuinely contemplate a purchase. This consumer is close to making a purchase but, if not deterred by price, may be put off by other characteristics of the product. Thus the shoes do not feel right, or the look is not just right. Another way to characterize this consumer is to say that he or she is neutral about a product. This shopper symbolizes indifference and indecisiveness. The lukewarm shopper is the bane of every salesperson. They are consumers who take up time and effort, but ultimately do not make a purchase.

At the third level we can identify consumer demand that is warm, that is, the consumer who is ready to make a purchase. This is the consumer who is prepared to buy something before he ever enters the store. These are the customers the salesperson loves. Not only are they keenly interested in the store's product, but also they are ready and willing to make a purchase. It is apparent to all concerned that if the right item can be found, the sales transaction will probably be completed. This consumer gives the go-ahead signal for shopping and is apparently eager to buy. She is warm or receptive to the salesperson's pitch. At the same time, the warm shopper is not emotionally involved with her purchase. She is still able to make a rational economic decision and if the price or the quality of the product does not suit her tastes, she will turn it down. From the retailer's point of view this is also the consumer who can be turned off by pushy or overbearing sales staff, and so what was almost a sure purchase can turn into a transaction that fails to get completed. The warm shopper is ready to buy, but conditions and goods must be just right. There is still an air of caution about this consumer.

Finally there is a fourth level of shopping, the one that characterizes the concept of shopping outside the box. This is the shopper who is emotionally inspired to buy a product and who has that *intense* level of demand that characterizes shopping at the highest level of demand. This consumer is hot, and there is virtually nothing that will deter him. If the store has the product he wants, he is determined to buy it, usually regardless of cost and other considerations. This is that perfect pair of shoes that one has been searching for, for days or weeks. This is that perfect set of golf clubs, that particular pair of designer jeans, or that ideal fishing lure. It's that new hit song, that big new movie, that hot new roller coaster. It's that car audio system. The shopper just *has* to have it. It's beyond reason and rational economic decision making. It's a decision that is ruled by *emotion*.

The hot shopper is the retailer's dream. He or she will make the purchase under any circumstance. This consumer *needs* the product in question, even though it may appear to others to be something that is optional or excessive. Shopping outside the box is about understanding shoppers' *needs*. It's about grasping why people have strong desires about particular products and services, and it's about pinpointing the nature of those desires. The hot shopper does not care if the salesperson is obnoxious or if the store is not quite up to par. It doesn't matter that the item is not on sale or that the price is higher than hoped for. All that matters is that he or she has found the Holy Grail—the item for which the search was under way. This is that perfect tennis racquet, that exact wristwatch, that just-what-was-wanted piece of furniture.

Retailers ignore the temperature of the shopper at their peril. While even cold and lukewarm shoppers can be coerced into making a purchase, the warm shopper is at the precipice of making a decision. Usually it does not take much to push the warm shopper over the edge and into the act of buying something. But caution is a watchword. The shopper can be turned off easily and must be treated with the utmost care. Usually some handholding is all that is required. For the retailer, the key is to have on hand the products that the hot shopper wants. This is a formidable challenge and one that every retailer faces.

Chapter 3

THE SHOPPING INFORMATION GAP

From a retailer's point a view, a major issue in shopping is trying to convey information to the shopper. Manufacturers go to great lengths to produce products that are competitive in the marketplace in terms of their features, quality, and price, but all is for naught if the correct message does not get through to the consumer. Unfortunately, one of the biggest problems in the shopping industry concerns the transient and incomplete information that gets across to the shopper. In spite of manufacturers' enormous efforts to put top quality *products* on the market, there exists a huge gulf between what the manufacturer knows about his product and what the consumer comes to learn. This *information gap* may be one of the biggest hurdles facing manufacturers and retailers in the current, highly competitive marketplace. In fact, the information gap may mean the difference between success and failure for the entrepreneur. What is the point of putting high quality merchandise on the shelf if you are leaving the consumer in the dark about the benefits of your product? Conveying an effective message about a product is not just as important as the product itself—it's more important.

Starved for information or, alternatively, overwhelmed by innocuous facts, the consumer is left wanting. There are two kinds of problems that can be identified. In the first place there is the fact that consumers are often given short shrift when it comes to getting the details on products. For example, the consumer shopping for an expensive product often leaves the store with less knowledge about that product than he desires.

He wants to feel that he is making an informed decision, but the retailer sometimes makes this all but impossible. A second issue is the opposite of the first, and is found in the situation where the consumer has too much scanty information about too many confusing products. At the end of the day, the consumer shopping for that expensive product will have been overwhelmed with too many small amounts of information from too many indistinguishable competing retailers. Thus the information gap problem consists of two components: *too little high-quality information* combined with *too much third-rate information.*

Is there anything more frustrating than trying to make that occasional purchase of a big-ticket item and not having enough information to go on? You know the feeling. You are interested in buying something like an audio system, a video camera, a computer, a big television set, or a vehicle, but the place at which you are shopping leaves you feeling like you want to know more. Just what are all of the features of that television set? How does it compare to the others you have been looking at? Which one has more features? Which one has the right features? How does that Panasonic compare to that RCA? And that Toshiba? And that Sony and that JVC? The shopper ends up bewildered and confused. The stores and the salespeople leave you, the consumer, starved for real information. Consumers get *too little* information. What do the stores provide? Usually the television itself will have dozens of features but the store usually provides nothing but a little sign on the shelf that lists the price. Salespeople are often of little help. Often they are so uninformed they have little additional information about the product and even if they do, you sometimes wonder if they know what they are talking about. You go home to contemplate your decision only to find that you are frustrated by the lack of comprehensive knowledge you have. If this is how you sometimes feel, you are not alone. Almost all shoppers are left wanting when it comes to collecting *valuable* information about major purchases.

On the other side of the coin is the problem of receiving too many of these scant bits of information. For example, even in situations where the salesperson seems to know his stuff, he typically *overwhelms* the customer with verbal information that is too voluminous to be remembered. Later on, when the customer gets home, the conversation goes like this, "Did that salesman at Acme say the sound system on that Sony TV for $1,199 was 10 watts or 100 watts?" And the answer is that no one remembers. Multiply that bit of confusion by the dozen other televisions at half a dozen other stores and you start to see how consumers not only feel overwhelmed by too much information, but are literally too confused to make a logical decision.

The same scenario is repeated with the sale of vehicles, houses, and other major purchases. The features of any one item become blurred together with others until no clear picture of any one product remains in the mind of the consumer. Anyone who test-drives three or four cars, inspects three or four open houses, or looks at three or four televisions will testify that they start to confuse the features of the individual items. Did the red car have the center console? Did the blue house have the built-in oven? Did the Sony TV have the luminous remote? And so on. Everything becomes a haze in the mind of the shopper, who heads back to his home in a state of utter confusion. Often the result is not to make a purchase, but simply to make no decision at all. That's the easy way out.

Is this what manufacturers, retailers, and salespeople intend to happen? Is there any advantage to be gained by having a customer with eyes glazed over as a result of a being literally swamped with poor-quality information? Salesmen talk and people appear to listen, but in actuality consumers are processing only a small portion of what that salesman says. If the salesman says, "This TV has Dolby digital," the novice consumer goes on to think, "What's Dolby digital?" Meanwhile that consumer misses half of everything else that the salesman says in the ensuing sales pitch. Everyone will be familiar with the fast-talking salesman whose banter goes by in a blur as one struggles to keep up with the barrage of information that is forthcoming. The salesman has every good intention, but his pitch is lost on the overwhelmed consumer. Normally the consumer is not only struggling to keep up with the sales pitch but is also trying to compare the product being talked about with one or more that were viewed earlier. The result is almost a complete failure of the salesperson to communicate with the customer.

The truth of the matter is that when consumers finally do make their purchasing decision, they probably often do it on the basis of something obscure or trivial about the product. Lost in the sea of confusion are the actual features that the manufacturer has worked so hard to incorporate into his product. Manufacturers would probably be amazed at some of the minor and inconsequential features that sway a customer toward, or away from, their products. The problem is that consumers are overloaded with too many small bits of information and any one manufacturer's product gets lost in the shuffle.

The results of a survey of automobile owners by J. D. Power and Associates were reported in the press. The survey was intended to rate vehicles according to which are most appealing, and it focused on the features of new cars identified by owners. The results of the survey are taken so seriously by the industry that new carmakers increase or decrease production depending on the place where their cars finish in the survey. Eighty-eight thousand car owners were asked what they liked most about their cars. What the results show primarily is that the features owners rate most highly are, to say the least, trivial. Owners of the BMW-3 series, the most appealing entry luxury car, for instance, did not rate the car highly because of its performance, comfort, or features. Rather, the number one reason given why owners liked it was because of the convenience of cup holders. Similarly, for the Volkswagen Passat, named most appealing sporty car, the feature the owners listed as most important was the illumination of its instrument controls. The Chevrolet Corvette was voted most appealing premium sports car but its owners rated it most highly for storage space. The list continues. The most appealing compact sport-utility vehicle, the Toyota 4Runner, was most highly rated for its smooth transmission shifts. The Dodge Dakota, voted most appealing compact pickup, was given its high rating because owners liked the convenience of its cup holders. Similarly the second most important reason given by owners for liking the Honda CR-V, the most appealing mini sport-utility vehicle, was the convenience of cup holders.

The survey results above are incredible. They show clearly that while major automobile manufacturers spend millions on research and design in order to imbue their cars with the latest technological features of performance and craftsmanship, the majority of people who buy those cars rate them most highly because their cup holders are convenient. There is no better proof of the extent to which the information that manufacturers hope to convey to consumers gets lost or diluted. The owners of the most highly rated, most expensive, most advanced cars in the world rate them highly for trivial reasons. Apparently all of the technological and performance features of the cars are unknown to the owners. Why else would they list cup holders as the most appealing features of their new cars?

This scenario described is probably repeated for virtually all major product purchases. Shoppers are so overwhelmed and confused by the information given to them by retailers that they lose track of it all, and instead apparently seek refuge in one or a few simple features of the products they are looking at, or own. If the features of the vehicles they buy confuse automobile owners, so too must owners of a multitude of other products be mystified and confused about those products. The results of the J. D. Power survey show that American manufacturers and retailers are unsuccessful in conveying product information to consumers. Consumers must be as confused about audio systems, televisions, video cameras, microwaves, wristwatches, refrigerators, VCRs, and just about everything else, as they are about cars. This is an excellent example of shopping in the new retail environment, where the traditional rules of retail are turned upside down. Where the trivial has apparently become important and the important has become trivial.

If nothing else, the results of the J. D. Power survey show that retailers and manufacturers are failing miserably in their attempts to get information across to the shopper. The shopping information gap is huge and major efforts need be taken to close the gap.

OVERCOMING THE SHOPPING INFORMATION GAP

One key to the problem of the shopping information gap is to realize that we need a better way of presenting and organizing information. Such a method is to organize information into different *levels,* where different amounts of consumer demand for information are presented at each level. Any shopper, at any point in the shopping experience, has a certain level of interest in products. Sometimes this level of interest is intense, where the consumer just cannot get enough, and sometimes this level is one of indifference, where the consumer is just browsing. The best way to convey information to consumers is to look at them as *shopping on a number of possible levels of interest* and to direct information to them according to their level. If a consumer has a high level of interest then more information should be available to him. Conversely, if a consumer is indifferent to a product, then he should not be overwhelmed with information.

The information gap pertains mainly to the purchase of big-ticket or more complicated items. It refers to the shopping decision that is normally not made on the spot, but rather where the consumer is *comparison-shopping* for a particular item, and takes time in making up her mind. Thus the shopper confronted with the information gap is typically shopping over the course of hours or days and is comparing items that have a relatively large number of features to assess, such as a vehicle, electronic component, a power tool, or a home appliance. Although consumers may go through similar periods of indecision with other items, such as clothing or shoes, it is usually the consumer's indecision, rather than a lack of information, that makes those decisions take a longer time.

In the first case of the shopping information gap, we can imagine the consumer who just gives products a *glance.* The glancing consumer is largely indifferent to the products in front of her and she may be best described as just browsing. Such a consumer has no need of further information and any attempt to convey more information to her is probably wasted. She scans the products she looks at but has no active interest in pursuing them any further. Her door of information receptivity is closed.

At the second level we might identify the consumer who gives products a look that shows *curiosity.* There is more than a glance; instead there is perhaps a sparkle of interest in the eyes, where this consumer's door of receptivity to information is opened just a crack. This consumer is responsive to further information if it is readily and easily available. This consumer may respond to more information about the product if it is on the shelf or she may react to a preliminary probe from a salesman. Her interest can be piqued.

At a third level we can pinpoint the consumer who is *actively interested* in the products at which she is looking. She wants more information and her door of receptivity is open. She is *seeking* facts and is anxious to learn more about a product. This is the consumer who should be catered to, the one that is more likely to pursue the product further if adequate information is forthcoming. Her interest is already piqued—it's up to the store to take advantage of it.

At the final level comes the consumer who is looking for *details.* This is obviously the consumer who is doing serious comparison-shopping and is ready to make a purchase. She is like a magnet for new information and just cannot get enough. This consumer may have narrowed down her product choices to just a few and is in the process of sorting out the final details before she makes a purchase. This consumer's need for information is huge and must be satisfied if she is to make a purchase.

The litmus test of this model of the four levels of interest is whether they make common sense to the everyday shopper. I think most shoppers can see themselves in glancing mode where there is little interest in getting any more information at all. This is the consumer who glances, for example, at electronics products on the shelf but does not even look at the information cards that accompany them. I think most consumers can also imagine themselves in curiosity mode, especially where a product catches their attention and where, at least for a moment, the door is open to more information. Similarly, all consumers will have experienced that mode of shopping where they are in actively interested mode. In this mode the consumer is looking enthusiastically at products and is eager for information. Finally, I think everyone can sympathize with the shopper who is in the quest-for-details mode. This is the stage at which the shopper is ready to make a purchase and is into detailed comparison-shopping.

Each of the four levels of shopping identified above requires different levels of information. Closing the information gap in shopping consists of targeting the correct level of information to the appropriate level of shopper. The key to success is to ensure that the ever escalating amounts of information that the consumer demands are available, as she needs them. In turn, this implies that retailers must make every effort to provide useful *levels of information to the consumer:*

Information Level #1—For the Indifferent Consumer. Apparently the indifferent consumer requires no information whatsoever. However, there is always the hope, on the part of the retailer, that the indifferent consumer will turn into a curious one. Thus product displays and product information should be as interesting and as visually appealing as possible. It is conceivable that an otherwise disinterested consumer will have her interest sparked by an innovative display or product and thereby become a more active or receptive type of shopper. Certainly most everyone has had the experience of going into a store with no product purchase in mind but having their interest piqued by an interesting product or product display.

Information Level #2—For the Curious Consumer. For the inquisitive consumer, there must be enough information to satisfy basic questions and perhaps to entice them into taking a more detailed look. This implies, at a minimum, that stores provide at least elementary amounts of information with each product. Although it sounds trite to suggest that stores should provide such basic information as the price of a product, every consumer is aware that it is often beyond the capabilities of many stores to provide even this simple fact. What is the product, how much does it cost, and what its two most important features are should be a bare minimum for product labeling, whether it is a VCR, a sport-utility vehicle, or a canoe. This is at least enough information to satisfy the curious browser and perhaps entice him into taking a closer look.

Information Level #3—For the Actively Interested Consumer. The interested consumer is like a sponge, waiting to absorb more detailed information. For this consumer, stores need to provide a higher level of information than that conveyed by Information Level #2. For the consumer who is genuinely interested in a product, knowing just two or three basic features is not enough. This consumer wants more, although she still is not at the level where she should be overwhelmed with information. Thus, at this level, stores might provide with each product a separate listing of five to seven features of the product. This should be *in addition to* the two basic features that were identified in Information Level #2. It is up to the store to take advantage of an interest that is already piqued and to provide the *discriminating consumer* with enough information to satisfy her basic questions. But this should not be too much information that will be easily forgotten. There is only so much that the consumer can absorb while she is standing at a product display. What is the point of listing 20 or 30 features of the product if most of them will be forgotten moments after the consumer walks away? Some retailers try to make the sale by listing a huge number of features in the hope that the very magnitude of the list will help to sell the product. This is a mistake—overwhelming the consumer *in the store* is a serious breach of shopping protocol.

Information Level #4—For the Consumer Seeking Details. This is the consumer who is *shopping for information. She should not be seen as shopping for an item but rather for knowledge about that item.* The best thing that the retailer can do with detailed information is send it away with the consumer so that she can look at it at her leisure. Thus the smart retailer is obligated to provide a fourth level of information which is intended to be read, or looked at, not in the store, but at the shopper's convenience. This implies that retailers of high-end items provide *walking-away information* in the form of pamphlets, brochures or information sheets. This walking-away information should be detailed and should list all of the features of the product, so that the consumer can compare the product with others when opportunity permits. This service is intended to satisfy the information-starved shopper who does the real comparison-shopping away from the store. When they make a major purchase, I think most consumers will agree that they do not usually make a decision on the spot, but rather they prefer to discuss and compare products with friends or relatives, or think about their decision in a moment of solitude. Usually this comparison-shopping is done, not in the store, but at a later time. This presents the wise retailer with the opportunity to have *his* detailed information in the consumer's hand at the real moment when decisions are being made.

The four levels should provide the consumer with escalating amounts of information as her own interest level increases. The key to success is to have the appropriate amount of information available at the appropriate time. The consumer who is just curious does not want to be overloaded with information, nor does the consumer seeking details want to be frustrated by a lack of information. A useful analogy to these cascading levels of information is to think of using a computer operating system such as Windows. Those readers familiar with Windows will be aware that as one seeks to find information or programs on the computer one proceeds through a number of levels on the screen. The same principle should apply to the consumer who is shopping for information. The start button should only be the beginning. From there the consumer should be able to point and click through a number of levels of information, each one more detailed than the last. In this way the shopper could be seen as proceeding up several flights of stairs, where each level provides more knowledge than the last.

In addition to the information sources described above, the technology of the Internet presents the retailer with yet another opportunity to provide detailed information to consumers. Rather than actual shopping on the Internet, *information gathering* may be one of the places where the Internet plays a key role in shopping. Studies show that one of the principal uses of the Internet by consumers is searching for, and gathering, information. For those consumers who are online, it would seem a certainty that when they are searching for information on products, they look to the Internet as a source. Thus *it is logical for retailers to provide four levels of information on the Internet as well as in stores.* The Internet is especially conducive to providing the consumer with detailed information about products and it is in this area that company Web sites should target themselves. Given that the Internet is usually found in the shopping environment of the home, it is only natural that consumers will seek out *detailed* product information on the Web, before or after they shop for those same products in the store. Many Web sites fail in their ability to provide such product information. The consumer who is comparison-shopping at home does not want just a cursory look at a product on the Web. She also wants details that can be used for point-by-point product comparisons. The Internet provides a valuable tool in overcoming the information-shopping gap.

Where does the on-floor salesman fit into the scheme of things? First of all, to the shopper who is just looking around, the salesman may be nothing but an annoyance. The consumer has no real interest in the products on display and the salesman is trying to create interest where none exists. On the other hand, to the curious shopper, the salesman can strike a chord of interest if he can notice a slight spark of attention in the shopper. At this point the salesman should strive only to pique the consumer's interest with a slight amount of information. At the third level, where the consumer is obviously showing an interest, the salesman can provide a valuable source of facts and guidance. However there is a very real danger of overloading the consumer by the overzealous salesman. The consumer must be given time slowly to absorb a small amount of information, a little bit at a time. Salesmen should be aware that too much information at this stage is just as bad as too little. At the fourth level of providing detailed information, the salesman should realize that he is dealing with a determined shopper and should probably go out of his way to provide detailed information *as needed* and, especially, to answer the questions of the comparison shopper. Once again the shopper has to be given time to hear and digest answers and information and can be easily turned off by an over-enthusiastic salesperson.

A few retailers already provide information in the form described here, whereby they address themselves to the four levels of information outlined above. Classic providers of information in this form are computer sellers, who usually take advantage of every possible level. In the first place, computers with on-screen displays can help to sell themselves. An on-screen demonstration can serve to attract the *indifferent* consumer's attention in a moment of opportunity. Secondly, computers usually have signs and stickers on them that portray in large type a couple of the really important features of the machine. These may describe the monitor size, the memory size, or the speed of the processor. Thirdly, computers usually have smaller stickers on them, which list many of the basic features of the machine. This helps to sell the machine to the *interested* consumer. Typically, sophisticated computer consumers have in mind a shopping list of these desired features, while novice buyers are probably often overwhelmed by the usually too-long list. Fourthly, computer sellers (because they have printers on hand) often also have walk-away sheets of information or brochures for consumers to inspect at their leisure. These lists or brochures usually provide still more detailed information for the consumer seeking comparative facts at a later point in time. In addition, most computer companies have Web sites, though not all of them provide the highly detailed information that the consumer is seeking.

Unfortunately, sellers of computers represent the exception rather than the norm. Most retailers of most products fail to provide information at the different levels that the consumer needs it. Most retailers put a product on the shelf or floor with a small sign indicating price and perhaps a few basic features and leave it up to the salesmen to take it from there. This is a fundamental error. Although the salesman can provide some information to the *curious* consumer and the *interested* consumer, he fails in providing the consumer with *detailed* information for comparison-shopping. Many salesmen try to provide such information verbally but almost all of it is lost on the beleaguered and overwhelmed shopper. If anything, the experience becomes a negative one, with the information overload serving as a turnoff to an otherwise interested consumer.

What are some of the major consumer product areas where the information gap exists, and what steps can be taken to relieve it?

HOUSES AND RESIDENTIAL PROPERTIES

There is probably nothing more frustrating for the consumer shopping for a home than looking at a series of open houses and coming away from the experience confused and bewildered. All of the features of the homes become confused in the mind of the shopper as information overload sets in. The locations of the houses, their styles, and their features become hopelessly jumbled in the consumer's mind. What should be a pleasurable experience becomes one more akin to a torture test. Is there a way to ease the information gap?

Some open houses send the consumer away with an information sheet that also includes a picture of the house. This is a bare minimum in this industry. Any sales agent who sends consumers away empty-handed is wasting his time—the house and its features will almost certainly be lost on the consumer and so will a potential sale. But a much better idea, when it's practically and economically feasible, is to send the serious looker away with a videotape or CD of the inside and outside of the house and its features. This might even require that the tape be borrowed and returned to the agent, but it is a sure way to send *serious* buyers home with *more information* to ponder. Buying a house or condo is a big decision and shoppers want as much information as possible. An information sheet only does a partial job. It does not allow consumers to *see* the features of the house over and over again, nor does it allow them to *find* features that they have forgotten. It does not cost much to make multiple copies of a videotape and offer it to interested buyers to borrow. It keeps the buyer's interest level up—as they go home the shopping experience continues—and it brings them back to the seller when they return the tape. It is not a common practice in the industry.

Of course, many consumers will have access to the Internet and for them the videotape can be supplemented or replaced by information about houses on a real estate Web site. Nevertheless, still pictures leave a lot to be desired and many consumers will not be able to access online videos with much degree of success. Thus videotape still provides a medium that is hard to beat, especially if the tape is professionally edited and done with voice over and music. This is an excellent way to sell houses and especially to help the consumer make a decision by providing as much information as possible. I think many consumers, if they are interested in a house, would prefer to go back immediately and look at it a second time. Since this is usually not practicable, videotape provides the next best thing.

SPORTS AND RECREATIONAL EQUIPMENT

For the consumer buying high-end recreational equipment such as golf clubs, jet skis, exercise equipment, hunting rifles, or even boats, there typically occurs a great deal of comparison-shopping. For this shopper it is often assumed that he will buy a product without having given it a trial or a test run. He is expected to buy the product and then have his first experience with it when he first uses it. If he is unhappy with the product, there is often little recourse open to him. An alternative way to provide this shopper with *more information* is allow him to test-drive the product before he buys it. It is possible to avoid the problem of consumer damage or adding wear to brand-new items by making available test versions or demonstrator models of the product. Although this is already done to some extent, there is a lot more room for more of it in the retail environment.

Why doesn't a local golf supplies vendor make available demonstrator sets of his clubs for free trial runs at a local golf course or driving range? Why not have test versions of jet skis available for trial runs at a local marina, or guns at shooting ranges? Similarly boats, Ski-Doos, all-terrain vehicles, and other such high-end sports products should all be available to the consumer for testing. How about a place where he can test-drive that new boat or all-terrain vehicle before he buys it? How about a local gym that provides a chance to sample that Stairmaster or treadmill for the potential buyer? What better way is there to provide the shopper with more information after he walks away from the showroom display than to provide him with the opportunity for hands-on experience before he buys? It's common practice for automobiles. Why isn't it used more widely for other big-ticket items?

For some top-end recreational equipment the idea of test use is impractical. As a consequence, the videotape or CD again becomes an absolute natural. Why not send the consumer home with tapes showing his five favorite motor homes and all of their features? Show the motor homes inside and outside, show them on the road and in the campground, and show *all* of the features of the vehicle, including perhaps many that the salesman did not have time to demonstrate. The tapes can illustrate not just the product, but even the RV way of life for the novice buyer. It is hard to imagine any better way of showing off this product. It should be up to the manufacturers to put together such tapes and make them widely available to resellers. They should be anxious to do so. The consumer can view and review the motor homes at his leisure, in the privacy of his home, and he will come back to the dealership for another look when it comes time to return the tape.

VEHICLES

Another place where the idea of the take-home videotape leaps to the fore is in the area of new vehicle sales. Anyone who has bought a new vehicle has had the experience of not getting enough information. The buyer takes several vehicles for a test drive but when it comes time to leave the car lot and ponder the choices, he is left wanting for information. Most dealers provide walk-away brochures, and they probably have no idea just how important those brochures are. Many new car sellers actually even fail to provide basic pamphlets. The car dealer who sends the customer home without extra information to ponder is making a big mistake. The decision to buy usually is not made in the test vehicle or on the showroom floor, but at a later time. The decision is typically made at the buyer's leisure and often with the advice and council of others, especially friends or relatives in the case of a single person, or a spouse in the case of a married couple. These decision-making units crave more information and it seems only natural to supplement a brochure with a company-produced videotape or CD. Such a video can demonstrate all of the features of the car, including those overlooked by the salesman, and it can show shots of the car in action and under a variety of conditions.

CONSUMER ELECTRONICS

Consumer electronics is a big field and in most cases with these products there is a demand for a relatively large amount of information. Almost all readers will have been frustrated by stores where there is not enough information posted, where the salesman is rushed or uninformed, or where there is no walking-away information. In addition, in such stores one often finds merchandise that is not hooked up or in working order, or products on the shelves that are missing parts, such as the remote control. These added inconveniences serve only to further frustrate an already disappointed consumer.

As the information era unfolds it is easy to imagine a not-too-distant future where there are small electronic monitors positioned beside each product on the shelf. Such touch-screen monitors could provide information to the consumer interactively and at a variety of levels. It is possible to imagine a series of screens of information where each one provides more detail than the last, thus satisfying every consumer, whatever their desired level of information. A natural approach is to have the monitors connected to the product's own Web site. This way the stores do not have to try to collect and present the information themselves, and the companies are free to demonstrate their products as they see fit. These monitors at the product Web site will also reduce labor costs by making it possible to sell products with fewer salesmen on the floor.

Imagine, for example, a product site display for a brand-name DVD player. Beside the product there is a small monitor with an active link to the company's Web site. By entering the model number of the product, shown on the product display, a series of screens come up presenting different information levels about the product, including a video clip of it in action. If the shopper desires more information, it is readily available on the Web site. Information is made available at every level, from the novice user right up to the technophile. The Web site not only answers the shopper's questions but also sells the product by demonstrating its best features and even comparing it to the competition. The Web site should leave the customer feeling satisfied and fulfilled, with all of his questions and concerns having been addressed.

More than anything, this idea suggests that Web site designers have a long way to go in making their sites more user-friendly, especially to the uninitiated user. Anyone, whether a 10-year-old child or a senior citizen, should be able to walk up and use the information monitor with ease and without assistance. The Internet will become the ultimate consumer information source of the future. It is user-friendly, interactive, presents information by levels very efficiently, and provides an individual with one-on-one dialogue. In addition, for the company selling the product, the Web site can be easily and instantly updated as products and prices change.

Part II

THE REASONS WE SHOP TODAY

Chapter 4

THE MINDSET OF SHOPPING

SHOPPING TO DEFINE ONESELF

People define themselves to the rest of the world by the things they wear, the objects they use, and the things they do. Clothing, jewelry, makeup, and hairstyles help to define the self. In addition, jobs, houses, cars, and recreational and other activities play a role in creating the persona that the world sees. As people go about defining themselves and the world around them, shopping plays a huge role. The things we wear, the goods we use, and the activities in which we engage are all part of our personalities. All of these involve shopping. From this perspective, shopping becomes much more than an activity we carry out in order to acquire goods and services. In fact, it becomes the most central event in people's efforts to define themselves as human beings. Self-definition is one of the most pivotal functions of shopping.

People define themselves through the things they wear. "Clothing makes the man," the saying goes, and nothing could be closer to the truth. Men, women, children, and teens make strong statements about themselves by the way they dress. A man who wears an expensive suit conveys a strong message about himself. Teens define their whole lifestyle by the clothes they wear, and everyone understands that particular social groups wear particular kinds of clothes. Preteens try to emulate their heroes in the way they dress. Parents dress their young children in a manner that conveys a sense of how they expect them to behave. A hooker has a certain look, as does the president of a bank. The Hell's Angels have a uniform they wear, as does a 13-year-old. Everyone wears a costume when they dress, and that costume says a lot about the person inside it. Clothes help to complete the person. Clothing is not only intended to send a strong signal to the rest of the world, it also helps people to achieve an inner sense of the kind of person they are, or hope to be.

Think of some of the other important ways in which clothing plays an important role in society. People wear special costumes for special events. Weddings and funerals, for example, demand particular types of clothing. There are unwritten social rules about many such customs that exist in our society. Does our modern society have culture? One needs only to look at the clothing being worn to a funeral to see culture in action. The workplace represents another important place in society where costuming is crucial. There are unwritten rules of dress in most workplaces, especially the office, and virtually everyone follows *the code* without a second thought. Casual Fridays provide a good illustration of just how restrictive, and adhered to, is the clothing code on the other days of the week.

Interestingly, people carry out a dual role with their costuming. On the one hand it is necessary for them to stay within the guidelines that society establishes, yet on the other hand it is important for them to express and define themselves as individuals. People go to great lengths to achieve these conflicting goals. For instance, the office worker will stay within the confines of the normal dress code for the office, but at the same time will try to define him- or herself by the unique clothes that he or she wears. A male worker may wear a defining tie or pair of shoes with a normal business suit, while a female worker might wear a dress that conforms to office code but also simultaneously reflects her style or personality.

People also define themselves to the outside world in other ways. Hairstyles are a crucial part of the look that any person wants to achieve. Boys and girls, men and women spend countless hours and countless dollars to achieve a particular hairstyle, a particular effect. Television and print media bombard us with a constant flow of ads for a seemingly endless parade of hair products, all of which promise not only a certain look, but also a lifestyle to go with it. The extreme example is found is the unusual hairstyles that some teens choose to wear. Clearly their intention is not only to make a statement about themselves, and to draw attention, but also to rebel against societal norms. Eccentric styles break the rules—they violate normal dress codes—but by so doing they illustrate with clarity that unwritten rules do exist. For most people, the goal is to express oneself, while staying within the rules that govern normal behavior.

Jewelry represents another significant way in which people costume themselves in the effort to self-define. Just like primitive tribal warriors, modern men and women decorate themselves with artifacts in an attempt to convey messages about themselves. Jewelry is truly an illustrator of the idea of self-definition simply because much of it is entirely non-functional. While clothing plays a necessary and anatomic role in civilized society, most jewelry is pure decoration. Necklaces, pins, earrings, bracelets, anklets, and so on play no functional role other than to decorate the self. What could be a clearer indicator of the nonutilitarian role of the shopping endeavor than the purchase of wholly decorative jewelry? Moreover, the significance of jewelry in self-definition is made patently clear by the huge expense and time that are expended on it. With jewelry, there are not only societal norms to follow, but also important rules to break. The preoccupation of teens with piercing is a clear indicator of the significant social role that jewelry plays in breaking rules and making personal statements.

By extension to jewelry comes the fad of tattooing. Try as we might to find it, there is probably no clearer demonstration of adornment for the purpose of messaging than in tattooing. Just like jewelry, it is a method of decorating oneself in order to define oneself. It conveys a message—sometimes explicitly—about the wearer. Even a tattoo that is hidden from sight is a form of self-expression. It says something to the wearer about him- or herself. It carries meaning about the self to the person who sports it.

Walk into any large department store and one of the first and most impressive departments you will see is the one for cosmetics and fragrances. This department always commands a huge amount of floor space and is clearly a big money maker. Cosmetics play a central role in self-definition for women. While there are general societal norms and expectations to which most women adhere, there are also opportunities to make statements about the self. Is the makeup for a night on the town the same as the make-up for the office? Is the makeup a single woman wears the same as that of a married woman? Clearly there are different opportunities and situations in which to convey different messages. An interesting question is whether women put on makeup primarily for men, or for other women. On the surface it would appear that women put on makeup to make their appearance more pleasing for men, yet if you ask men they will almost all claim that they really do not notice makeup. Presumably most makeup is worn in order to conform to societal conventions, those being set by men and women. Nevertheless, makeup is another important part of defining the self. How much of it is worn, how it is worn, and on what occasions, helps a woman to define herself to others.

Perfumes and fragrances also play a significant part in defining oneself to the world. Both men and women employ scented products that are intended to give off an aroma, and presumably a message, about the user. Sometimes the goal is to attract members of the opposite sex, but more often than not people simply wear a fragrance as a way of saying, "This is me." Why else would people adorn themselves with an odor other than as another form of self-definition?

The conclusion to be drawn is that clothing and costuming in society play an integral role in human self-definition. How we define ourselves, and how we see others, depends to a large extent on the clothing and other decorations that people wear. The very act of shopping for clothing and accessories becomes an exercise in self-definition. People are not just buying clothes; they are buying an image of themselves. They are trying to construct a self, a persona, by buying costumes, hairstyles, jewelry, and makeup that reflect accurately the inner self. Shopping for these things is almost akin to a religious experience and this helps to explain the huge amount of time and effort that people are willing to invest in creating an acceptable look. It is part of the very essence of being human.

When the fully dressed and costumed consumer inspects himself in the mirror, he gains a strong inner sense of who he is and a perspective on the image he wishes to project to the world. Shopping provides the route to this world of self-definition and contentment.

There's more to defining the self through shopping than just clothes, jewelry and makeup. There are also the external things in our lives that we use to help define the self. The kinds of vehicles we purchase say a lot about ourselves. Compare people of equal means, one of whom drives a huge, brand-new sport-utility vehicle, while the other drives a beat-up car that is ten years old. Each of these people has a different message to convey about themselves, as conveyed by the vehicle they drive. Consider the middle-aged manager who buys a sports car, or the young stockbroker who buys a luxury sedan. Each one has a purpose in buying such an automobile, and in each case the important point is not the vehicle, but rather the statement the vehicle makes about its owner. Wearing a particular automobile is just like wearing a set of clothes; the medium is the message.

We also define ourselves by the things we do. Sports, recreation, leisure activities, vacations, and social activities all play a role in defining the self. These activities involve purchasing an item or a service, and as a consequence the act of shopping is inexorably mixed together with the act of defining the self through one's activities. Investing in a scuba diving trip to an exotic island, buying a membership in a golf club, or riding on a thrilling amusement ride is analogous to putting on a cloak of self-definition. It sends a message: "This is what I do. This is who I am." The really interesting part of this concept is that most people assume that they participate in most activities just because they like them. Little are they aware that a big part of their motivation is not just to enjoy the activity, but also to send a message about who they are. A weekend of downhill skiing, water-skiing, hang gliding, or skydiving brings with it the Monday morning bragging rights at work. A two-week cruise, a trip to Disney World, owning a cottage, or even a camping trip allows the shopper to brag about his experiences. Similarly, attendance at a play or a concert, a visit to a sports event, or even a trip to a movie provides the purchaser with boasting rights. A big part of the whole process of carrying out many such activities is to be able to talk about having done them. In fact, it may not be too far out of line to say that the *principle* motivation of a large amount of people's recreational activity is wrapped up not in the activity itself, but in obtaining the bragging rights to it. That Monday morning boast is usually *purchased* by the owner and forms another crucial part of the process of defining the self through one's shopping.

A further important component of the process of self-definition is found in the places people live. The apartments and homes that we rent, and the houses that we buy, also send a strong message about ourselves to others. One of the key components here is in entertaining guests, for it is on those occasions that we display our residences, and another part of ourselves, to others. Of course there are the inevitable bragging rights that come with size—the larger the residence, the more impressive, and the greater the display of wealth. But there's more to it than that. The style of a residence, the decorating, the furnishings, and the geographical location all have something to say about the owner. A large, expensively decorated executive home in an upscale neighborhood does not just represent an ostentatious display of wealth. It also makes a strong statement about the owners and where they see themselves fitting on the social scale. It enables them to define their place in the social and economic worlds and it helps them to create a feeling about who they are. Similarly, a small, sparsely decorated inner-city apartment also makes a statement about its owner. And it's not necessarily just an economic statement. Although the owner may be able to afford to live in more luxurious surroundings, he or she may wish to make a statement that says, "This is me. This is what my lifestyle is about." Perhaps more than any other form, shopping for a place to live is literally shopping for a lifestyle. It ultimately represents the idea of shopping to self-define.

It was said in the introduction that shopping is a form of self-expression and that people define themselves through their shopping. People express their inner-self—their personality and their sentiments—through their shopping. Items that are purchased create emotion—feelings of pleasure, of satisfaction, of achievement. Whether it is clothing, jewelry, makeup, recreational activities, vehicles, or houses, people set the boundaries of their lives through the things they buy.

SHOPPING AS A FORM OF PERSONAL SELF-REWARD

Life is tough. People work hour after hour, for months and years on end. They drag themselves out of bed, day after day. They faithfully trudge into work and back again, fighting the traffic or the other commuters. They work hard at their jobs and they put up with a lot. But at the end of the day, what do they get for their efforts? How often does anyone pat them on the back or thank them for their efforts? More often than not, if they do want to be rewarded for their work, they are going to have to do it themselves.

How do they accomplish this? They buy something. But not just anything. It has to be something special, something upscale, and something extra. A good example is the office worker who treats him- or herself to some fashionable new clothes on Saturday. At another level, consider the worker who buys himself a new fishing pole, even though he already has a perfectly good one. It is his way of paying himself some dividends.

Shopping as a form of personal self-reward is one of the most important but least understood aspects of the shopping endeavor. In fact, it may not be an understatement to suggest that outside of shopping for needed goods and services, the personal reward component of shopping is the most significant of them all. People have a deep-seated need to reward themselves as they go about their day-to-day activities.

A great deal of self-rewarding behavior is work-related. As the examples above imply, there are few perks or obvious rewards for most employees most of the time. It falls to the employee himself to provide the extra rewards for working. Usually, after someone has put in a tough week at the plant or the office, they like to be rewarded in some special way for their efforts.

Self-rewarding shopping does not just result from work however. Most people seem to find it necessary to reward themselves regardless of what they are doing. There appears to be a psychological need for people to pat themselves on the back as they go about their business. Whether one is doing everyday shopping, tending to errands, or just going about the daily routine, there seems to be a need to self-administer rewards by buying things for oneself.

One common example of self-rewarding behavior is found in the average woman shopping for the week's supply of groceries. After going through the effort of hiking up and down the aisles of the grocery store and fighting her way through the crowds, the customary shopper is typically ready to reward herself for her efforts by buying something extra. Ordinarily, this reward item is not a required item or even a household necessity, but rather something superfluous, something that is a luxury or an indulgence. This usually consists of something as simple as a houseplant, a cookbook, a food treat, or a bunch of flowers. The extra item is something that is over and above the regular basket of groceries, and something that says to the shopper, "Here's an indulgence in exchange for your hard work." It's a personal reward.

As another example, consider the stereotypical man shopping in a hardware store or building supply store for a list of yard, plumbing, and home improvement supplies. Here again our shopper is often prepared to indulge himself in buying something extra—and needless—as a form of self-reward. This might consist of an unneeded tool or gadget that is simply a form of self-indulgence. It's a way of patting oneself on the back for a good effort, deserved or not.

The irony should not be lost on the reader. In both of the examples above we have *shoppers rewarding themselves for doing a good job of shopping.* But there is much more to self-rewarding shopping behavior than that. People also reward themselves in many other, grander ways. As was indicated above, the most usual form of this behavior is when people reward themselves for the work they do. This type of self-reward can take on several forms.

It is important to specify that the magnitude of the purchase can vary widely for the self-rewarding shopper. One working employee may reward himself with a coffee and a doughnut while another might buy a new car. The amount shoppers are willing to spend depends a lot on their disposable income, but it also depends on the level of their need for self-gratification. Some shoppers will treat themselves to a shopping spree every weekend, while others will be satisfied to go on such a spree occasionally.

Another important aspect of the idea of shopping to reward oneself is that most people are not aware of the fact that they do it. Instead, it is just part of subconscious shopping behavior that takes place in the shopper's mind.

Shoppers who are looking for an item that will reward them are typically seeking something out of the ordinary, something that is above and beyond the everyday, or the mundane. The special or unique item is a key ingredient of shopping as a form of self-reward.

One ad that is characteristic of the item being described here is an ad for a woman's hair care product that uses the line, "Because you're worth it." That ad captures the essence of the idea of shopping as self-reward. The ad is effective because it plays on the shopper's ego and self-esteem. It conveys the message to the shopper that they are special and deserving of the special treatment promised by the product, whatever the cost.

SHOPPING IN THE ZONE

An interesting question to ask is why we frequent some stores but not others. Everyone has favorites—stores where they shop regularly and which earn their repeat business. What is it that draws a consumer back more than once? What is it about some stores that makes consumers never go back to them, having visited or shopped there once? Better yet we can ask: When are shoppers *in the zone* when it comes to shopping?

Perhaps one of the most important concepts of all is the general comfort level of the shopper. People like to feel comfortable. Presumably making a purchase implies a mental and psychological condition where the consumer is otherwise at ease. It is difficult to imagine a consumer who is feeling distracted—by unusual people, strange surroundings, or behavior—buying a product. The focused shopper has his or her mind on the business at hand, and on the goods or products on display.

Many things will influence the comfort level of shoppers. While things like the degree of crowding of displays or the amount of aisle space may have some bearing on comfort levels, more important are the psychological and environmental cues in the shopping area. How intrusive are the store staff or the security cameras? How crowded is the store? How many people are there around who are not there to shop? How much traffic is there? These are some of the crucial factors that will influence a shopper's mental state.

The distracted shopper is easily lost as a customer. It is difficult for her to shop if she is not in the correct frame of mind, and it will not take much to shift a shopper's focus away from the job at hand. Just imagine the situations that a female shopper might find herself in, for example, where she encounters a suspicious-looking group of teens wandering through the women's clothing section of a store, or a leering man in the lingerie section. Similarly, she might be distracted by too much passing foot traffic or by sales staff that are too overbearing. Her comfort level is a delicate thing and it can be destroyed easily by the slightest provocation. If it is, her concentration on the shopping will be lost. She is more likely to move on to another store or department. Everyone has had experiences like this in a store and everyone will agree that under such distracting circumstances, further serious shopping is difficult to carry out.

A good example of this phenomenon comes from a local department store where women shoppers have nicknamed one of the saleswomen the "Bra-Nazi." This pushy saleswoman barges into the fitting rooms and attempts to help the local ladies get into the bras they are trying on. Her reputation is such that local shoppers have started to avoid the store altogether in hopes of not having to deal with the overly "helpful" saleswoman.

Familiarity probably has a lot to do with a customer's general comfort level in a store. We tend to frequent the places that make us comfortable and so the amount of repeat business a store generates can be taken as a good indicator of the level of comfort it achieves for its customers. The more times we visit a place the more comfortable we are with it, and so it is important to try to generate repeat business. Promotional events that encourage repeat trips do more than just bring customers into a store. They also create a pattern of behavior that may persist through time. People are creatures of habit and it is essential to create the habit of shopping at a particular store.

It is important to realize that the comfort zone extends outside the store as well as inside. Shoppers must be made to feel at ease while they are parking, or walking to or from a store. The store manager's job is to create a complete shopping comfort experience that makes the shopping itself the number one priority. The comfort zone of the shopper should not be disrupted.

Shoppers need to be in the zone if they are to shop successfully. A shopper who is in the zone is comfortable, relaxed, undistracted, and able to center attention on a product. For a brief time the shopper is caught up in the shopping experience and is oblivious to the world around him. Being in the zone may last just a moment, as when a shopper is comparison-shopping for something simple such as clock radios, or it may last an hour, as when a shopper is comparing more complex products. In either case, the key is that the product has the shopper's undivided attention for a time because it is during this time that the shopper is making a decision. The decision-making part of the shopping experience is the most crucial one and the shopper must be able to devote a significant part of his or her mental energies to this task.

Putting shoppers in the zone requires that storeowners create the appropriate shopping environment. While there is nothing much that can be done with respect to rude or inconsiderate shoppers, there is at least an onus on the retailer to create store spaces where the shopper's attention is not distracted by unnecessary foot traffic or unwanted intruders. In addition, store sales staff should be aware that it might well be inappropriate to interrupt a shopper who appears to be in the zone. Such a shopper will take little comfort in having her train of thought and her decision-making process disturbed by an unwanted intrusion.

The shopper usually demonstrates a great deal by his or her body language and behavior. Salespeople would be well advised to pay much more attention to the subtle clues of body language than they currently do. Most salespeople barge into the shopper's domain rudely and bluntly without paying any attention to the behavioral cues that the shopper exhibits. How often does a salesman intrude while the shopper is deep in the zone, absorbed in comparison-shopping? How often does the average shopper attempt to divest himself of a pushy salesperson, only to have him or her persist in his efforts to provide assistance? Putting and keeping a shopper in the zone is a difficult process that requires tact and subtlety. It is where salesmanship becomes an art unto itself.

The bottom line is that there is definitely a zone into which shoppers go mentally when they shop. There is a time when the mind is deeply preoccupied with the shopping decision at hand and when it is important to let the customer have his thoughts to himself. People get emotionally caught up in shopping and there is no doubt that their concentration is sometime so focused on the shopping experience that other environmental cues or stimuli are completely blocked out. During this moment the shopper's mental faculties are centered on the products under consideration, and this is a crucial time during the shopping experience and decision-making process.

IN SHOPPING, TIMING IS EVERYTHING

Being in style has a lot to do with timing. Part of the phenomenon of being in tune with the latest trends, fashions, and fads has to do with having them at the right time. Whether it is clothing, an entertainment event, a trip, or a restaurant, part of the value of a purchase involves having made it when it is at its highest value. For example, an item of clothing is only in style for a limited time. Knowing *when* to buy is often as important as knowing *what* to buy.

Importantly, there is a competition factor at work. While fashion-conscious teens will strive to be the first to own a new style, so too will adults make an effort to compete with their friends, relatives, and neighbors by being the first to own the latest innovation. This might involve being the first on the block to own a new style of vehicle or the first in the family to visit a new theme park. There is not only the satisfaction of being the person who is the trendsetter among peers, who is at the cutting edge of fashion, style and innovation, but there is also the advantage of being able to boast about one's farsightedness, willingness to innovate, and ability to stay on top of the latest trends. Thus the *timing* of purchases is critical to their perceived value in defining the self. The worth of a purchased innovation to family and friends reflects in large part the *time* at which it was obtained. There's not a lot of bravado to having been the last one on the block to go to Disney World, nor is there much of an impression made when you are the last among your peers to drive home in a sport-utility vehicle. In shopping, timing is everything.

One must demonstrate the ability to outshop family, friends, and neighbors. This involves not only being the first to get something but sometimes also requires paying an exorbitant price to get it. It's the price people are willing to pay to be innovators. Usually when the latest fad hits the streets, it costs more at the outset. In fact, that may be a part of the mystique of owning it. Whether it is the latest teen clothing or the newest adult fad, it is usually more expensive when it first comes out. For teens, think of how the cost of personal CD players or video games has dropped over time, while for adults one can consider the downward-sliding price of home DVD players. Once again it becomes clear that even though shopping is about a lot of things, one of the last on the list may be practical quality and value.

A great deal of the importance of having purchased the right thing at the right time relates to the bragging rights. People like to be the first to buy or experience something because it gives them the ability to talk and discreetly brag about their ability to stay ahead of the game. Being the first to see a local stage production, or the first to own the latest fashion, allows one to parade one's farsightedness before others. This is part of defining the self through shopping. One is able to say something about one's innovativeness through one's purchases. Bragging rights may be entirely silent: showing up at a social event or a party wearing a chic evening dress may be all that is required. This is where the mystique of shopping is so interesting and so profound. For most people there is sense not only of accomplishment, but also of utter joy in being able to show off, brag about, or wear something that demonstrates one's ability to keep ahead of the times, or one's ability to afford the latest items. Most people believe it says a lot about themselves.

Part of the retailer's job is to stay ahead of the trends, to have the correct merchandise available at the correct time. This can be an onerous task. Trends change quickly and the hottest item today may be unwanted next month. Because the teen world of fashion and style changes faster than the adult world it will be particularly difficult to keep up with trends and fads within this demographic. Teen tastes are often described as being fickle. This unfair criticism misses the mark. To adults, the teen world of fashion seems to change too quickly simply because teens have a different perspective on time than adults. To a teenager, the four years of high school seems like an eternity, whereas to the adult, four years goes by in a flash. In the time world of teens, fashion changes at a pace that is suitable to their perspective on the speed of the world. As a result, adult manufacturers and retailers have difficulty keeping pace with the rapidity at which change takes place. No sooner do the latest fashions arrive in stock, than they are demoted to the out-of-style, on sale rack.

Timing is especially crucial for the preteen and teen demographic, but it is also important for the adult groups as well. Adult consumers demand that the goods they want be available when they want them. Fashions and trends in clothing can dissipate while the clothing is on the rack. The same argument applies to nonclothing items. Adult shoppers demand the latest home theater systems or furniture. Adults are just as fickle as teens when it comes to trends and fads; they just do not like to think of themselves that way. For example, how many adult golfers do not own the new oversized clubs that are all the rage?

It is important not only to own the right things, but also to own them at the right time. The price of an item on the shelf reflects not only the value of the product but also the time at which it is available. All shoppers are willing to pay more to get what they want, when they want it. Defining the self is not just about having the right things—one's sense of timing is also on display, and must be shown to be in tune with the world.

GOODWILL

There exists an important but intangible element of every shopper's world that is created by his experiences with retailers. This is the subtle element of goodwill that exists between a store and a shopper. Goodwill is hard to define. It is about the potentially good attitude that a customer has about a particular store. A store earns the goodwill of its customers by the way it treats them and by the things it does for them. For instance, a store may earn a customer's goodwill because it has always been easy for the customer to return items there. Or goodwill might be earned by a store because of past instances of helping customers with excellent service. Similarly, goodwill might be earned by a store whose efforts to please a customer have gone above and beyond levels that are normally expected. Every shopper will be able to relate stories of stores or salespeople that have earned their praise for exemplary services.

The most important result of goodwill is the creation of a *loyal* customer who will give a retailer his repeat business. Customer loyalty may even be so important that shoppers will ignore competitors' lower prices or competing products in order to patronize the store that has earned their trust. Imagine a hardware store that has earned a customer's loyalty through many years of helpful advice and assistance with product selection. Many consumers will be tempted to continue to patronize such a store even when they know that the prices there may be a bit higher than the competition's. The store has earned the goodwill of the customer, and it is a bond that is difficult to break.

Some stores have made positive customer relations a high priority for many years and it has paid off for them royally. A good example of a store with a high degree of goodwill is Sears. It has earned an excellent reputation for high-quality customer service and a no-hassle return policy. The financial value of the goodwill that Sears has earned is beyond calculation, but it is a hugely important part of this retailer's success. How does one put a dollar value on the reputation and level of customer trust that such a business earns over many years?

Most retailers are acutely aware of the importance of goodwill in creating a successful, long-term bond between a store and a customer. Just think of some of the areas of shopping where customer trust plays a crucial role in buying patterns. Sometimes a customer is loyal to a company, regardless of the products they sell, as is the case with Sears. At other times a shopper is loyal to a particular product, as might be the case with vehicles. Automobiles come to mind as a good example of a situation where past experience plays a big role in future customer decisions. A car buyer's decision often very much reflects his past experiences, not only with a particular brand of vehicle but also with the quality of service and customer care that he received. Vehicle sellers are well aware that customer goodwill is critically important to repeat business.

From the retailer's point of view there is a cost to establishing strong customer goodwill. It usually requires the hiring of extra staff. It also implies in many cases that there is an added cost of hiring and keeping older, seasoned staff who may be more helpful and especially understanding of customers' needs. Hiring cheap, inexperienced staff has its short-term cost savings, but in the long run there may disadvantages in having a young and indifferent sales staff that may be unresponsive to customer needs. There is more to sales experience than just basic familiarity with product lines. There is also life experience that often makes the difference between a turned-off customer versus one who has an enjoyable sales experience. How many young adult to middle-aged shoppers have been turned off by teenaged salespeople who make it abundantly clear that they would rather be doing something else?

Chapter 5

MOTIVATIONS FOR SHOPPING

BARGAIN HUNTING

There is a shopping mall in Las Vegas that is one of the best known in the world. Visitors to Vegas go out of their way to make a trip to this mall when they are in town. Gambling, shows, swimming pools, amusement rides, and other entertainment features are temporarily ignored so that visitors can go shopping for the day. With all of the other entertainment options and attractions in Las Vegas, you would think that the last thing people would want to do is go shopping. Yet this mall pulls them in to the tune of $8.5 billion in retail sales annually. What is it that drives people to spend the day shopping even when they are in the entertainment capital of the world?

The answer is bargains and brand names. Las Vegas is home to Belz Factory World Outlet, America's largest factory outlet mall. This mall consists of 580,000 square feet of space leased to more than a hundred stores, including some of the best-known chains and brand names in the world. It is 2.5 miles south of Las Vegas and within easy reach of 15,000 hotel rooms. Here's a look at some of the retailers located at Belz:

Bose	London Fog
Casio	Nautica
Fila	Oshkosh B'gosh
Hush Puppies	Reebok
Nike	Calvin Klein Outlet

Rockport
Royal Doulton
Waterford/Wedgwood
L'eggs/Hanes/Bali/Playtex
Bugle Boy
Buster Brown
Chaps Ralph Lauren
Danskin
Esprit
Vans Shoes
Designer Fragrance
Fragrance Outlet
Perfumania
Prestige Fragrance
Geoffrey Beene
Haggar
Jockey
Levi's Outlet

This is not a regular shopping mall, but a factory outlet. Bargains are to be found everywhere on brand-name and designer-label shoes, clothing, and accessories. Most prices start at 30 percent off and continue from there. Merchandise is brand-new. Here are some of the kinds of bargains to be found. Wool sweaters at Calvin Klein for 75 percent off. One hundred percent cashmere sweaters at Saks for 70 percent off. Cotton shirts at Esprit for 85 percent off. And so on. When it comes to designer labels, this is a bargain hunter's paradise.

Why do people shop at Belz? Because there are *bargains.* Everyday items become prized pieces. The fact that people will spend far more money than planned for because they have found bargains is one of the most interesting aspects of shopping. It's fascinating. It illustrates that shopping is part common sense but that it is also irrational. The bargain hunter is a strange creature, buying things that were not anticipated, and are not really needed, but buying them because the price is too good to pass up. How does one explain or understand such unusual shopping behavior?

Why are people drawn to bargains? Why do people buy stuff they really do not need just because it's available at a good price? It was pointed out in the introduction that about two-thirds of everything that people buy is unneeded and unnecessary from a basic economic point of view. The same is true of most of the products bought at Belz, yet people just cannot help themselves. The high-quality, brand-name merchandise is at such bargain prices that they feel they just *have* to buy it. Why? Is the reason purely economic? Probably not.

The principal reason why people feel helpless in the face of a real bargain is that buying the items in question provides a sense of accomplishment. The bargain is not just about saving money. It's about feeling that you've accomplished something extraordinary and beat the odds on prices. It's almost like gambling.

Shopping at a place like Belz is literally exciting. People get a real adrenaline rush as they encounter designer-label merchandise at prices never seen before. There is actually a thrill to encountering and discovering such merchandise and sharing the experience with a friend or loved one. An interesting psychological study would measure the adrenaline levels of shoppers as they encounter things like Nike shoes at 70 percent off! This is exhilarating to the shopper. This is as good as it gets when it comes to shopping. It is the ultimate bargain hunter's shopping experience, a veritable nirvana of designer labels and low prices. Shoppers boast to their companions about the bargains they have just found. They say, "Look at the price on this!" and "Do you believe the price of that?" They snatch up bargains and are in an actual state of euphoria over the merchandise they are finding. Never mind whether the items are really needed. These prices are just too good to pass up. All readers will be familiar with the experience of seeing prices too good to be true and with sharing the excitement of such discoveries with others.

Shopping at Belz is not shopping for fun or entertainment. It's hard work. People literally spend hours and hours trudging through the mall looking for merchandise and they shell out hundreds and hundreds of dollars in doing so. The intensity of the activity is implied in the very phrase bargain *hunting.* Shopping for bargains is for the modern shopper what hunting for wild animals was to our cavemen ancestors. It's a *hunt.* It's a heartbeat away from the excitement of stalking prey in the wild. It's the shopper stalking the designer-label merchandise of her dreams. Look again at that list of stores above. It is truly a shopper's paradise. What better place for it than in the most unreal of all entertainment cities, Las Vegas?

Not all bargain hunting has the same level of excitement or energy as does Belz but the common denominator of all bargain shopping is the same. Usually much to their surprise, people encounter items on sale at prices low enough that they are impressed. This might be a lawnmower at Sears or a perfume at Fragrance Outlet. Whatever it is, its combination of price and quality is enough to get the shopper's attention. Once hooked, the shopper is confronted with making a decision on whether he wants or needs the item, and this is the point at which irrational behavior sometimes takes over. In other words, sometimes the price of the item is so attractive that the consumer is seduced into a purchase regardless of whether he really needs the item or not. Occasionally a shopper will find a good price on an item he was already looking for and so the bargain is just what the consumer wanted anyway. But most often the real bargain is found on an item that was not really needed or wanted and so the consumer is faced with a dilemma. To buy or not to buy. It is important to note that there is a difference between a true bargain and just a good price. The bargain presents a price so low to the consumer that he or she is *surprised* by the value being offered. A true bargain should represent more than just an everyday sale price.

Retailers are well aware of bargain hunters, as demonstrated by their habit of putting inflated regular prices on merchandise that is subsequently marked down to the bargain price at which they wish to sell it anyway. Consumers need to be wary of this ploy, though it is often difficult to retain one's sense of perspective when an item that has a supposed regular price of $200 is apparently marked down to $50.

Bargain hunting represents one of the significant reasons why people shop. It's all about the excitement of finding merchandise at surprisingly low prices and being able to take advantage of such discounts. The thrill of bargain hunting motivates shoppers and gives them a feeling of winning over the retailers, in much the same way that a gambler feels like he has won. It's an important part of the shopping mentality and one that retailers could probably take better advantage of. How many retailers set out with the explicit goal of literally raising the adrenaline levels of their shoppers by offering prices that are truly unbelievable or exciting? This is surely one way to spur sales and increase the interest of shoppers. Everyday sale prices are not the same—the bargain must truly stand out in the consumer's mind as a good deal that is just too exceptional to pass up.

One phenomenon that bargain hunters should be aware of is the well-known concept of the *loss leader.* This is usually an attractive single item that a retailer will advertise and sell at a loss in order to attract customers into a store. A loss leader acts like a lure, drawing consumers into a business who might not otherwise go there. It's a good idea from the retailer's point of view—it brings in customers—but shoppers should sometimes be wary of deals that appear too good to be true.

SHOPPING VICARIOUSLY

One of the great advantages of shopping is that when shoppers have run out of things to buy for themselves, they can always shop vicariously for other people. How many times have you found yourself saying, "Mom would sure like that" or "I'll bet the kids would love to have that"? You are not alone. A very big part of the retail market consists of people shopping for other people. This is not always active shopping. People will just browse for things that they think other people close to them would like to buy. Consider a typical example. You know that Mom is looking for a new dress or that your brother-in-law is looking for a new set of skis. It is not uncommon for people to go out of their way to shop for these items, even though they have no intention of buying them. Rather they see themselves as being collectors of useful information that will be of interest to the third party that actually wants the item. Such shoppers will tell Mom that they saw a perfect dress for her at a particular store downtown, or they will tell their brother-in-law that they saw particular skis on sale at the mall. This is *surrogate shopping*—getting enjoyment out of the experience of shopping even though there is no intention to buy anything. It is getting pleasure by pleasing others, by helping other people to shop and find what they want. Notable among vicarious shoppers are family, friends, and relatives.

Why do vicarious shoppers shop? The vicarious shopper helps to explain one of the mysteries of those shoppers who appear to shop intently, but then do not buy anything. Such shoppers may pursue products vigorously, even asking the sales staff many questions about items, only to turn and walk away from what seemed to be a potential sale, without explanation. The message for the retailer is that someone who may appear to be a likely candidate to make a purchase may in fact be doing advance work for someone else and so should be treated as an important customer. This shopper may be likely to return with a third party in tow for whom the purchase is really intended.

It's not hard to imagine that vicarious shoppers make up about one-third of all shoppers in stores. This behavior is much more common than most people would believe and is an experience that just about everybody has had. Sometimes vicarious shoppers are easy to spot. Middle-aged baby boomers at the Gap, or grandparents at Gap Kids, for example, may be dead giveaways that surrogate shopping is at work. Similarly, one can imagine that women browsing among hunting gear or men looking around in an arts and crafts section may be surrogate shoppers. We are not talking here about gift giving. The surrogate shopper has no intention of making a purchase. He or she only sees him- or herself as helping to find things for other people.

Men shop surrogately for men. A man will advise a friend of a good price on that boat motor he's been looking for. Women shop for women. A friend will inform a friend that the sweater she has had her eye on is on sale. Teens will inform other teens of new clothing that has just arrived at the mall. Almost everyone likes to surrogate shop and it is one of the frequent reasons for shopping. For the surrogate shopper, it is a way to enjoy the pleasures of shopping without spending any money. At the same time it is seen as a means by which one can help others and bring pleasure to them.

SHOPPING DREAMS

An interesting question to ask people is what they would do if they won a million dollars. Most answers to this question involve shopping. People will often speculate that if they became instant millionaires they would buy the car or the house of their dreams, or other similar luxury items. In spite of never winning a million dollars, many such shoppers live out their dreams vicariously by shopping for and looking at things they cannot possibly afford. If you cannot own the objects of your dreams you can at least look at them, and that is just what many people do.

There are many ways in which people shop their dreams but one of the most common is to go out and look at items that are put on display for the general public. This helps to explain the popularity of auto shows, boat shows, motor home shows, and so on. Such events enable shoppers to have a closer look at the products they lust after without having to go to the places where such products are usually sold. Similarly, people will attend open houses of homes just to have a look at what they might someday own.

People also shop their dreams in stores. Almost everybody likes to go out and have a look at the products they cannot possibly afford. People just love to look at high-end products and to ogle the price tags on outrageously expensive items, whether it is furniture, clothing, or other extravagant items. "It doesn't cost anything to look," they say, and most people are driven by curiosity to have a look at all kinds of fantasy products.

Some retailers are aware of the propensity of people to shop their dreams, and so they sometimes deliberately include products in their displays that are outrageously expensive. They do not expect to move such items but they do hope that they will serve to draw in traffic that might otherwise pass by. As an example of this, imagine an auto dealer who puts on display an extremely expensive sports car. His goal is not normally to sell the sports car outright, but to bring in lookers, who will then inspect his other products. This strategy will work in just about any retail environment. The goal is to arouse the curiosity of shoppers.

There is also an extremely practical reason why people like to window-shop stores and products that have outrageous prices. It makes them feel good about the things they have bought themselves and instills a feeling of common-sense practicality about their own purchases. When people look at an evening dress that costs $2,000, it makes them feel good about the comparable one for which they paid $200. Similarly, if people see a big-screen TV that's selling for $15,000, they feel better about the similar one for which they paid $1,500. Looking at shocking price tags gives most people a sense of contentment about their own, more practical shopping experiences.

SHOPPING AS COMPETITION

Shopping is a form of competition. It's serious business. When people shop, a very important aspect of their behavior is that they are competing with friends, neighbors, coworkers, and relatives. This competition takes place on a number of levels and in a variety of ways. It is one of the most significant motivators for shopping, and retailers and advertisers ignore it at their peril. Consider the average consumer who purchases a new, high-end product, for instance, a sport-utility vehicle. Elsewhere in this book a number of reasons have been suggested for such shopping behavior. It rewards the self, it provides self-recognition, and it satisfies the ego. But one huge motivator is that people shop to compete. In many respects life is a competition. We gauge our success and our accomplishments in life by how they stack up against those of other people. A key element in measuring levels of success is found in the things we own or buy.

How frequently do people gauge themselves against others? This probably happens far more often than we like to admit, and probably forms a more important part of our lives than most people are ready to acknowledge at a conscious level. Consider that sport-utility vehicle again. Although almost everyone would like to believe that they would make such a purchase for reasons of *self*-gratification, it is probably true that the purchase of such an outwardly visible manifestation of personal success is overwhelmingly motivated by competitive reasons. In other words, half the point of buying such a vehicle is to let other people know you own it, and to be seen driving it. The buyer wants his neighbors to see his SUV. He'll park it in the driveway just to put it on display. He wants his friends and coworkers to be aware of his ability to buy such a vehicle. He'll talk about it at work and when he's socializing, just to make sure everybody knows he bought it. Equally important is the idea that family members be aware of the purchase. The buyer will let his dad know he bought the vehicle and he will probably also make sure that his brother-in-law hears about it too. A big part of the reason for buying such a vehicle is to acquire the bragging rights that come with it, and there is almost no end to the lengths to which people will go to exercise those rights. The buyer of that sport-utility vehicle wants the whole world to know he bought it, and it's precisely that competitive factor that motivated him to buy it in the first place.

The idea that shopping is ultimately a competitive process applies to many of the things we buy. In fact, it is possible to divide everything that we buy into two categories: those things where we compete and those where we don't. When it comes to shopping for everyday things like those in the grocery store or drugstore, there is little room for competition. But when it comes to just about everything else we buy, it is clear that there is a competition factor at work. Whether we think about houses, electronics, vehicles, furniture, vacations and leisure, or a host of other things, we can usually see that people compete with one another through their purchases. Is your neighbor's house bigger than yours? Do your relatives have better furniture than you do? Does your coworker have a better audio system than you do? Does your brother-in-law have a bigger boat than you do? Do your friends take better vacation trips than you do? These are just a few examples of the myriad ways in which we compete with other people through the things we purchase. Pretension is essential in this process and once again we see that people measure their worth and their success in life largely through the things that they are able to buy. Shopping helps to define one's station in life, and the very heart of shopping is found in the way in which it defines our competitive success as human beings.

Competition among women will be with respect to those things that are important to them. To some women, for example, home furnishings and home decorating will be a source of competition with neighbors, friends, and relatives. It is not important to have expensive furnishings but rather to show a sense of style and decorating taste that surpasses that of others. The way in which the home is decorated is seen to be a reflection of the owner and thus it is important that it be discriminating. It's a status symbol, and countless shopping hours will be devoted to it.

Men are generally considered to be more competitive than women are and this shows quite clearly in the wider range of products over which they are able to compete. The list is almost endless. Men will compete over sports equipment, tools, vehicles, houses, recreational vehicles, electronic equipment, and so on. Just about anything is fair game. The battle is usually over who has the biggest, the fastest, the most powerful, or the best of anything. Women are subtler in their competition, while men are more blatant. It's important to have a boat engine that has more horsepower than the other guy's, and it's important to have a sound system that has more watts than the competition. Men are relentless in their drive to compete, and very often the cost of products is not much of an obstacle when it comes to winning a competition. In this regard men are as just as serious when it comes to shopping as women, if not more so, and the stereotypical idea that women love to shop while men hate it proves to be incorrect. Men love to shop for the things they like, and they may be far more diligent and competitive shoppers than women.

One of the principal levels at which intense shopping competition takes place is with respect to personal attire. When people buy clothing, shoes, and accessories they are, in effect, in competition with all of the people with whom they associate. People shop to belong when it comes to clothes, but at the same time they shop to compete. Every individual wants to dress better or look better than his or her colleagues, friends and relatives, and this is a central motivator when it comes to buying clothes.

At the office, it is important not only to look good and to fit in; it's also usual for men and women to try to outdress their coworkers. Thus there is the woman who somehow manages to wear a new outfit to the office just about every week. Similarly, there is the man who seems to have an endless number of different new suits. If nothing else, employees must at least make an effort to keep up with office norms and office trendsetters. Conforming to office dress codes is an expensive proposition, and as trends and fashions change, many employees are hard-pressed to keep up with the times. Nevertheless, there is a definite air of competition and there always seem to be some employees who are more determined than others to keep up with fashion trends. There are personal bragging rights to be had by being a trendsetter and these can be achieved through appropriate dress.

In addition to everyday competition over clothing styles, most people also think that personal advancement and on-the-job success are at least partly attributable to personal dress and grooming. Moving up the corporate ladder often requires that employees look the part when it comes to advancement. Thus when it comes to shopping competition in the workplace, there is often more at stake than simple bragging rights. As employees jockey for promotion and advancement at least part of their strategy usually involves the manner in which they dress. Imitation, they say, is the sincerest form of flattery, and there is no better way to flatter the boss than to dress in a way that is similar to his or her own. One not only demonstrates one's willingness to become part of the group, but one also demonstrates a willingness to conform and thus become a trusted coworker. How one dresses at the office says a great deal about one's attitude toward one's job. Most workers understand implicitly the significance of dress codes, not only for fitting in but also for promotion and advancement. Shopping for clothing is a central part of working and is one of the major reasons why people shop for clothing as intently as they do.

In addition to clothing, there is also serious competition when it comes to hair and makeup. Men and women compete with one another on a number of fashion fronts, but when it comes to hair and makeup, women set standards of competition that are theirs alone. Social standards dictate that for formal occasions women must get their hair and makeup done, thus implying the purchase of a hair stylist and a makeup professional. It is seen to be absolutely appropriate to spend hundreds of dollars to achieve a look, if only for a few hours. So intense is the competition to look good that almost any expenditure of time and effort is justified. There is probably no better example of the idea of shopping for competitive reasons than that of women's purchases of hair and makeup services. There are certain social expectations that must be met when it comes to formal wear and usually the cost of such personal services is little deterrent, if any. Those in the hair styling and cosmetic industries understand that there is a high price to be paid for vanity, and as a consequence the industry thrives on reputation and image, rather than on cost cutting. For the retailers of such services it is imperative to convey the idea that although their services are not necessarily cost competitive, they are *competitive with respect to social rivalry.*

Another area where shopping competition for clothing is rife is among preteens and teenagers. Elsewhere we speak of the teen's need to fit in and to coordinate with peers when it comes to clothing, but at the same time it is important to realize that there is a serious competition effect at work. Every teen, just like most adults, wants to be at the forefront of fashion. This means that there is a high personal payoff to being an innovator and being among the first to adopt the latest fashion trend. If there is a hot new style or item on the market, every teenager wants to be the first to have it. Once again, there are bragging rights to be had and most shoppers are willing to pay a premium price to acquire them. There is a shopping competition factor at work. The winner is the shopper who gets the new innovation first. The implication is that intense shopping pays off because it will lead the determined shopper to a reward of being the fashion trend winner. Smart retailers are able to stay at the leading edge of fashion and by so doing can gain an edge on the competition. It's important to create the belief in the shopper that the product he or she is buying is novel. The shopper needs to be convinced that he or she will win the competition to be the most innovative if the product is purchased. The advertiser and the retailer want to persuade the shopper that their product is at the leading edge.

Teens also compete when it comes to members of the opposite sex. The girls compete for the attention of the boys and the boys compete for the attention of the girls. Shopping is key. It is important to show that you are in tune with trends but it is also important to show that you are an innovator. Although many people do not want to be the first to adopt a new trend, neither do many want to be last. Timing is everything, and a great deal of shopping is usually necessary to stay in step. The teens compete intensely among themselves for the attention of the others, and one of the surest ways they know how to compete is through their clothing, hair and, for girls, makeup. Shopping for these products and services is intensified by the fact that there is a strong competition factor at work, and when it comes to making oneself attractive, cost is seldom much of a barrier. It is obvious that advertisers should emphasize that their products make the buyer attractive to members of the opposite sex, but they would do well to remember that the shopper sees him- or herself in competition with peers. Thus a successful strategy will emphasize that the product not only makes one attractive, but also that it makes one more attractive than competitors.

Are advertisers and retailers acutely aware of the competition factor when it comes to merchandising? Are they cognizant of the crucial role that rivalry plays when it comes to shopping behavior? One suspects not; otherwise the role of competition would form a central theme in the promotion of many more products than it does. The world is a competitive place and a very large proportion of that competitiveness is expressed and exhibited through people's shopping. People shop to compete and every retailer and every advertiser should be aware of this ever-present dimension of shopping. Not only is it unavoidable, it is one of the most significant aspects of human shopping behavior.

ADVERTISING—THE SHOPPING APHRODISIAC

Advertising is considered to be the engine that drives consumer sales. Just think about the number of ads that people see or hear in an average day. Between television, radio, computers, magazines, billboards, labeled clothing, signs, newspapers, and other media, the fact is that advertising at virtually every waking moment is bombarding people. Indeed, innovative advertisers have plans to pitch ads at you when you're standing still for a second at a cash machine, waiting in your car for your gas, and even when you are going to the washroom. There is no moment of the day that they will leave you alone. What does all of this do for shoppers? How does advertising work? Does it motivate shoppers?

Take the Coke test. You're standing at a cooler of soda pop with several different brands staring you in the face. It's a hot summer day and you want a cold drink. Which brand do you pick up? Marketers work day and night to try to get you to pick up their product. Do you make your decision unconsciously? Probably. Choosing a soda is just a minor decision and most people would agree it does not deserve a moment's thought. But does advertising affect your choice? Are you more likely to choose Coke if you've seen a dozen Coke ads in the last five days? Are you more likely to choose Coke if you've seen 1,000 Coke ads in the last five years? The answer is, "probably." Marketers know that exposure means sales. The more they get the name of a product out there, the more the product will sell. Yes, they do know that they can influence your behavior and that when it comes time to choose that cola they can make you pick up their brand. It works. It works whether we like it or not.

The choice of the Coke is a small decision, but an important one in its implications. Take the Coke example and generalize it to hundreds of other decisions that shoppers make. There you have the essence of advertising. The bottom line is to get the consumer to react, to choose one product over another. Advertisers pursue the mind and the heart of the consumer in their efforts to sway decision-making behavior. And it is effective. If surveys are carried out about products, virtually all people will have brand preferences for every kind of product, from toothpaste to laundry detergent and from beer to potato chips.

From the point of view of the beleaguered shopper, advertising serves three purposes. First it *informs* the consumer of the availability of products, especially new ones. That ad on television for a new cleaning product lets the shopper know what is available. Second, ads serve a *competition* purpose; to sway the shopper, to get him or her to choose one product over another. There may be more than one version of that new cleaning product on the market and the consumer likes to comparison-shop the competition. Third, there is the element of *persuasion,* the idea of trying to coerce the shopper into buying a product. Here the advertiser tries to convince the shopper that she really does need the new cleaning product.

How does advertising work? What does it do to one's mind? Quite simply the goal is to create desire, and then turn desire into want and even need. An ad just doesn't draw one's attention to an item. Rather, its most important function is supposed to be to portray the product in a light that will create in the consumer a desire to buy the product. It is not only about introducing new products to the consumer but also about wooing the customer away from existing products and about creating new demand for existing products. The logic of the business is that there is a consumer wallet out there, and it's a competition for the consumer's mind share and wallet share.

Shoppers are decision makers and advertising aims to affect that decision-making process. Other parts of this book have illustrated the great complexity of the shopping enterprise, so it is no surprise that it is difficult for advertisers to understand shoppers. People shop for personal reasons, for emotional reasons, for selfish reasons, for unselfish reasons, and for all kinds of other reasons. Trying to convince a shopper to buy this product or that product is about as difficult a task as one can imagine and yet companies pour millions of dollars into advertising agencies in the quest to tempt the elusive shopper. Sometimes ads that are cute or memorable are absolutely useless for increasing sales, while at other times ads that seem too simple or annoying are actually a boon to sales. Advertising is one of the great mysteries of our times and no one really understands what makes a great ad.

No two shoppers are the same and no two shoppers have the same motivations. Short of understanding that consumers have definitive brand preferences, advertisers are able to shed little light on the psychology of shopping. The dizzying array of commercials that we see pays testament to the elusive nature of the consumer, and the inability of advertisers to figure out what that consumer wants. The only measure of the effectiveness of an advertisement is in its effect on actual sales. Although this provides concrete evidence of the results of an ad, it does not really provide us with any greater insight into the shopper. The truth of the matter is that there is nothing that one can put one's finger on that defines the average shopper or makes clear their intentions.

Shoppers endure ads. They do not like them and they do not really pay too much attention to them. In today's time-stressed world people have enough things to deal with in their lives without letting ads distract them. Shoppers view ads as part of the price they pay for living in a free-enterprise economy. Other than that, they are largely indifferent to the efforts of advertisers and prefer to go about their daily business without the complications that ads offer.

Smart advertisers are aware that shoppers do not care what they say and are cognizant of the fact that shoppers are mostly indifferent to ads. In the battle for the hearts and souls of shoppers, the biggest enemy is indifference. A consumer watching television during the evening, for example, is bombarded with hundreds of advertisements. How many does he pay attention to? How many does he remember? How many have any real impact on him? Advertisers face an uphill battle in their desire to compete for the attention of shoppers and are hard-pressed to achieve victory. They use drama, they use humor, they use sex, they try to entertain, they try to grab interest, but despite their best efforts consumers, for the most part, appear to remain largely unmoved.

Yet, when it comes time to choose among the colas, consumers do make a choice among brands. And it is at that moment that advertisers achieve success. If they can make the shopper choose one product over another, they succeed in their goals. In spite of the apparent indifference of consumers to ads, consumers do make shopping decisions and somehow those ads do play a role in the process.

By far the most interesting aspect of advertising is in the creation of new demand for new products. This is all about making shoppers shop. In this regard it may be instructive to look at the past. In particular it is fascinating to consider the long line of home appliances that have been invented over the years. Consider the bread maker, the pasta maker, the home cappuccino machine, the slow cooker, the toaster oven, the food processor, the microwave, and so on. Manufacturers have done an outstanding job of devising a long line of innovative home appliances that created new demand where none previously existed. This list serves to demonstrate that it is virtually always possible to create new marketing niches and that consumers are usually willing to buy innovative products. More importantly, it illustrates that there always seems to be room for shopping in new areas of unexpected demand. This is an economic mode in which consumer demand for products is virtually insatiable, where new demand can always be created for new or existing products. It is the economy where demand is not a function of what people really need, but where it is a want, *manufactured* as needed. It is the economy where consumers never have enough, where there is always something else that one feels a need to buy.

A very big part of the pursuit of creating new demand is found in the business of advertising. The message is that new demand can be created where none previously existed, simply through appropriate and intense advertising. In fact one must wonder, when one considers the long line of highly demanded consumer products that are available, where the demand comes from, if not from advertising. The point is that consumer demand can be created for nontraditional things and for nontraditional reasons. Advertising can spur shoppers to buy products that are outside the realm of normal purchases.

When advertisers create demand they create a motivation for shoppers to shop. People who own a perfectly good television may be motivated to shop for a new big-screen television by the forces of advertising. People may be motivated to go out and look for the latest items of fashion by ads that they see in a magazine. They may be persuaded to go shopping for a new car because they like the look of one they saw in an ad. Sometimes the message does get through and sometimes people shop just because advertisers are creating the desire to shop. The long list of appliance products above that have been invented over the years pays testament to the fact that shoppers will shop for new products. Advertising has the power to motivate people to shop and has the added feature that it can create demand where none existed before. It can be a powerful motivator to the shopper.

Chapter 6

SHOPPING FROM THE HEART

IT'S THE THOUGHT THAT COUNTS

Buying gifts is one of the most important reasons for shopping. It is also where some of the most extreme and illogical shopping behavior of all takes place. People exhibit the most unusual and uncharacteristic behaviors when it comes to buying gifts. They will overspend their budgets, they will go into debt, and they will buy almost anything it takes to please the intended recipient of the gift. People will spend far more effort and money to please another person with a gift than they will spend shopping for themselves.

Why are people so anxious to please others? Why will a man buy a woman an expensive diamond that he cannot really afford? Why will a woman buy a man a ring or a watch that is incredibly expensive? The answer is that people try to make a strong statement about their emotions toward other people when they give them gifts. When you give Uncle Bill a birthday present, it's not just to celebrate the occasion. Rather it is a way of telling Uncle Bill what you think of him. The emotion or expense put into a gift is a measure of one person's esteem, respect or love for another. Though the amount of money spent is often used as a barometer of the intentions of the gift giver, time or effort can also easily be used as an indicator of emotions. The child who spends an hour drawing a picture for her mom is putting her emotions for her mother into a physical form. The person who spends hours and hours looking for that perfect gift for a friend or relative is making an emotional commitment to the recipient. The grandfather who spends hours in his workshop crafting a gift for his grandchild is investing his feelings for the child in a tangible form. Gifts are important. They are not just items to acknowledge special events; they are indicators of what one human being thinks of another.

It is no wonder we get so emotionally involved when we shop for gifts. It is often said that artists express their deepest feelings and emotions through their work. What is not noted is that everyday people do the same thing when they purchase gifts for other people. A gift is an expression of the very deepest human emotions that people have for one another, expressed in the form of a physical entity. A simple box of chocolates can carry a huge emotional message that is conveyed from the giver to the receiver. It can say, "This is what I think of you," or "I think you're special," or "I love you." Couples in love cannot always find the words to express their feelings toward one another but they can buy each other gifts that are intended to convey their feelings.

The greeting card business taps directly into this fertile emotional ground by providing the words that accompany gifts. Tapping into this reservoir of emotion was one of the greatest marketing innovations of all time. Imagine that no one had ever thought of greeting cards and that people had to literally write down their thoughts and emotions about one another. This multibillion-dollar industry makes its money simply from effectively and briefly expressing emotions for people.

People can agonize over the purchase of greeting cards. They will spend an enormous amount of time searching for just the right words to convey their thoughts. It is usually an embellishment to the emotional statement that is being made with a gift. Together the two are intended to convey silent passions or feelings to the recipient. The greeting card section in a store can be likened to an emotional buffet. People move along, looking at the selection of items, in an attempt to find what suits their emotional needs the best. It is truly one of the most unusual places in all of retailing, where feelings are quite literally for sale.

"It's more than words can say" is an expression that sums up the sentiment of gift giving. Sometimes a gift conveys a message other than one of love or passion. Sometimes people will attempt to say, "I don't care" through a thoughtless gift. Sometimes feelings are mistaken; sometimes an inexpensive gift will be appreciated, while at other times an expensive gift will be unappreciated. The gift giver has an enormous emotional investment in a gift and so can be very pleased or very disappointed by the reactions of the recipient. The onus is usually on the recipient of a gift to react appropriately and to acknowledge the intent of the giver.

A gift is as much for the giver as it is for the receiver. Although the giver typically *thinks* that the emotion of a gift is directed entirely toward the recipient, in actual fact there is an enormous investment of the self in a gift. The giver of a gift is not altogether altruistic; he or she expects some payoff. Who has not experienced the tide of emotions that prevails when someone opens a gift? Usually the giver waits with bated breath, anxious to see the positive emotional reaction of the recipient. Retailers should be aware that the purchase of a gift is as much about the giver as it is the receiver. For example, when a young man purchases a diamond ring, he is as much concerned with his own emotions as he is with pleasing the recipient. This suggests that when it comes to gifts of all kinds, retailers should be aware that the customer is seeking reassurance that the given gift will bring him as much emotional satisfaction as the person for whom he is buying it. When you buy that special someone a gift, your aim is to bring emotional release to yourself as well as that person. Gifts are ultimately self-indulgent.

Gifts are also a place where extravagance is not only understood and tolerated, but is also sometimes expected. Irrational expenditures are seen to be logical by others if a gift is being purchased. Retailers are aware of this phenomenon and are more than willing to exploit it. Many luxury and other gift items are irrationally priced because the retailer understands that shoppers are willing to pay a premium price for presents. As an example of this, consider an item like cologne or perfume that is often intended as a gift and usually comes with a highly inflated price. Indeed, the toiletry section is often seen as the cash cow in many department stores. Even if it does not make economic sense to others, it does make *emotional sense* to spectators and participants alike.

Gift giving is one of the most mysterious areas of shopping. Irrational behavior is almost the norm in this area of consumer spending and it is tolerated, expected, and even encouraged. Gift giving is less about shopping and more about the emotions of the shopper. This helps to explain the extreme nature of gift shopping and the illogical nature of the whole process. From the consumer's point of view, shopping for gifts is an emotional process that one gets caught up in. It is an area where the laws of supply, demand, and price go out the window as anxious shoppers do their utmost to bring pleasure to another person, and thereby, to themselves. The shopper shopping for gifts is the most susceptible of all shoppers. Smart retailers are ready to take advantage of the defenseless and emotionally vulnerable gift buyer. Meanwhile, the shopper knows he is vulnerable, but he is also unwilling to defend himself. Pleasing the recipient and conveying the intended emotional message are often more important than the price.

Another interesting area of gift giving is the one that involves holidays and special occasions. Mother's Day, anniversaries, and Valentine's Day especially come to mind as big shopping days when buyers are forced into a must-buy situation. In economics this is known as a situation where demand is inelastic—that is, unbendable—where the male shopper must make a purchase. Sons, husbands, and boyfriends find themselves in a situation where not buying something is unthinkable. One very interesting aspect of these occasions is that much of the shopping on these days occurs in specialty stores, that is, those that sell flowers, jewelry, chocolates, and so on. Such specialty retailers would be wise to cater excessively to the male shopper in search of gifts because very often, high prices are not really an issue. It is considered only appropriate that male shoppers spend an outrageous amount on a small gift, as this demonstrates to the gift recipient that when it comes to love, price is no object. This is another of those intriguing areas of shopping where it is more appropriate to spend *more* than one really wants to, because the purchase is driven by emotion rather than common sense. Does anyone really shop around for bargains when it comes to buying a dozen roses? Not really. The male shopper who is desperate to purchase a token of love for the object of his affections will pay almost any price to get what he wants. And very often, the higher the price, the better, as the amount of shopping extravagance is equated with the degree of emotional caring.

CHRISTMAS

If there ever was a reason for serious shopping it has got to be the annual ritual known as Christmas. People get carried away at Christmas. They are full of emotion and they go shopping with an attitude that is unlike that at any other time of the year. Many people will literally spend themselves into bankruptcy at Christmastime, putting huge and unanticipated purchases on credit cards that are already strained to the limit. Christmas is supposed to be a time of joy and celebration, but to many it means a time of unabashed, relentless shopping.

What happens to shoppers at Christmas? Why do they get so emotional over shopping and buying? Why do they go to extremes that are unheard of at other times of the year? The answer is that the Christmas season imparts a special sense of obligation to please those for whom the gifts are being bought. It's a special time of year and so special gifts are in order. The shopper goes to great lengths to try to delight and satisfy the recipient of the gift. *People are anxious to please others.* How else do you explain the parents who search the whole city for that one special toy? How do you explain the husband, wife, son, or daughter who frets endlessly over the choice of a gift for a relative? How do you account for the girlfriend or boyfriend who hunts tirelessly for a gift for a loved one? People like to please other people—it gives them great pleasure to do so—and the determined Christmas shopper knows almost no bounds in the quest to delight the recipient of a gift.

The act of extreme Christmas shopping is also selfish. People get pleasure themselves out of giving appreciated gifts to others and *it is this pleasure that is one of the primary motives of the Christmas shopper.* In effect, the supposed pleasure that is being given to others is really directed to the self. The gift giver wants to feel the egotistical pleasure of giving, and wants to be praised as generous and thoughtful by the recipient. The gift giver wants to earn the affection of the person receiving the gift. Giving a Christmas gift is usually not an unselfish act of kindness, but rather a self-directed method of rewarding oneself by earning the adulation of the recipient. Does not everyone experience a sense of excitement when watching a recipient open a gift? Is there not a real feeling of pleasure, delight, and emotion that pours out of the giver when someone unwraps *their* present?

There are two factors at work. When a wife buys her husband that power tool he has always wanted she is anxious to please him. She will save her money so that she can buy the product and she will shop relentlessly, if need be, to find it. Her goal is to please him. But at the same time it is important to realize that the wife is also pleasing herself by the very act of giving the gift. She hopes to earn the praise and gratitude of her husband, and is anxious to feel the pleasure herself of the joy of giving the gift. Christmas gift giving is a two-way street, with emotions directed both at the recipient of the gift as well as at the giver. This helps to explain why people are so obsessive when it comes to shopping for Christmas. Their motives are not entirely unselfish.

The difference at Christmastime is that the motivations for gift giving are heightened by the emotion of the season. Christmas presents psychological conditions that are nonexistent at other times of the year. In many cases, Christmas may be the one and only yearly occasion on which someone buys another person a gift. It represents one person's annual statement to another that says "This is how I feel about you" or "This is how much I care about you." The emotional content of just a single gift can be enormous, and it is no wonder that people are driven to distraction by the shopping that is expected during the Christmas season.

From the retailer's point of view, Christmas is also the most important time of year. Very often the difference between bankruptcy and success is determined by the sales that are made over the holiday season. Retailers are anxious to exploit the emotions of shoppers and will do everything in their power to try to boost sales. Obviously, an important retail strategy is to ensure the buyer that his or her gifts are sure to please the recipient. This is an indirect way of helping to ensure that the shopper's own emotional needs are met when the gift is given and opened. It is important for advertisers to emphasize that the gifts and products available are sure to earn the praise of the people receiving them. That's what it really is all about.

Christmas is an emotional time of year. It brings out shoppers like no other season. It is a time when shoppers are vulnerable emotionally and when retailers can do their utmost to spur sales. Shopping traffic levels reach their peaks at Christmas. Everything, including shopping, is at an excess at Christmas and many shoppers, in spite of the gross commercialization, cannot help themselves when it comes to excess buying. Expectations of both shoppers and buyers are unrealistic, yet this acts as little impediment to determined shoppers.

Determined Christmas shoppers will go to almost any lengths to find what they are looking for. At the same time, shoppers who are desperate will buy almost anything that qualifies as an adequate gift. Everybody knows that perfume and cologne are the gifts of the despairing, yet record sales levels continue to be set for these products every Christmas. Such is the nature of desperation-driven holiday shopping.

Shoppers get carried away at Christmas. There are certain expectations that must be met. If you bought Uncle Fred a sweater last Christmas he will expect a gift of at least equal worth this year. Otherwise the wrong message will get sent. Similarly, if you bought Aunt Mary a present last year, you will have to get her one this year or she will think that your opinion of her has changed. Children who opened 25 presents last year will be disappointed if there are only 15 this year. Everybody has hopes and high expectations at Christmastime, and the only way to ensure they are met is through shopping.

In spite of all of these good intentions, disappointment is almost always guaranteed at Christmas. Children have higher hopes than are reasonable, and they are usually disappointed by the absence of one or more hoped-for item. Even adults have certain expectations about what others will buy them, and they are usually somewhat discontented by the gifts they ultimately receive. We all learn early in life to be gracious gift recipients and to feign pleasure at the receipt of a gift, no matter how far off the target it is. As folks gather 'round the Christmas tree it is a time for faking it, in order to ensure that the pleasure of the gift giver is not foregone.

Christmas is quite clearly one of the strangest times of year for everyone concerned. The extreme emotional involvement of people in buying and receiving should not be underestimated. It is not only a frantic time of year but also one that is fraught with passion, sentiment, and other profound psychological baggage. All of these feelings are intricately tied up with shopping, and it is an understatement indeed to say that Christmas more than anything demonstrates the enormous emotional investment that people put into shopping.

SHOPPING AS SOCIALIZING, COUNTERFEIT SHOPPING

Shopping is an event. There is more to it than just the act of walking through a retail environment. Shopping requires planning. Most shopping takes place in a group and so requires that the participants plan their schedules to allow the event to take place. Shopping normally requires travel, and so the act of traveling, as well as the socializing that accompanies it, becomes a part of the shopping event. Whether by bus, car, subway, or other means, the trip is part of the event. At the same time, other activities are woven together with shopping. A shopping trip often involves a luncheon date, coffee, beers, or cocktails as another part of the experience.

Shopping is social. It presents a chance to go out with friends, acquaintances, or relatives and to socialize while one shops. Socialization is probably one of the most important functions of shopping. The shopping event provides a medium through which socializing can take place. One only needs to look around a typical store to see the truth of this argument. Although there are a lot of individual shoppers, they are usually outnumbered by shoppers in groups. Women friends, men friends, groups of teens, couples, and families all shop together.

People will use a shopping event as an excuse to get together for reasons other than shopping. The conversation may never drift anywhere near the issue of shopping, other than at a superficial level, because the real purpose of the event is to converse and socialize about other things. Groups of teens, men, or women may spend hours together shopping when they have absolutely no intention of buying anything. Sometimes the social purpose of shopping may be purely innocent, but at other times there is some ulterior motive. When a mother wants to just spend some quality time with her daughter, or else grill her about her new boyfriend, shopping presents a perfect facade behind which to carry out the task.

We can label such behavior *counterfeit shopping*. Counterfeit shopping has ulterior motives and is not really shopping at all. It is socializing in the form of shopping, with little or no intent to make a purchase or even look seriously at merchandise. It is a common occurrence.

Many people will go shopping in the company of others as a form of emotional support. Whether one is buying a new dress or a new lawnmower, it is usually easier to make a decision when the advice and opinion of another person can be solicited. Sometimes this support role is truly genuine. People really do require the counsel and guidance of others in making a purchase.

Shoppers may enroll the support of friends who are perceived as experts in some particular area—for example, sound equipment—or, alternatively, people may enlist the help of others simply as a means of providing a second honest opinion concerning the latest fashions. Couples often make purchasing decisions in the face of a shared, limited budget, and so they need to debate the merits of a purchase. In all of these examples, the need for support is perceived by the shoppers as being authentic—they really do value, and take into account, the advice of another person in making a decision.

Often the support role is purely emotional. A person may have already made up his or her mind to make a specific purchase but simply needs the verbal affirmation of a friend or relative to carry out the actual purchase. One can imagine a shopper looking for a more expensive item having already made their decision to buy. When it comes time to make the actual purchase, however, such a consumer may be unable to complete the transaction without the psychological support of a third party. This might be called *enabled shopping*. The enabled shopper just cannot make the big purchase without moral support. One imagines that part of the reason for this is that it enables the shopper to shift the blame for a misguided purchase to the other party. This is probably especially true of purchases by couples.

When it comes to shopping decisions, retailers would be wise to pay attention to the group dynamic, for it is often the group as a whole that is making decisions. The individual shopping with a companion may be more swayed by the companion than by the salesperson. Thus the shopping group or duo should be viewed as a single decision-making unit.

This may be especially true of couples who tend to decide about purchases as if they are one.

Shopping is a form of recreation. It is often an activity that is pursued to fill time or to be done at one's leisure. Like many leisure activities, part of the mentality of shopping is that it be carried out with others. It is important to share the experience with others. The social experience extends well beyond the store itself and includes the *preshopping warm-up* and the *postshopping analysis*. The preshopping warm-up involves the excitement of planning for the trip and the anticipation of shopping together. In addition it includes the trip to the shopping destination and the high hopes that prevail. It is the beginning of an event that is expected, perhaps more than anything, to be a fun social outing. The postshopping analysis includes the experience following the social shopping trip. Shoppers will compare notes following shopping trips and will review and mentally revisit the merchandise they saw together. These are important aspects of the shopping experience and the purchasing decision.

IMPULSE SHOPPING

We've all done it. You're walking through the mall to buy some nondescript item, like a birthday card for Aunt Mary, when you unexpectedly get the urge to take a stroll through a clothing store. Suddenly, there it is. The sweater of your dreams. It's the perfect color and size, and the price is not too far out of line. The last thing in the world you had in mind was to buy a sweater, but you soon find yourself at the checkout, buying this must-have item. This is *impulse buying*. It does not have to be clothing. People will buy anything on impulse, from a pair of earrings to a new car. While one's personal budget may determine the price of impulse items, there is not a shopper anywhere who has not given in to the desire.

Why do we shop on impulse? What is it that gives people the urge to suddenly make an unanticipated purchase? Part of the answer is that people *indulge themselves* in buying an item on impulse. It is part of the psychology of rewarding the self. By making an impulse buy, the shopper compensates himself; he pays himself a self-indulgent bonus. But shoppers can reward themselves by buying things anytime. What is it that distinguishes the impulse buy from an ordinary purchase? The answer is that it is the very impulsiveness of the shopper that is its own reward. The fact that an impulse buy is an *unplanned and unanticipated* purchase adds to the excitement and pleasure of the experience. It's a bit of bad-boy behavior, that feeling of being naughty, or of doing something unpredictable and unexpected. There's a bit of an adrenaline rush to genuine impulse shopping. The shopper gets an emotional charge out of the experience and comes away from it feeling exhilarated. Impulse buying, and the emotional lift it provides, afford a clear demonstration of the important and deep psychological nature of shopping.

Retailers hope that people will buy on impulse and they go out their way to try to make sure that it happens. They are aware of the emotional lift that impulse buying provides to shoppers. Almost all stores are designed with the impulse shopper in mind. If you go into a convenience store, for instance, you will find that the things you really need, like milk, are always located at the back of the store. The retailer hopes that you will buy the other merchandise—the chocolate bars, chips, and pop—on impulse as you pass by. The same design principle holds true in department stores. If you are looking for underwear you will undoubtedly pass by the perfume section, the men's wear, and the ladies wear on your way to it. Walk into a home electronics shop and you will find the impulse items on display at the front of the store. Pass by a store in the mall and things on display at the front will be those that the retailer hopes will sell on a whim. Virtually every store follows this kind of design layout. In addition, of course, attractive store displays are intended to coerce the impulse shopper. Colorful arrangements of items and special lighting are intended to draw the shopper's attention to merchandise that will be purchased out of self-indulgence.

People also feel guilty about impulse shopping. They will try to justify and rationalize such purchases. They may claim that they really needed the item anyway, that they would have bought such an article eventually, or that the deal was just too good to pass up. Some people may buy merchandise on impulse just to make worthwhile use of their time. If someone is going to go shopping on their lunch hour, it only justifies the time expended if they buy something. Why invest 45 minutes in shopping and come away empty-handed?

Retailers can do their best to indulge the impulse buyer by making purchases seem justified. Letting the buyer know that "she deserves a break today" is one of the classic examples of such an approach to merchandising. It is important to tell the shopper that her impulse buy is justified, that she has earned it and is entitled to it. It's critical to have the shopper feel good about a self-indulgent purchase and to heighten the feelings of well-being that emanate from such a shopping experience. Telling the shopper that she has earned the right to a reward, and that she should not feel guilty about indulging her whims, should be a top priority in advertising and marketing. Make the impulse buy a good feeling that the shopper will want to repeat.

Whether we are talking about the most fashionable, high-end boutique, or the everyday grocery store, shoppers are constantly engaging in spontaneous, self-indulgent buying. An interesting product mix, a high rate of stock turnover, and a fresh and well-organized display will go a long way toward enticing the shopper's desires. Buying something gives shoppers a sense of accomplishment. When they have no items left to buy that they really need, an impulse buy will satisfy this need.

WINDOW-SHOPPING

Window-shopping is an age-old idea. Ever since there have been stores, there have been displays of products, and people have amused themselves and passed the time with browsing the merchandise. Window-shopping is an odd idea. It indicates that shoppers are interested in just looking at products when there is no possibility of buying them. It suggests perhaps that enjoyment or pleasure is obtained simply from inspecting merchandise that is available. That is an important idea. It implies that there is value and purpose in shopping, even when there is nothing to buy.

The idea of window-shopping originated with storeowners putting products on display in order to entice customers. Perhaps surprisingly to storeowners, the tease provided by the displayed merchandise worked whether the store was open or closed. People would entertain themselves by walking around and looking at the latest merchandise. Storeowners hoped to fuel demand for their products by putting them on public display, little realizing that they would provide a source of free entertainment to passersby. The age-old tradition continues today, with shoppers in downtown urban areas still taking the time to browse the displays that retailers make available.

The fact that people will window-shop at all says volumes about the psychology and mindset of shopping. Why do people want to look at inventory even when they cannot buy it? First and most simply, it is just a form of entertainment. People have a natural curiosity about things and storeowners take advantage of it by putting products on display. Presumably, what is put on display usually represents the latest products, so that window-shoppers are able just to see what is new. Secondly, window-shoppers are collecting information about goods and products for use at a later time. The window-browsing consumer is taking stock of products and prices as he or she window-shops. Presumably this information is filed away to be recalled at a later date. Third, there is a location factor at work. Window-shoppers are adding to their stock of personal information about what's available and *where it is*—they are adding information to their mental maps of the shopping environment.

From the retailer's point of view, the purpose of window displays is simply to arouse shoppers' curiosity and to bring them back to the store at a later time. Window displays are ultimately a form of advertising, where the ads consist of literal, real merchandise. It is the ultimate virtual advertisement. Retailers should keep in mind, however, that window-shoppers are also stockpiling information for a later date. Displaying unique items is a way to let the consumer know that these items are available in a particular store and is a way to create an association between a product line and a location.

DECISION TIME AND THE PRIVACY OF SHOPPERS

One of the most crucial components of the shopping experience is found in the issue of the personal privacy of the shopper. From the point of view of the consumer, privacy in shopping is something to be treasured and guarded inasmuch as it is a key element of the decision-making experience. From the point of view of the retailer, the privacy of the shopper is a delicate aspect of consumer relations that should be handled with care. Whether we are talking about individual shoppers or shoppers in groups, there is an important, private moment in the shopping experience that can be called *decision time*. This is that period of time, anywhere from a brief moment to up to 15 or 20 minutes, or even several days, during which the consumer makes the actual decision to make a purchase.

Privacy in shopping comes to the fore as a crucial variable when groups of consumers are involved in decision making. This facet of shopping is closely related to the idea that shopping is largely a social event. Decision-making units are usually composed of groups: groups of teens, couples, women with women, men with men, or relatives. These units usually make choices about purchases by discussing the item or items in question. This might involve women pondering a pair of shoes, men talking over the purchase of a computer, teens discussing a CD, or a couple trying to decide on whether to buy a microwave oven. In every case, the decision-making group normally requires a moment of privacy in order to discuss the purchase. Indeed, the whole purpose of not shopping alone is more often than not to gain the input of others in making decisions. This group decision making may be the most crucial part of the shopping expedition, and yet eager sales staff can disrupt the privacy required for it.

Privacy is also important to the individual shopper. Even when the decision to purchase is made in the absence of a group dynamic, the individual shopper still usually needs some quiet time, even if only a second, to make up her mind about a purchase.

People often like to look at and evaluate a product in private. When they are in a group they like to judge a product by discussing it in comparison with others. This often involves *criticism of the product* and therefore people want to do it in private, out of earshot of the salesperson. Typically people might wish to discuss the fact that a product is too expensive, of poor quality, or does not compare well with competitors' versions. In any case, these are things that people want to talk about among themselves. They do not want to share such criticisms with store staff.

For less-expensive items, for example clothing, usually only a moment of privacy is required. But for more costly items, such as furniture, people will usually require a greater amount of time. In fact, for very expensive purchases, such as automobiles or houses, people might take days or even weeks to make a decision. Here people often employ a wait-and-see strategy. They accomplish this by looking at items, then leaving the sales area altogether to discuss the purchase, and then returning to the sales area later. A closely related type of purchase is the one where the product remains under the supervision of the sales-person, such as buying jewelry enclosed in a glass case, where it is difficult if not impossible to steal a moment of privacy. The wait-and-see strategy is an excellent illustration of the lengths to which people will go to achieve an element of privacy in their conversations.

There are of course exceptions to the rule. Sometimes people will make a decision to purchase in the immediate presence of a salesperson. This practice is the exception, not the norm, and in most cases people prefer some privacy while pondering a purchase. Many people would assume that they often make shopping decisions in the presence of a salesperson. Even though a shopper may appear to do so, in many cases shoppers will actually make the decision to buy when they have a moment to collect their thoughts and/or discuss the purchase with the other person(s) with whom they are shopping. Experienced salespeople are aware of the need for privacy and will often excuse themselves for a moment to allow it.

Salespeople are notorious for invading privacy, especially by approaching groups of shoppers who are in the midst of what they feel is a private discussion of a product. The well-worn phrase "We're just looking" is often a signal that shoppers really just want some privacy. This strategy puts shoppers in a quandary when they really do want the help of the salesperson. By asking for that help, they often put themselves at risk of having the salesclerk linger, and thereby lose their privacy.

There is a whole interpersonal dynamic that takes place between salespeople and customers. It is an incredibly complex and exceedingly subtle relationship that could form the basis for innumerable psychological studies. The key element of the relationship is the appropriate mix of the salesperson's desire to provide sales assistance, balanced against the shopper's need for privacy.

Chapter 7

THE PASSIONATE SHOPPER

THE THRILL OF THE CHASE

A large part of shopping involves the thrill of the chase. Everyone has had the experience of getting emotionally involved with a potential purchase and being completely absorbed in tracking down and buying a product. A typical scenario involves a husband and wife who are looking to buy a major item such as a car, a boat, a cruise, a cottage, a motor home, a home theater system, and so on. Typically it is a major purchase, but one that is optional. It is a product for which they do not have an immediate or desperate need. Usually there are a series of steps involved in the purchase of such a product.

Initially we might consider where the idea to buy such a product comes from. Perhaps it originates with advertising; perhaps it comes about because a friend or relative has purchased the same product. Whatever the case, there is a preliminary desire to buy a new product—the seeds are sown, and it is only a matter of time before the idea for purchasing the product becomes a shopping reality. At the second stage, there is a period of superficial browsing. The couple does not go out of their way to look for the product, but they do show an interest in it when and wherever it is encountered. Their level of interest in the product slowly grows as more information is accumulated. They will also tend to seek out information from friends and relatives. At the third stage, there may be a period of time when interest in the product is high enough that the couple starts actively to seek out and search for the product and for additional facts. Thus they go out of their way to visit places where the product is available and start actively to look for further information. Once this stage is reached, their appetite is whetted, and the fourth and final stage of the process unfolds. This is when the couple is actively and wholeheartedly in pursuit of the product, to the point that the search may literally occupy almost all of their attention. Demand and interest levels are piqued and the couple is *driven* to pursue the product until the final purchase is completed. This fourth stage represents the experience that almost everyone has had—the thrill of the chase—followed by the actual buying experience. It is during this chase that shoppers put all of their energy into finalizing the process of buying the product.

The fourth stage of the shopping experience is intense. Emotions can be high. The shopper wants the product and can be desperate to acquire it. The shopping process suggests that the shopper can go past the point of no return. In other words, it can be said that at some point the shopper commits so much time and effort to the product search that a purchase becomes inevitable. There is no turning back. There is a mental commitment. Retailers should be aware that shoppers can reach this state of intense demand for a product, where a sale is virtually a foregone conclusion, if the buyer's basic demands can be met. Shoppers in this final and heightened state of shopping awareness are prepared to make the purchase and are almost frantic to do so. They are ready to buy and they desperately want the process to come to its inevitable conclusion.

No one can deny that a certain excitement level is reached when one is about to make a major purchase. If the retailer could measure the customer's heightened state of emotional arousal, he would be surprised to see that the customer is brimming with excitement and anticipation and probably has a higher-than-normal level of adrenaline. There is a thrill to buying a major product and, as much as people might like to deny it, they get excited emotionally when they make a major purchase. If the retailer can sense this emotional state he can tap into it and take advantage of the customer's elevated arousal level and weakened defenses. Normally, however, the consumer's raised level of shopping interest is difficult to discern and is not evident to the retailer.

From the retailer's point of view, an extra element of fascination in this shopping process is trying to gauge the shopping stage that a consumer has reached. Any given shopper may be shopping at any one of the four stages of the process, and the seller usually will not be quite sure where the mindset of the shopper lies. Nevertheless, if the retailer can estimate the level of the shopper, he or she can respond to the shopper accordingly. For instance, a shopper at the second stage wants only a brief look and cursory information about a product. Anything more than that may turn her off. Meanwhile, a shopper at the fourth, final, and ready-to-buy stage may have an almost insatiable thirst for product information. In this latter case the retailer should be ready to spend whatever time it takes with a customer who is close to making a buy.

Although this example has emphasized major purchases, there certainly exists a thrill-of-the-chase factor for many other products. People get just as excited when they find a particular item of clothing they have been looking for, or that special Christmas toy they have been pursuing. The thrill of the chase applies to all ages and all kinds of shoppers. It is a universal human feeling that is part of the shopping experience.

It is easy to make the argument that man is, at base, a hunter, and that very often shopping is a substitute for our basic instinct to hunt. There is no denying that human beings experience an increased level of exhilaration when they finally corner their shopping prey. And, once the hunt is completed, there is a sense of accomplishment and victory that is difficult to describe with words. How does one put into words the thrill of driving that new car off the lot, launching that brand-new boat, or taking possession of that new cottage? The point to be emphasized is that *these are intense emotional human experiences that result purely from the act of shopping*. There is nothing else quite like it.

The thrill of the chase can lead ultimately to the situation where the hunt itself becomes more important than the product being pursued. This may be especially true when people get caught up in a bidding war. Consider, for example, the situation where people are bidding against other people in the quest to buy a house, or even when people are bidding for a product at an auction. After a point the search for the quarry becomes such an intense competition that people lose sight of the product they are bidding for, and instead find themselves caught up in a bidding war that they are determined to win at almost any cost. The same kind of frenzy also grips people when they find themselves searching relentlessly for a simple product, whether it is a particular pair of shoes or an item of clothing that has been exceedingly difficult to find. The hunt becomes intense, so much so that the shopper becomes almost obsessive about finding the product. Who has not found themselves driving all over the city looking for that one particular item even when the effort has become totally exhausting?

There is an idea from psychology that applies here. Studies show that when people stand in line waiting for something for a long enough time they start to feel that they cannot leave the line. The idea is that they have so much time already invested in standing in the line that they are not about to give up that investment and quit. The same idea applies to the thrill of the chase in shopping. If someone is looking for a particular item they will invest time in the search. Once a substantial amount of time has been invested, shoppers will feel they have no course of action open to them except to continue the search until success is achieved. Everyone will have experienced this feeling of steadfast determination to find a particular item, regardless of how long it takes or how much effort needs to be invested.

THE BANDWAGON EFFECT

Have you ever found yourself buying something, like a bread maker or an espresso maker, because it is the latest rage and everyone else you know seems to be buying one? What about a treadmill or a Stairmaster? Have you ever found yourself buying a particular style of clothing because it seems to be what everyone is wearing? If you have done any of these things you are not alone. People chase popular trends and fashions and in doing so they follow the crowd.

One of the most important reasons that people buy things is because they are imitating the behavior of others. Men see a new style of vehicle on the street and this makes them want to buy it. Teens see all of their friends with a new style of shoes and they are envious—they want to own the same thing. Women see other women with an attractive new item of fashion and they are desirous of it themselves. People copy and imitate other people, and this is one of the primary motivators of shopping. We call this a *bandwagon effect*. The history of the idea is interesting.

In olden days a parade used to proceed down the street of a town, and one of the main components of such a parade was the appearance of a musical band playing on a wagon that was pulled along by horses. Crowds would gather and would follow along with the parade. Children and even some adults would clamor to hop on the bandwagon to become part of the parade themselves. Eventually people in the town were attracted not so much to the parade itself, but to the commotion and spectacle created by the crowd. Eager spectators would wonder what all the excitement was about and would follow the crowd, having been drawn to the excitement generated by the whole process. The event would get larger and larger, as more and more people joined in the chase.

The bandwagon effect is illustrated by the behavior of people who are attracted to a crowd and who follow along with it. People climb on board when there is a popular new fashion or style. In fact, it is the bandwagon effect that makes fads or fashion trends work. People see a demonstration of a product they are attracted to and some of them buy it. Still more people now see the new trend and still more buy it. This leads, in turn, to ever greater numbers of people seeing the trend and adopting it. What started with a few trendsetters can become a national or global trend as more and more people adopt it.

Ultimately, this snowballing effect of a new fad or craze is one of the more essential components of shopping behavior and is a big source of sales of most products. The key is that there is a demonstration effect at work. People see other people wearing or using a product—it appears to look good or work well—and they want it themselves. Demand is created by a copycat effect. People imitating friends, relatives, and strangers spurs sales.

Often demand is created for a product whether people really need it or not. New demand is fabricated in new marketing niches. The bread maker is a perfect example of this. Here is a product for which a huge national demand was created, and where market saturation has reached extremely high levels, yet before its invention no demand existed for it at all. It was a brand-new idea that caught on quickly, as everyone jumped aboard the home bread maker bandwagon.

One can imagine how the bandwagon effect works for a product like the bread maker. Consider a group of women who work together. An innovator in the group will be the first to get a bread maker. As she talks it up and boasts about its capabilities, others may be tempted to buy one for themselves. Soon there is a *group* of women talking about their bread makers, sharing recipes, trading cooking tips, and so on. Before long, other people in the group want to become part of the bread maker social circle and so they too buy the machines. Normally it will not take too long until everybody in the group owns one and is able to join in the socializing.

Having a bread maker, like many other products, signals that one is a member of the group and shares its interests. This is an important idea. It helps to explain *why* the bandwagon effect works as well as it does. People are not just attracted to the product that is the focus of interest; rather, they are attracted to the whole social and psychological atmosphere that the product creates.

The bandwagon effect is what drives fashion trends that are portrayed in the media. Magazines and television often serve to act as initial demonstrators in the hope that readers or watchers will start to adopt the trend that is illustrated. Fashion magazines and fashion editors, for example, go to great lengths to try to start fashion snowballs rolling that will eventually help the sales of their products. It is important to create a spin, to create an excitement about a particular product or product line, in the hope that it will catch on and become the catalyst for a fashion trend that will sweep the markets. For consumers it is about being in tune with style; for fashion houses it is about the bottom line—corporate sales and profits.

Jumping on the bandwagon of a particular fashion trend or style means conforming. It means following the norms for one's demographic. Teen fashion trends sweep the globe every few weeks, while adult ones swing by every few months. Millions of shoppers are always at the ready to join the latest initiative. An excellent example of this phenomenon was the fad of cargo pants that swept the teen and preteen worlds in 1999. For a time, it was virtually impossible to find a teen on the street, male or female, who was not wearing cargo pants at that moment in time. Literally millions of pairs of pants that were not cargo style were discarded in favor of the new style. Wearing the pants was not just a matter of keeping up with trends, however. It was also a matter of signaling that one was a member of a group, even if the group had fifty million teens in it. It was an exclusionary thing. Adults were excluded, as were the few teens who failed to grasp, or did not want to embrace, the trend. If nothing else, the cargo pant phenomenon pays testament to the shopping power and market significance of teens. They are able to discard perfectly good clothing in favor of new, in-style apparel. This says volumes about the economic significance of this demographic. It also says a lot about the apparent willingness of parents to pay the price to enable their children to keep pace with fashion and to keep abreast of the latest bandwagon trend.

There is a definite pattern to the way in which a population adopts new products. There is a well-known idea that says new trends and fashions go through three stages as they become popular. In the first stage, there is a slow pattern of adoption of a new innovation—just a few shoppers are buying it and these tend to be the leading edge, fashion trendsetters. Few retailers will stock the product and those that do are taking a chance that it will become a big seller. At the second stage, interest in the product literally starts to explode and hordes of people begin to buy the new product. Here, growth in sales is fast and retailers are hard-pressed to meet demand for this hot new product. Finally, there is a third stage in which market saturation takes place. Just about everyone who is going to buy the product has bought it and the keen interest in the product has started to wane. Retailers that were anxious to bring in supplies of the product suddenly find themselves overstocked and unable to move this merchandise that has reached the end of its shelf life. Generally, retailers are able to raise prices in the second stage, when demand is high, and must lower prices in the third stage, when consumer interest has fallen.

As an example of the three stages of life that many innovative products pass through, consider the children's phenomenon of Pokemon. Here was a product based in Japan that, in its infancy in the United States, was a novelty that a limited number of trendsetting consumers were aware of. Initially sales were slow and interest was limited. Suddenly the product became a hit, and sales took off. Kids just could not get enough of the Pokemon product. Retailers scrambled to stock shelves and manufacturers made Pokemon products of every imaginable sort. Finally came the saturation point, when everybody had had enough and the product lost its mass appeal. Sales fell off and buyers lost interest. Readers will be able to create their own lists of other such fad products: Cabbage Patch dolls, Beanie Babies, Furbies, and so on. In every case, the product follows the three-stage history that is typical of such items.

The same three-stage pattern applies to virtually every innovative product on the market. No one is more aware of the three-stage sequence than the average retailer who goes through this chain of events over and over again with almost every product that comes along. Fashion and clothing trends, vehicles, sports gear, designer labels, footwear, rock bands, rap groups, toys, and so on—the list is endless; almost everything that sells, goes through a product cycle of the type described here.

The bandwagon effect comes into play primarily at the second stage of the product cycle. Anxious shoppers have an unquenchable thirst for the latest innovative items, and there is almost a feeding frenzy as millions of people seek out the latest products. Many consumers, for example, will be aware of the furious shopping that comes into play as people search for that elusive but highly popular item that is in hot demand at Christmastime. Such is the nature of the bandwagon effect.

There are repeated waves of consumer demand for products, and retailers must be prepared to catch the wave if they want to be able to cash in on trends that wash by. The demand of shoppers for products is not a constant through time, but varies according to the stage that the product is at. From the shopper's point of view, waves of innovation make for interesting shopping. There is always something new or exciting to be looking for. No sooner does the consumer's interest in shopping wane, than along comes another innovative product to catch his eye. Every wave brings another demonstration of the bandwagon effect as people try to get on board with the latest hot trend.

IS SHOPPING ADDICTIVE?

Is shopping addictive? That's a good question. On the one hand, there are some shoppers who will look upon a major shopping expedition as a tiring event that is to be carried out as seldom as possible. These people may look at shopping as an enjoyable pastime, but at the same time they see major shopping occasions as situations where enough is enough. A big shopping trip is something they want to undertake only once in a while. On the other hand, there are undoubtedly other shoppers who just cannot get enough. These are the people for whom a major shopping trip serves only to whet the appetite for still more shopping, and where every trip leads to another. Thus there may be some shoppers who can be considered to be hooked on shopping, especially those who find that they just never are finished shopping—where there is always one more store or one more mall that just has to be visited.

It may be best to imagine that there exists a bell curve of shoppers where the majority, in the middle of the curve, are those normal shoppers who think enough is enough. This would include most average shoppers who probably take some pleasure from a major shopping trip but get tired of it after awhile. Although interested in shopping, they do not feel compelled to continue to "shop 'til they drop" and are able to put shopping in a proper, balanced perspective. These *bell curve* shoppers form the silent majority.

At one extreme end of the bell curve we find those people who utterly hate to shop. These are people who take absolutely no pleasure from shopping but find it instead to be a boring, mundane chore that has be carried out whether one likes it or not. These *shopping exiles* hate to be in stores and would rather do just about anything other than go shopping. There is no distinction among the sexes here. Men and women are equally likely to be unenthusiastic shoppers and little if anything will change this attitude. Often, when they shop, these are the run-and-gun shoppers who try to get in, get what they want, and get out again as fast as possible. They take no pleasure in browsing or just looking around and regard shopping as something akin to torture.

At the other end of the bell curve we find those shoppers who just love to shop. Shopping is their favorite pastime and they are always happy to do more of it. Everyone knows someone like this. They never tire of shopping but seem to literally thrive on an experience that most people find exhausting. These are the *super shoppers,* and there is little if anything that will stand between them and the next shopping opportunity. They love to shop.

What is it that drives the addicted shopper? For the super shopper, shopping becomes an end in itself. It is not the results of the shopping that matter—there are only so many things that a shopper can use or wear. Rather the very act of shopping—the searching and the finding of items—becomes the object of the shopper's attention. Really addicted shoppers can start to run out of things to buy and must sometimes start to shop for items for others. Such shopping is directed to finding things for friends or relatives. But the one thing that super shoppers can shop for almost endlessly is clothing. It does not matter how many clothes you have; you can always buy more. Thus addicted shoppers are able to shop for clothing, shoes, and accessories to their heart's content and are never at a loss for something else to shop for.

In extreme cases we get shoppers like the legendary Imelda Marcos, wife of the former leader of the Philippines. Imelda's extravagance as a shopper was revealed to the public when it was reported that she had collected 3,000 pairs of shoes, 2,000 ball gowns, 1,000 pairs of unopened tights, 200 girdles, and 500 bras. There exist all kinds of shoppers like this, perhaps not to the extreme of Imelda, but to the extreme nonetheless. How many people are there who have shoes, tops, shirts, suits, sweaters, and so on in numbers that are simply beyond reason? There must be a lot of them, and most of them, rather than admit their addiction, will go right on shopping for even more items. Thus we can identify two kinds of extreme shoppers. There are those who simply shop a lot and go to extremes when buying things. Then there are those who shop to extremes—who shop to the point that the number of things they have is indicative of a personality disorder that is manifested through shopping. The everyday super shopper does not have a problem. It is only the individual with the severe form of shopping affliction that may be in need of help.

Sometimes we all behave like addicted shoppers. This may be especially true around the holiday season when shoppers are looking for gifts for loved ones. What starts out to be an innocent shopping expedition for a few Christmas presents can easily turn into an obsessive quest to find more and better things, as the shopper strives to do his best to please friends and relatives. This effect is probably most true of parents shopping for Christmas presents for young children. In their desire to please their children, most people typically go overboard when it comes to

Christmas shopping. One or two days of shopping suddenly becomes weeks, and the shopping budget that was planned for goes out the window as the number of gifts and toys grows and grows. Almost every parent is guilty of excessive Christmas shopping at one time or another, and when they are in this state they can claim temporary addiction to shopping. Most people have experienced this and so know what it feels like to be addicted to shopping, if only for a short time.

THERE'S MORE TO BROWSING THAN MEETS THE EYE

Have you ever found yourself looking through a store at merchandise even though you have absolutely no intention of buying anything? If you have, you are not alone. Most everyone shops just for something to do. This is shopping as entertainment and it is probably one of the most common features of society. On occasion, everyone likes to browse and just look around. People are fascinated by the diversity and novelty of products available and can make an evening or afternoon out of shopping just for entertainment purposes. This form of shopping behavior is very important to retailers for two reasons. The casual shopper often ends up buying merchandise that he did not expect to buy. Most people cannot resist the lure of the innumerable products on display and frequently find themselves making an impromptu purchase. This form of *spontaneous shopping* is very enjoyable to most people and there is often a real pleasure in buying something for oneself even though the item is probably unneeded, or at least unplanned for.

All retailers are intimately familiar with the significance of walk-in traffic. The idea is that all consumers that just happen to innocently stroll through a store become potential customers. The greater the amount of traffic that one has moving through a store, the greater the amount of impulse buying that will take effect. There is no greater proof of the importance of browsing to the retailer than walk-in traffic. What the retailer should realize is that shopping for entertainment purposes easily turns into shopping for products, provided the merchandise displayed is able to grab the attention of the shopper. What grabs the attention of the shopper? Usually a display or product that is different or unique is enough to make people take a second look. The impulse buyer has to have her attention seized by something that is peculiar, uncommon, or just plain attractive.

Informal browsing is important because, whether they like it or not, consumers are taking a personal inventory of merchandise, and are therefore subtly planning for future purchases, every time they wander through a store. Thus a browser may see a shirt he likes and although he does not buy it immediately, it may enter his personal inventory as a likely future purchase. Browsing consumers not only become familiar with a store and its layout, but they also take stock of inventory and file it away for future reference. This is important. It says that the browsing, apparently indifferent consumer is very important and should be treated with the utmost care. Many times a consumer on a first pass through a store will simply be sizing up the place, its merchandise, and the sales staff. Once this browsing consumer has become familiar with the store, she is much more likely to make a return visit, if the store piqued her interest in the first place. Thus the browsing consumer is to be not only welcomed, but encouraged to go about just looking at merchandise. Most consumers like to reconnoiter a store before they mentally commit themselves to serious shopping there. This is true whether we are talking about a clothing store, an electronics store, or a grocery store. People gradually acquire a familiarity with a place and this increases their comfort level. In turn, an increased level of comfort means that purchases are more likely.

The message of shopping for entertainment purposes is twofold. First, the browsing consumer should be encouraged, if only for the reason that they may make an impulse purchase. Second, browsing is more than just looking. It implies taking stock and acquiring familiarity. Both of these are extremely important features of shopping. Seldom do consumers walk into a store or chain cold and make a major purchase. Many of them like to achieve a certain level of comfort and familiarity with a store before making the emotional commitment to buy something.

FLYERS, FLOATERS, AND AISLE RAGE

Some shoppers are on a mission. These are the active shoppers, the *flyers*. They know what they want and they are determined to get it. They have no time for browsing—there is a job to be done and they have a duty to accomplish it. They have a goal, an assignment. They even have a list. They get into the store, get what they want, and then they get out again. Shopping is a basic chore to be finished—a routine task that is treated as something to be completed as quickly as possible.

Some shoppers are *floaters*. They are the passive shoppers. They have no specific goals or desires. Their intent is merely to wander the aisles looking at the merchandise. They have plenty of time—they do not have anything else to do and they are not on a mission to accomplish anything in particular. They are happy to just be shopping. They stay in the store as long as they like, meandering about with no particular purpose. If you ask them what they are doing they say they are "Just looking around."

Flyers hate floaters. Floaters get in the way, they clog up the aisles, they stand around and they walk too slowly. Floaters always frustrate flyers. Flyers have a purpose and floaters always seem to be interfering with their ability to get their job done quickly. There is nothing more frustrated than an antsy flyer who is stuck in an aisle behind a dallying floater.

It is tempting to say that floaters and flyers have different personality types. One can imagine flyers having well-organized, well-kept houses where everything is in its proper place. All shopping needs are kept on orderly lists and items are replaced well before they are used up. These are the kinds of people you love to hate. Meanwhile, floaters can be imagined to have disorganized houses and disorganized lives. Shopping lists are the last things they would use. Floaters run out of everything and never have replacements on hand. Their lives are as disorganized as their shopping habits.

The truth of the matter is probably somewhere in between. Who among us has not dashed into a store to grab something in a hurry and found himself frustrated by slowpoke shoppers? At the same time, who has not been caught standing in the aisle, dawdling over some foolish item, only to incur the wrath of a frustrated flyer breathing down her neck? Everyone shops like a floater sometimes. Everyone shops like a flyer at other times. It is only when the two meet that the ultimate shopping conflict arises.

Floaters and flyers produce their own in-store special kind of frustration—*aisle rage*—the anger felt at being stuck behind slow-moving or immobile, ambivalent shoppers who coast along, plugging up the aisles and forcing faster shoppers into department store tailgating. For the impatient flyer, or just about any regular shopper, the glacially moving floater is a source of frustration, leading to dirty looks, sighs of disdain, and head-shaking contempt. For the floater—who has all the time in the world and is engaged in relaxed browsing—the rage of the flyer is usually unseen or else treated with indifference. It goes with the territory.

Short of widening store aisles, there is little that can be done about aisle rage. It is probably best regarded as a symptom of the times, when too many people have too many things to do and not enough time in which to do them. Aisle rage represents an overreaction to a common and largely unavoidable situation. Many instances of aisle rage result from the fact that the elderly sometimes do not move as fast as younger people would like them to. Most consumers who experience it would undoubtedly be better off to relax. It is, after all, just shopping.

HUNTING AND GATHERING

In prehistoric days, families managed to survive by carrying out two basic activities—hunting and gathering. Wildlife was hunted, while nuts, berries, fruits, and other edible flora were gathered. The modern family still hunts and gathers today, but this is accomplished in the form of shopping at the mall or grocery store. The behavior is much the same as it always was, that is, searching out and seeking cherished prey or desired items. It is truly amazing that much basic human activity remains almost exactly as it was thousands of years ago. Walking through the ancient bush picking fruits and berries was little different from walking down the aisle at the modern grocery store selecting fresh fruits and vegetables. In spite of mankind's protestations that he is a truly modern being, a great deal of his everyday activity is literally identical to that of his caveman ancestors.

There is one interesting way in which we can distinguish the hunting and gathering of the modern shopper from that of his forebears. Using the pyramid of shopping needs, it can be suggested that much shopping for everyday items—mostly items that are low on the hierarchy of needs—consists of gathering. When the modern shopper heads out to buy everyday items such as groceries, he or she can be said to be merely assembling the items in question. Not a lot of thought or energy goes into the process—it is simply a matter of picking up all of the basic necessities that are desired. Virtually every item that is desired is readily available. The choice of products in our society has become so all encompassing that seldom is there any desired product that the shopper cannot find. Usually such everyday shopping is also convenient to the shopper. The stores with such items are close at hand. Other than in the time expended, everyday gathering is a mostly mindless activity that is relatively easy to carry out.

Then there is hunting. The hunting of the modern shopper presents a whole other set of possibilities. Like his or her ancient ancestors, the modern hunter is in search of elusive prey. That perfect dress or pair of shoes. That perfect car or house. That perfect furniture or jewelry. Those perfect golf clubs. That new toy the kids want. The hunter is after something that eludes him. He must stalk his prey, intently tracking it down until it is finally found and captured. It is a difficult and time-consuming process. Sometimes it takes hours, days, weeks, or even months to find that perfect, evasive item. But like the hunter pursuing an animal, the shopper-hunter usually follows her quarry until she brings it down for the kill.

There are analogies to the caveman shopper. Unlike the shopper-gatherer, the shopper-hunter usually has to travel farther from the home base to find what he or she wants. More time, effort, and inconvenience are required. Unlike the gatherer, the hunter also requires a scent—a strong desire for some elusive product or item that he knows is out there. The hunter is more persistent—less willing to substitute one product for another, less willing to accept second best. There are few things in this world as tenacious as the determined shopper-hunter in search of her prey.

We have all had the experience many times. There is some particular item you want and either you know exactly what it is, or else you have a clear mental image of it. You do not go out shopping for such an item in the usual way you go to gather groceries. There is an extra dimension of tension and desire, a determination to find the item you are looking for, almost without regard to the time or effort it takes. How many of us have driven all over the city, looking for that one special item, at one time or another? Usually we persist in our efforts, sometimes to the point of exhaustion, in the hope of finding *exactly* what it is we are looking for.

A startling element of the shopper-hunter's approach to his target is that the cost of the item becomes less and less significant as the search continues. As people hunting for an elusive item get more and more desperate to find it, the amount they are willing to pay for the item usually continues to escalate. There is such a thrill in ultimately finding the product that the cost of it becomes secondary to the thrill of the hunt. How many of us have paid far more than we ever intended to for an item because, after a long search, we finally found what we had been so desperately seeking?

The clientele of most shoe, jewelry, or furniture stores for instance, would consist of hunters. Similarly, the customers of most grocery or drugstores are primarily gatherers. Many stores, however, fall in between the two extremes. Most department and big-box stores, for example, such as Wal-Mart and Price/Costco, can be seen to contain both hunters and gatherers at any given moment. Gatherers will roam the store with carts, stocking up on the necessities they want, while hunters will tend to be more directed in their efforts. They will forego a cart and will tend instead to shop with more precision, looking quickly for just the item they want, and moving on rapidly to another shopping venue. Gatherers tend to buy more, lower-cost items, while hunters buy fewer items that typically are more expensive. It is easier to please gatherers than it is to please hunters. Hunters are on the prowl for that perfect item.

For the fortunate hunter, there is a feeling of accomplishment when that elusive product has finally been found. The efforts of the hunt can pay off in a prosperous mission. There is a feeling of completion, and almost a sense of exuberance and exhilaration. The successful hunter returns home triumphantly with her trophy. For the unsuccessful hunter there is a feeling of failure and remorse. All of the effort goes for naught and the hunter returns home empty-handed. Everyone has experienced both sides of the hunt, and everyone knows all too well the intense emotions, both good and bad, that so simple an act as shopping can produce.

Chapter 8

EMOTIONAL REWARDS

SHOPPING IS EMPOWERING

Shopping puts people in control. Everyday shopping is largely about making decisions, and when people shop they make a multitude of decisions, thus gaining a feeling of power and of control. Consider the housewife or househusband who is on a routine grocery-shopping expedition. The entire trip through the store requires an endless stream of decisions and represents an opportunity to be in charge, to be the one making those decisions. Shopping puts the power of decision making in the hands of the shopper. And it does not matter whether the person is otherwise largely powerless in his life—in the store the shopper is king. Shopping can put power in the hands of people who do not otherwise have it. Shopping, in other words, is empowering, whether it is for everyday groceries or for buying a new house.

People grow up with the message that shopping provides power. The young child buying penny candy in a convenience store is empowered by the fact that she has money and is able to make purchasing decisions. In fact, this may be the first real experience in life where independent decision making, on a limited budget, takes place. It gives the child control of her purchases and puts the power of her money at her disposal. The 50-year-old clerk at the store responds to the child's wishes and bends to her demands. For the first time in her life the child has power over an adult, and the message is a strong one. Money provides power, and shopping provides the outlet where one can exercise that power.

All participants in shopping become decision makers. Whether the shopper is buying a pair of socks, a carton of milk, or a new vehicle, she must use her mental abilities to make a decision. That decision is usually a very complicated one involving a great many factors. Even in choosing a product as simple as milk, one must consider the size of the container, the type of container, the type of milk, the brand of milk, and the expiration date. All of these factors, as well as price, must be weighed in the brief moment in which the shopping decision is made. The more complex or expensive the product, the more complicated the decision. If simple milk is a complex product to buy, consider the number of factors involved in buying a house, car, or other major item. Not only must one gauge the product, its features, and its competitors, but one must also make such decisions in the context of their importance as major financial decisions. People sometimes agonize over big shopping decisions. Clearly, shopping presents one of the most difficult challenges that people face in their everyday lives.

The phrase we are all taught from childhood onward is that the buyer is always right. The implication is that the shopper has power. There are two forms of this power. In the first place, there is power over the shopkeeper or salesclerk. The interaction between the shopper and the salesman is such that the consumer is the one who is supposed to be in control. It is the shopper who should place demands on the salesclerk and who should dictate the course of the sales transaction. Of course, this is not always the case when it comes to pushy salesclerks and high-pressure salesmen. But by and large, the salesclerk is taught to demur to the customer's whims, wishes, and desires. If the customer wants to try on more clothes, drive another test car, or see another television, the salesman is usually happy to oblige in order to keep the customer happy and, eventually, make the sale. The power is in the hands of the customer, who holds the sword of the potential purchase over the salesman's head. This is especially true in those situations where the salesperson gets a commission when he or she makes a sale. This is also true whether the shopper is 7 years old or 70 years old.

But there is also another form of power in shopping. Being able to own the biggest, or best, or newest of anything has traditionally been associated with power. The logic of this relationship is easy. Wealth is power. That power is exercised through possessions. Wealthy people demonstrate their power and place in society by the results of their shopping. The wealthy usually have the biggest houses, the best furnishings, the most expensive vehicles, and so on. Shopping is the means whereby people are able to express their station in life through what they buy.

Whether one drives a brand-new Lincoln Navigator, or a 15-year-old Toyota Tercel, one is displaying one's financial accomplishments in life. A person's possessions are taken as one important measure of that individual's success in life, and whether we like it or not, wealth is ultimately equated with power. Thus the shopper also has power over the salesclerk by virtue of his assets.

Although the wealth of the shopper is not always evident to sales personnel, very often the means of the shopper can be estimated by the very nature of the products she looks at or the stores she frequents. The low-end shopper frequents the discount stores and bargain outlets looking for low-priced, everyday merchandise. Meanwhile, the high-end shopper patronizes shops that are upscale, in search of goods that are sophisticated and out of the ordinary. The everyday shopper fights the crowds. The sales staff is overworked, underpaid, and sometimes indifferent. At the same time, the wealthy shopper frequents expensive boutiques where the sales staffs are attentive, knowledgeable, and eager to please. The wealthy consumer is likely to buy more and spend more, and thus has the undivided attention of store staff.

Part of the logic of the power relationship in shopping comes from the idea of the commissioned salesman. Everyone has had the experience of the too-pushy salesman, and most people assume this means that the salesman is on commission. But what does the commission accomplish? In essence it *gives the shopper more power.* The salesman working on commission is at the beck and call of the customer: such a salesman is more anxious than others are to make the sale, and as a consequence this puts more power than normal in the hands of the shopper. Often the shopper sees a salesman on commission as being pushy, when in fact the customer should view such occasions as a chance to exert greater than usual control over sales personnel. Of course, this is easier said than done, but the fact remains that the commissioned salesperson is more desperate to make a sale and should be seen as such.

Perhaps the best example of the way in which shopping is empowering is seen in the low- to middle-income shopper. This is the average couple who both have regular jobs where they carry out the same repetitive tasks from day to day. It may be a boring job but it earns a decent income, puts food on the table and earns its owner a healthy measure of self-respect and pride. Most such working people take orders from someone else all day long, every day, and are seldom put in any position of decision-making authority. For such people, life consists of a job where the boss is king. But there is a major exception to this rule. The one big exception is shopping. In the evenings and on weekends when it comes time to shop, the regular working man or woman is suddenly given the power to make decisions. Some of these are small, and others are large, but shopping gives the average working person a chance to be in control and make important decisions. This is the primary empowering capability of shopping and its significance should not be overlooked. Shopping levels the playing field and gives everyone the power to become important.

A case in point is found in the teenager who is shopping for clothes, shoes, and accessories. When these teens are younger their clothing is purchased for them, and chosen for them, by their parents. But there comes a time when preteens start to want to buy their own clothes and, more importantly, want to start to make *their own decisions.* Part of the blossoming life of the young preteen comes from *attaining the power* to do one's own shopping. This is usually a difficult time in life for adults and children alike. Parents who have always traditionally been in control of what their children wear suddenly find themselves faced not only with a rebellious preteen but also with a loss of decision-making power. Children wrench this power from their parents whether the parents like it or not. It is part of growing up. Similarly, children who have always been dressed by their parents start to resent the lack of control they have over how they look and start to resist the power of their parents in deciding what they will wear. Battles ensue. Although these often appear to be about clothing and appearance, they are actually about power. Who has the power to decide what will be worn, the parent or the child? Right or wrong, the preteen wants the *power* to make his or her own shopping decisions. He or she wants this measure of independence from parental control. *The clothes themselves are secondary*—the main point is for the preteen to begin to earn his or her independence as an adult by making his or her own clothing-shopping decisions.

There are not many areas of life in which a preteen or teen can assert independence or make decisions. They are surrounded by authority figures, such as parents and teachers, virtually every minute of the day. Their life is highly structured and seldom do they get to express themselves as individual and unique human beings. Yet they are at a stage in life when this is very important to them. They are searching for the means to be able to declare themselves as unique and important people who are not just clones of their parents' desires. They want to become individuals. Shopping lets them accomplish this.

Little children wear exactly what their parents want them to, and so are just reflections of how their parents see them as people. Their choice of dress has little to do with how they see themselves. Preteens break free of the shackles of their clothing servitude by rebelling against the control that their parents exert and by making their own shopping and dress decisions. In the highly constrained life of the teen and preteen, clothing is one area where individual expression is maximized. This is one of the few areas where the teen is able to declare, "This is me. This is who I am as a unique individual." This is very important in life, and adults, teens, and retailers alike should be aware that it is an essential component of growing up. This is not just shopping—this is a crucial part of the transition from childhood to adulthood. It is one of the most important reasons for shopping.

Advertisers would be well advised to take this perspective into account when they target preteen and teen audiences. The message should be that buying a certain product is not just about fashion; rather, it is an assertion of personal independence. In a life that is otherwise highly structured, clothing, shoes, and accessories should be marketed as items that provide the means to assert oneself as a person, rather than as a clone of one's parents.

In order for parents to understand the teen's point of view, one need only remind adults of the freedom and power they have with their own shopping. If adults get the urge to purchase a particular piece of clothing for any reason whatsoever, they are usually free to do so. They are free to open their wallets and make a very personal decision about what to buy and what to wear. Imagine if those same adults could only buy or wear what someone else approved of—and that someone else had very different ideas about what they should wear. Teens and preteens are looking to have the same freedom to choose that adults have. Wise parents should remember that when it comes time to do battle over clothing, teens are simply looking for the same freedom that they themselves already have.

From the retailer's point of view, the empowerment of shopping should be seen as a powerful aphrodisiac to the consumer. Put the buyer in charge; make him feel important and at the center of power. Make him feel like it is his turn to make a big decision and that the power of the situation rests in his hands. *Shoppers like to feel the power at their disposal*—they do not want to be treated like they are inconsequential—and anything the retailer can do to empower the shopper will surely add to the shopping experience and the likelihood of a successful transaction. This is true whether we are talking about the sale of a minor item or a major purchase.

The classic example of a shopping situation in which the customer likes to feel empowered is the usual dickering that goes on when someone is buying a vehicle and coming to a price on it. It is standard practice, of course, that the sticker price on a vehicle is not the real price and that it is necessary to bargain with the salesperson to arrive at a deal. Surprisingly, surveys of car buyers show that they *prefer* to dicker over prices, rather than just pay a price as listed. To the crafty car salesman, the essence of the dickering process is to make the customer feel that he has won the bargaining process. This is accomplished by giving in to the customer's demand for a better price and by letting him believe that the price he is getting is very good, that it's just above the break-even price, that it's the best deal that the manager can give, or that not everybody gets a deal like this. Whatever the scenario used, the point is to make the consumer feel like he got the best of the salesman in the deal, regardless of the price he actually pays. Savvy cars sellers start high and leave themselves lots of room to cave in to the customer's quest for a good deal. The process empowers the consumer and makes him believe that he bested the salesman. The important idea is that the customer is made to feel that he prevailed—that is, that he succeeded in outmaneuvering or outwitting the salesman. He walks away as a happy customer.

SHOPPING AS BELONGING

Sociologists tell us that one of the important human needs is to feel a sense of belonging to one or more groups in life. Thus the average person may feel that they belong to a number of groups such as with coemployees, with social groups or friends, with community groups or sports teams, with neighbors, and so on. In essence, we all belong to a number of different social groups and the sense of belonging and camaraderie that is created is important to our mental well-being. Shopping is a key to many group memberships, whether they are formal or informal, and a big part of the feeling of belongingness that people need is often achieved through buying things.

Very often membership in a group implies that it is necessary to *purchase* items to establish affiliation with that group. There are many subtle and not-so-subtle ways in which people establish group membership, but almost all of them involve the purchase of something. Consider membership in a sports team, athletic club, exercise group, and so on. Items such as clothing, equipment, or membership fees usually need to be purchased in order to belong to the group. For instance, a man who is a member of a sports team will need to acquire equipment, a uniform, and perhaps a team jacket to become part of the group. He will also probably need to pay user fees or membership dues to be able to participate in an activity. Thus, group membership comes at a price and usually part of that membership requires the purchase of several things. Similarly, a woman who is a member of an aerobics class will need to purchase appropriate work-out clothing and will need to pay a membership fee in order to become part of the group.

Sometimes membership in a group is defined by the very things that the participants own. Car clubs, gun clubs, model clubs, craft clubs, and so on are associations where ownership of the appropriate equipment or materials is essential to participation in the group. Group identity comes from belonging to a collective with shared interests, but more important than the interests themselves is the sense of belongingness and camaraderie that is created. Thus, owning certain things, and buying certain things, ultimately leads to the achievement of a feeling of membership in a social group. Shopping for these items is a means to an end.

There are many more subtle and interesting ways in which people purchase group membership. One of the more important ones comes through the way in which people dress. For instance, in the working environment of an office, there is usually an unwritten dress code for employees. People usually follow such an informal dress code rigorously, and by so doing they define group membership for themselves. Employees at different levels of seniority may define their different group membership by their dress code. For example, men in middle-level management may find it adequate to wear a tie and sports coat, while upper-level managers may find it appropriate to wear suits. This type of dress code behavior creates an environment where group membership is quite clearly defined by the clothing people wear. Lines of authority and communication reflect the boundaries set out by the different clothing styles.

Clothing defines group membership much more broadly than just within the confines of the workplace. All people define themselves and their group memberships by the way they dress. In extreme cases, one can imagine members of motorcycle gangs or religious sects where group membership is clearly defined by the style of clothing that members wear. The same is true, more or less, of everyone. People define their place in life, and their group affiliations, by the way they dress. Shopping for and purchasing particular clothing entitles one to informal membership in a group. This is true whether one considers a group of men playing golf or fishing, a group of women playing golf or hosting a baby shower, or a group of teens going to a movie together. In all of these cases, there is a commonality of dress code that makes the wearers feel that they belong to the group they are with. This feeling of belongingness is very important in life and is brought about in large part by the clothing, shoes, and accessories that people purchase everyday.

There are many levels for which shopping time is invested in creating a sense of belongingness. Most people belong to a large number of different groups, both formal and informal. The middle manager who dresses her role at work may belong to a fitness club and a sports team in the evenings, and she may also belong to a community association and a church choir on the weekend. Every one of these activities requires a different and unique dress code, and shopping effort will be expended to satisfy the demands of each group.

The idea of shopping to belong applies demographically as well. People often try to dress their age or at least try to dress according to the unwritten rules for their age group. Most people, most of the time, endeavor to dress like their peer group and try to follow the rules for their demographic. At the same time, however, there are some people who attempt to demonstrate that they belong to a younger age group by the clothes they wear and the things they buy. Who has not noticed the middle-aged adult who tries, usually unsuccessfully, to dress like a teenager? The goal of such a cross-dresser is to redefine him- or herself as belonging to a younger demographic than is the case. One of the more common occurrences of this crossing of the demographic boundaries occurs when older or middle-aged shoppers strive to buy things—like sports cars—that make them feel that they belong to a younger age group. This kind of shopping behavior is very common and is indicative of the shopper trying to belong to a group that is outside of the realm of what is normal for his age. Similarly, one can imagine teens, especially girls, who try to look older than they really are by the way they dress. This is another good example of people trying to belong to a different demographic group.

WHEN HIGH PRICE IS IMPORTANT—THE BEAMER EFFECT

In spite of most shoppers' desires to find bargains and save money, there is also another psychology to shopping. This is found in the quest of some shoppers to spend larger amounts of money than necessary. There are a large number of products that are vastly overpriced. We all know what they are. Designer shirts that cost $500. Sunglasses that cost $300. Cars that are $100,000. Fragrances that are $200 a bottle. And so on. Everyone knows that such products are overpriced, yet there is huge demand for them. It is almost as if the usual laws of economics were reversed, so that the *more expensive* the item is, the greater the demand for it. There is a simple explanation for this phenomenon; we call it the *Beamer Effect.*

The Beamer Effect says that overpriced products are attractive to people because they come with bragging rights. The owner of a BMW does not buy the car primarily for its performance advantages or other features. The principle reason to own such a car is for the bragging rights that it produces. It is a luxury item. More importantly, it is a status symbol. The high price is in fact an important part of the mystique of owning the product. The product carries a certain aura about it because everybody knows it is expensive. And that's the reason for the owner wanting to own it in the first place. Buying a BMW enables him to flaunt his wealth, to boast about his success, and to demonstrate his prosperity. Multiply that phenomenon by the hundreds of such products on the market and you have the Beamer Effect in its full glory.

Not all products have the Beamer Effect. There is a limited set of brand names that are able to carry it off. Many of the brand names are well known; with automobiles, the brands include Lincoln, Cadillac, Lexus, BMW, Mercedes, Audi, and so on. With perfume there is another such list. For clothes there is another. For sports equipment there is still another. And so on. Adults can recite the names for adult products, and teens can recite them for teen products. Every age group has its own set of Beamer Effect products.

Companies that carry out market research have as one of their specific goals to discover the brand names that carry enough of a mystique to be able to pull off the Beamer Effect. Many products aspire to this level of accomplishment but not that many attain it. It is very difficult to launch a new, high-end, outrageously high-priced product and have it capture the fancy of the buying public. But it happens all the time. There are always new products coming on board, if only for a limited time, that are simultaneously shockingly priced and in high demand. The Lexus is a good example of a relatively recent product that achieved this goal.

Interestingly, the Beamer Effect works with some products but not others. For example, it is quite conceivable that a particular brand of perfume be positioned in the market so as to have the Beamer Effect. A designer-label name, together with an extremely high price for a very small amount of perfume, is a well-known and everyday occurrence of the Beamer Effect at work. But if a company were to try the same thing with a musical CD, the effort would fall flat. Imagine a big-name musical group trying to charge double the usual price for its latest CD. The Beamer Effect just would not work. Why not? The effect only works when the product is *perceived* to have a difference or mystique that sets it apart from the competition. An expensive pair of designer jeans, an exotic sports car, or a costly perfume can be seen to have properties that set them apart from the competition, whether they really do or not. The difference is not in the product, but in the mind of the consumer, who wants to believe that there is some justification for paying the outrageously high price that is associated with the product. A $200 Ralph Lauren shirt is perceived to be a better shirt than its $20 counterpart at Wal-Mart, even though the actual quality may be the same. Beauty, they say, is in the eye of the beholder, and so too is the perceived quality of many consumer items. Teens will willingly pay $300 for designer-name sunglasses because they really, truly believe—they have a genuine perception—that the product is better than its $30 competitor.

This genuine belief in the mystical qualities of the Beamer-type product is given further impetus by the fact that those products impart power to their owners. That Ralph Lauren shirt is expensive so it must be good. The buyer who buys that shirt shows off not only his ability to afford such products but also his supposed shopping astuteness. There are bragging rights not only to the shopper's wealth and prosperity but also to his shopping acumen. The teen who buys Oakley sunglasses is just as concerned about making a statement as the middle-aged buyer of a Rolex watch. Both products say something about the shopping intelligence and economic success of their owners, and that is just what their owners want them to say.

The Beamer Effect is one of the most interesting elements of shopping. As was indicated above, part of the mystique of Beamer-type products is carried in the reputations they carry. A key ingredient in this is that almost *everyone* must be aware of the name of the product for the effect to work. And there are all kinds of products in existence whose reputation is well known. In fact, the very value of many products is linked solely to their reputations.

Is a Mercedes automobile, for example, really worth the price its owners pay, or are they really paying for the reputation behind the name? Everyone knows a Mercedes is expensive, and that is part of the very attraction of owning one. When its owner climbs in, what does he feel? Is there a sense of self-worth and personal satisfaction? Is there a sense of wealth and success? Is there a sense of superiority and accomplishment? The answer to all of these questions is a resounding "yes." But one wonders how a simple automobile can achieve all of these things for its owner. The answer is that the Beamer Effect is much more than just an outward statement of success and wealth. It is also a way in which people measure their lives.

Products are often classified according to their functions. Cars serve a transportation function, while sunglasses serve the function of protecting the eyes against the harsh rays of the sun. But what is the true *function* of a Mercedes car or a pair of Oakley sunglasses? It would appear that the time has come to define anew what we mean by the function of a product. Beamer-type products clearly serve a higher function than is implied by their basic uses. Thus the function of expensive designer cologne, or costly brand-name sports gear, is only partly to serve the practical use for which it was intended. The primary use of such products is *to serve the emotional needs of their users.*

This is an important concept because it changes our perception of the role of products away from the physical needs that they satisfy to the psychological needs that they fulfill. The essence of shopping for many products has little or nothing to do with their physical usefulness as consumer durables and everything to do with their use as psychological accessories. This is an evolutionary concept in shopping and one that cannot be emphasized too strongly. It says that the consumer walking into a store or a showroom is not really always looking for a physical product, but rather is looking to buy a form of emotional support and assistance.

These are important concepts. Although retailers may wish to stop short of putting a sign outside the store that says "Emotional Accessories on Sale," the main point is to emphasize that the shopper is often after something that is not immediately obvious to the seller. Advertisers and retailers have to be more cognizant of, and more responsive to, the psychological needs of their customers. How much is an emotional accessory worth? What's a fair price for the psychological well-being of a customer? How can the subconscious needs of the shopper be satisfied? How do you sell a customer psychological support? How do you know when a customer is looking not for a product, but for emotional sustenance? These are the new kinds of questions that the modern advertiser and retailer need to ask.

The answer to many of the questions raised above is contained in the very products the retailer is selling or the advertiser is promoting. An advertiser should not be so naïve as to believe that a customer buys a Lexus because of its practical automotive features. A retailer should not expect that a customer buys $200 perfume because she likes the smell. When a customer is contemplating the purchase of a Beamer-like product, there is a message in the very act of shopping. The customer says by his actions that he is shopping to fulfill the psychological needs that the product satisfies. For the retailer, this implies that the product should be promoted on the basis of its *emotional features* rather than its practical ones.

A case in point is found in the current promotion of high-end vehicles. The popularity of traditional vans and sedans has fallen as people have shown greater interest in sporty trucks and sport-utility vehicles. In fact, the automotive industry has taken to calling the latter "lifestyle vehicles." The sales pitch becomes one that focuses on the lifestyle associated with the vehicle rather than with the vehicle itself. Customers are led to believe that the vehicle they own says something about their personality and the kind of life they lead. This is a profound idea, for it says that the features of the product itself are secondary in importance and that the buyer is really *purchasing a statement about his lifestyle.* The president of the Center for the Study of Automotive Transportation at the University of Michigan sums up this point of view when he says this about lifestyle vehicles: "They say that you like to go hiking on trails, for instance, even if you never do." The Beamer Effect says that retailers can charge premium prices for such lifestyle vehicles because they are selling more than an everyday, practical product. Just as with the Mercedes, the Lexus, and the BMW, they are selling a product that directs itself primarily to the psyche of the customer.

CLOTHING IS PERISHABLE

Sometime in 1999, all of the light blue, faded denims in all of the teen closets of the entire world expired. It was almost as if all of those blue jeans had an *expiration date* on them—"Best before year 2000"—and all of the teens decided at once that they would throw away the defunct product and replace it with dark blue denim. This was an amazing event in its scale and its degree of widespread acceptance. It was a major coup by the fashion industry. Literally millions of pairs of denims were suddenly tossed aside for no other reason than that a strong current of fashion suggested that it be done. It became *entirely* inappropriate, almost immediately, for anyone under twenty to be seen in faded blue jeans.

Usually when people think of perishable items they think of things such as milk, meat, and vegetables. The blue jean event is the best indicator that we should also think about clothing, shoes, and accessories as being perishables. When an item of clothing gets too old it is seen to have outlived its shelf life and, just like a bunch of overripe bananas, is relegated to the scrap heap. The mass expiration of the blue jeans is just one dramatic indicator of the idea that clothing has a limited life span and is regarded, when purchased, as an item that goes beyond its "best before" date.

Years ago, many items of clothing were used until they were worn out. Pants would be patched, socks would be darned, and clothes would be handed down from one sibling to another. Not anymore. As affluence has increased, and especially as the fashion industry has hit its stride, the idea that clothing should be used until it is actually worn out has become obsolete. Everyone, young and old alike, has closets full of expired clothes, items that have seen daylight for the last time. Nowadays all clothing has a limited shelf life. Even socks and underwear have achieved a sense of style and fashion that is unprecedented in the industry.

People of all ages will pay incredibly high prices for clothing without regard to shelf life. Teens and adults are willing to pay hundreds of dollars for a new coat or pair of shoes, for instance, even though they know they will last for only a year. Such purchases indicate quite clearly that it is the sense of fashion that the item declares that is far more valuable than its practical worth as an item of clothing. Smart marketers are able to convince people to buy their high-priced product because their brand name implies high quality, even when it is obvious that the items purchased will be retired long before they are put to any practical test of their quality.

It helps to assuage the guilt of throwing away perfectly good clothing if people have a ready outlet for their used, or expired, clothing. Organizations such as the Salvation Army and other similar groups help to alleviate the guilt by providing a place where people can dispose of otherwise perfectly good clothing. Similarly, having friends or relatives who will accept hand-me-downs is easier for most people to accept than taking those expired clothes and throwing them in the garbage.

People do not like to admit that clothing expires. It makes their purchasing decisions seem like mistakes. What could be worse than to have to admit that those $200 shoes one is buying will simply be valueless in six months? When one is making a purchase it is most important to feel happy with the decision *at the moment the choice is made.* The future is not an issue. The truth of the matter is that when people are buying things they often do not consider the longevity of the item in their purchase. This is another important key for manufacturers and retailers. It says that while an appearance of durability and quality may seem to be important product virtues, in the long run most shoppers reach their shopping decision *based on the emotions of the moment,* not according to the product's fashion expiration date.

Not just clothing is perishable. All items have a sense of style or fashion, and so all such items have a limited shelf life. For teens, a brand of bicycle may expire, while for an adult, a video camera may go past its socially acceptable date. Even big-ticket items like furniture and houses expire. Manufacturers and builders are constantly updating their products in an endless effort to make older models look obsolete. Take automobiles for example. Clearly, those cars on the street that are ten years old have "expired" written all over them. The manufacturers want them to look old and out of style, and they have been doing their best to accomplish this goal for 60 years now. One need only look back at the changing and extinct fashions of the last 40 years to see how virtually everything has an expiration date. Shag carpet, record players, eight-track tapes, mini skirts, and all the rest have paraded by in an endless stream of product obsolescence.

People like the fact that purchased items expire, especially clothing. It gives them an excuse to shop. Wouldn't it be boring if you had to wear clothing until it wore out? The manufacturers and retailers do their best to accommodate the enthusiastic shopper. Every season brings a new line of clothes, in new styles and colors. One's wardrobe has to be updated to stay in tune with the times. Boots, shoes, coats, jewelry, accessories, hairstyles, and formal wear—everything runs past its prime and into the fashion abyss. People just keep buying and shopping, in the endless cycle of chasing the ever elusive goal of keeping up with popular fashion. All purchases should be looked upon as temporary and fleeting. One is buying primarily the temporary sensation that the item creates, rather than the item itself.

Chapter 9

SHOPPING IN THE DEMOGRAPHIC STAGES OF LIFE

Shopping is a behavior that people carry out in order to define themselves as human beings, but at different stages of life, people will have different priorities about what is important to them. In fact, it is possible to identify the life stages at which different demographic groups have different shopping needs and desires. Every age group has preferences that are unique to it. Identifying those demographic preferences is an important component of understanding the concept of shopping as a form of defining the self. It is also a very important aspect of retailing and advertising.

By understanding demographics, predictions can be made about what people will do, where they will go, how they will shop, and what they will buy. Knowing that a group of shoppers is male and 45 years of age tells us something important about them. If they are busy executives at midcareer we can guess that they do not have a lot of time to spend on shopping but that they do have a pretty good income. Such information provides some key insights for the retailer or the advertiser that is hoping to target this group of shoppers. Similarly, predicting the behavior of shoppers is easier if we know they are female and 16 years old. That tells us that these are shoppers who are primarily interested in clothing, fashion, and entertainment. It also says that they do not have a lot of money for shopping but they do have a lot of time for it. Simple age and sex tell us a lot about how shoppers will shop, and about how the retail market should be targeting itself toward them.

WOMEN SHOPPERS

If there is any one point that needs to be made with respect to the demographics of shopping, it is that about 75 percent of all shopping is carried out by women. Various studies show that this is the norm for shopping of all kinds, and especially mall shopping. Why is this so? What does it mean?

The stereotypical role of males and females is that the male is the hunter and the female is the gatherer. The logic of this arrangement is that in prehistoric days the women needed to stay closer to home and the children. There is perhaps also an argument that women lacked the testosterone needed to be successful, competitive hunters. This is the folklore that dates from the days of earliest human settlement. Move forward in time to the 1950s, and the same kind of pattern still held. Women tended to stay home, tend to the children, and do the shopping. The simple explanation was that they had more time available to carry out these duties. Men went to work. Fast-forward to the early twenty-first century and what do we find? Most women are in the workforce, holding down full-time jobs, but at the same time, in most relationships they are still expected to carry out most of the shopping duties as well. This is not surprising, considering that almost all studies of domestic life show that women also continue to carry out most of the other household chores, just like their sisters from the 1950s. Apparently, the same rules apply to shopping as to the other household tasks. Whether it is shopping for clothing, groceries, or everyday household needs, it is up to the woman, in most cases, to get the job done.

Shopping is one of those issues in a relationship that rarely gets resolved. Even though the woman might dislike being imposed upon with almost all of the shopping duties, she knows if she does not do it, it will not get done. Shopping falls into the same category as doing the laundry or cleaning the bathroom. Most men just will not take a hand in these jobs, and, just like their fathers, they leave it up to women to get them done.

When do men get involved in shopping? For the most part, we can suggest that this seems to occur when big decisions need to be made. If the household is buying a car, a major electronic appliance, or other such major item, then hubby involves himself in the decision making and the shopping. When less important shopping decisions are being made, about groceries and cleaning supplies, for example, the man is content to let the woman make the choices. This is a highly sexist approach to shopping but one that seems to be the norm for most couples. Men do 25 percent of the shopping, so there are lots of them out there buying diapers and cleansers, but by and large the majority of men leave everyday shopping chores up to women.

CHILDREN AND SHOPPING

In childhood, self-definition comes through one's parents. Primarily by the clothing they buy, parents try to define their children as human beings. This starts in infancy, with the traditional distinction between pink and blue clothing. Thus even when children are just a few days old, parents start to define their children's lives through the manner in which they dress them and shop for them. The pattern continues. Even infant clothes can carry messages, for example, of sports or learning, that may indicate the early desires and goals of the parents. Shopping for these items becomes more than an exercise in wishful thinking on the part of the mother and/or father. It also sends a clear message to other people about how the infants are seen in the eyes of their parents.

Beyond clothing, children's lives are most certainly defined by the other things that their parents buy for them. This shopping is not just about acquiring needed items; it is about defining little human beings. By their purchases, parents make conscious or unconscious decisions about the direction that they hope their children's lives will follow. Do they emphasize educational toys or sports toys? Do they focus on toys for the mind or toys for the body? Shopping is about defining the self, but in the case of parents, it is about defining their children. Parents express their very deepest desires for their children through the things they buy, even though most of the things they purchase may often appear, on the surface, to be just toys. The importance of this behavior should not be underestimated. Shopping for infants and young children is very much an effort at trying to define personality.

An interesting aspect of parents' shopping for young children is the amount of money that parents are willing to spend. Very often this will reflect not only the income level of the parents, but also their level of concern with being in style. At one extreme are the parents who try to economize on their children's clothing by buying at discount or department stores and by buying non–brand names. At the other extreme are the parents who buy only at specialty stores and buy exclusively the latest in designer names and labels. What is the message the designer-label parents are trying to convey? The children are too young to understand the consequences of their clothing, so in addition to the obvious message of ostentatiousness, such parents must also be endeavoring to impart a sense of their own fashion awareness. Designer-label clothing on young children sends a message to *other adults* about the extent to which *the parents* are in-vogue with fashion. It is an extension of the self—it is dressing the children for one's own self-definition, rather than for the children themselves.

Parents also try to define the lives of young children through the entertainment, and especially movies, that they purchase for them. A significant part of the movie business revolves around young children's movies, and parents are anxious to indulge their children in the fare that is offered. There's more to this than just seeing the movies because that could wait for the video or television release. Rather, there is a tradition of young parents taking young children to the movies, apparently reflecting a desire on the part of the parents to recreate something that they themselves experienced as children. Moreover, there seems to be a belief that seeing the movie classics somehow creates well-rounded children. Movie retailers should be aware that parents are not just taking their kids to a movie. Rather they are buying *the experience of the movie theater.* By this experience, parents are striving to give their children pleasure and to define them as people. The urgency with which parents approach these goals is witnessed by the fact that very often parents take very young infants to children's movies well before they are able even to comprehend them.

The same line of thought follows with the purchase of other forms of children's entertainment. Whether it is the Ice Capades, a concert by a child entertainer, or a trip to Disney World, the parents' purpose is to give the child all the possible benefits of life by exposing them to as much entertainment as possible. These experiences are also seen to shape and mold the child's development as a person, and buying them is seen to be a crucial part of child rearing. Sellers of such children's entertainment emphasize the educational and experiential value of the event rather than the amusement aspect of it. That's what parents are shopping for. With young children's entertainment, parents are also competing with other parents. They do not want their children to be the only ones on the street who have not been to Disney World. Just like themselves with other parents, they want their children to be able to compete successfully with other children in terms of the bragging rights to events.

PRETEENS AND SHOPPING

At a very young age, children start to want clothing that is in style. In fact, other children at school will literally make fun of them if their clothing is not in tune with current fashion. This helps to explain why even young children can seem so desperate to have particular clothing. To the parents, the premium prices to be paid for brand-name clothing can seem absurd, but to the young child, such clothing can mean the difference between being accepted at school and being a social outcast. The fashion industry has done an exemplary job of creating brand awareness in even very young children and their parents, and the demand thus created prods even the youngest children to look for designer labels. It represents capitalism at its best, and at its worst. Parents are driven to search for whatever their children want in order to satisfy the huge pressures placed on children to conform to fashion norms. This is modern shopping at its finest. The shopper, with child in hand, shops for brand names, and especially fashion labels. Quality, value, and price become secondary to style and fashion, and parents and children alike are willing to pay virtually any price to achieve fashion goals. Smart retailers are aware of this phenomenon and are more than willing to take advantage of it. Shopping to define the self, even at a young age, implies that *perception is more important than substance.*

Some parents face a seemingly endless struggle with young children and preteens over what is and is not acceptable clothing. If it is not a struggle over style, then it can often be a battle over paying high prices for clothing that is otherwise available at a discount. Such parents cannot see the sense in paying double to get an item with a designer label on it, while most children just will not tolerate anything less. On the other hand, many parents are anxious to indulge their children's fashion desires and are more than willing to pay a premium price to ensure that their children are happy about their clothing.

Unlike teenagers, young children and preteens are not all that concerned about defining themselves as human beings. Rather, the focus is just on being in style, where that style is often dictated by heroes in the media or by older teenagers. Although there are certainly some children and preteens who are concerned about projecting an image to adults, most of them are concerned primarily about how they look to their peers. Having a sense of fashion means blending in at school and among friends, and conforming to trends. Gone are the innocent days of childhood of the pre-designer-label era. Young children have been made very brand aware by advertisers and retailers, and never before have their been such pressures to conform to fashion at such early ages. As most parents are well aware, kids know what they want. Far from being the innocent young children of the past, preteens are now among the most demanding shoppers. Imitations and knockoffs will not do. Clothing has to be *exactly right,* whatever the cost and whatever the effort required.

When it comes to shopping for entertainment, children and preteens are at an awkward age. Parents still want to define for them what they should see and do, hoping to foster an environment of wholesome and healthy enjoyment. Parents see them as little children and want them to be entertained accordingly. The kids, however, have other ideas. They want to start to go to more grown-up events, such as teen movies or rock concerts, and are embarrassed to be seen with their parents at Disney-type movies or events. As the children head into the teen years and start to want to define themselves through their activities, the parents struggle with the transformation that takes place. The children are becoming shoppers in their own right, and it is with movies and entertainment that they first start to make their own, self-defining choices. Teen idols and teen movie stars become extremely important in marketing entertainment to this young group that just cannot wait to grow up.

THE TEEN DEMOGRAPHIC

Everyone would agree that teenagers seem to be obsessed with their clothing. Why is this so? Most people would simply say that it is a stage that teens go through. In fact, there are good reasons for the obsession with clothing, not the least of which is that for the first time in their lives teens are starting to define themselves as people without the guidance, or interference, of their parents. As teens set out to establish themselves, and by so doing start to break free from the control of parents, their very first opportunity to express themselves as individuals comes through choosing their own clothing. Thus, teen clothing represents much more than style, fashion, or fad. In truth, it represents the very first authentic opportunity for teens to self-define.

Why do teens seem to wear exactly the same clothes as their friends wear? Because as they define themselves, they have two goals. One is to belong, to be part of a group, while the other is to be an individual, distinct from others. Wearing the so-called uniform of their peer group, while simultaneously expressing individualism, accomplishes both goals simultaneously. They all seem to wear the same thing but, much like adults, they each declare their uniqueness by the subtle variations (color, cut, style) in what they wear. Teens like to be unique. Although it may not appear that way to adults, teens will define themselves as unique individuals by the clothes they wear. A special necklace, a unique pair of earrings, a different watch, or a distinct hairstyle can all serve to make a statement about individuality, in spite of trends to conformity.

Why teens and *clothing?* The answer is simple. It is not that teens are necessarily obsessed with clothing per se, it is just that clothing is all they can afford in order to define themselves. Adults can buy houses, furnishings, vehicles, trips, and other big-ticket items in order to make statements about themselves and their lifestyles. Teens must define themselves on a limited budget, and when you are that age, clothing is all you can afford.

Food and entertainment represent the other big areas where the teen demographic spends its own money. Teens have a very limited disposable income and therefore like to get good value when it comes to buying food and beverages. This explains the natural affinity between teens and fast food. Fast-food outlets provide the optimum combination of quantity, quality, and price when it comes to serving food, so they win the teen dollar away from sit-down restaurants that have higher overhead costs. Teens care little about ambiance or atmosphere—all they want is good quality and a filling meal, at a reasonable price.

Entertainment is huge. The movie industry is booming like never before, and the teen market for movies is enormous. Look at the range of movies being offered. Hollywood is making movies especially for the teen demographic. Teen movies and teen movie stars are big business, and the top ten is becoming ever more dominated by the teen market. In this market, movie quality is easily offset by what's popular, and trends play a huge role in determining what will be a success. As new releases hit the theaters there are certain pictures that become big hits, and in fact one would be hard-pressed to find a teen who has *not* seen some particular must-see hit movies.

The size of the teen demographic is growing in importance. The children of the later-born baby boomers are now entering the marketplace in huge numbers, and the dollar value of this segment of shoppers is not insignificant. Retailers and entrepreneurs of all kinds are responding. Teens make up a significant percentage of the shopping demographic and their spending power is on par with just about any other segment of the market. Retailers on the cutting edge respect this important group. Brand loyalty is important. These teens will soon be acquiring credit cards and shopping as adults.

The children of the baby boomers have far greater access to their parents' cash than any generation before them. As a consequence they are in the market for higher-end items than most analysts give them credit for. Teens not only are buying audio systems, portable music systems, televisions, and other electronics, they are also shopping in a big way for computer supplies. It is crucial to remember that this is the first generation to be raised on computers, and on the Internet, and as a result many teens are much savvier than adults are when it comes to shopping for the latest computer technologies.

Teens are also big spenders in other ways. For many people, gone are the days when the family purchased on old car for a teenager. Today many teens get brand-new cars, fresh off the showroom floors. The wealthy baby boomers like to earn recognition, and nothing is too good for their kids. Those kids are not going to have to drive an old wreck like dad did. The midcareer boomer can afford the best.

Just looking at the size of the teen demographic is misleading. Its impact is far greater than its size, and indeed the teen demographic can be said to be extremely influential when it comes to deciding how the family dollar is spent. Teens are not only important shoppers in themselves but they play a major role in other major shopping decisions. Adults hear from their teens when it comes to buying many major items, such as vehicles and computers. Shopping decisions are not made in a vacuum, and the teen member of the household is likely to make his or her influence felt when it comes to many major family shopping decisions.

THE YOUNG ADULT SHOPPER

The next demographic to appear after the teen years is the young adult. This is the postteen group that is *single* and working. This is an interesting demographic that has time to shop, money to spend, but a very limited repertoire of merchandise in which it is interested. This is the stage at which young adult shoppers are able to buy all of the things they longed for as teenagers. Thus there is a demand for things like expensive audio equipment (for the home and car), sporty cars, short adventure-style trips, high-end sports gear, expensive jewelry, and more and better clothing and accessories. This is the shopper with a fairly large amount of disposable income who is not yet ready to make the big purchases—homes, furniture, boats, cottages—that adults make. This demographic probably represents one of the most underserved shopping groups that exist. These shoppers have disposable income and plenty of time to shop, but the number of items available for purchase is limited largely to the dreams of high school. They are anxious to define themselves as young adults, but beyond items such as those listed above, and especially the sporty car, they are very limited in the range of items they wish to buy.

The single young adult represents an enigma to the retailer. What do you sell to a 25-year-old who does not really need much? The answer is that there exists with this demographic an opportunity to create new demand. What is needed is to get this shopper beyond the aspirations of high school and into a new realm of shopping. Retailers and manufacturers need to invent marketing strategies that will make single young adults strive to buy more adult products. Since most of these young singles rent their accommodations, an obvious marketing opportunity is in the home furnishings and appliances markets. When was the last time you saw a furniture ad that was targeted to young singles in apartments? When was the last time you saw home appliances, or even cleaning products, marketed to the young adult demographic? This is a huge segment of the market that is destined to become ever more important as the children of the baby boomers age, yet scant attention is paid to it as a demographic force. The advertising message needs to be conveyed to this demographic that it is growing up and needs to spend its money on things other than adolescent fantasies.

THE BUSY DEMOGRAPHIC

There is another demographic group out there that is the one that is really going to power the stores and malls in the years to come. This is the group that is younger than the baby boomers, the 25-to-40-year-old demographic. This young group is at the busiest time of life when it comes to work. They are trying to establish careers and so are working longer and harder than many older coworkers. This demographic group is also one that has a huge number of activities outside of work. They are in the childbearing and child rearing years and so participate in all of the activities that are associated with young children.

Where demographics make a big difference for the young married adult group is with respect to time. Most young and middle-aged professionals, and families with young children, live in a *time-pressed* world where there never seem to be enough hours in the day to get things done. Jobs are demanding, extended hours of work are expected, and other daily activities demand attention. Children need to be driven to piano lessons, soccer practice, and swimming classes; there is the PTA meeting to attend, and shopping for groceries and clothing needs to be done for that dinner party on the weekend. Never mind that report that needs to be written by Monday. The time-pressed adult has less of one thing available to her (time) and more of another thing available (money). As a result, she is looking for time-saving products and services wherever they are available. A good example of this trend is in the growing use of professional housecleaning services, which more and more shoppers, especially women, are taking advantage of. Similarly, some clothing stores are now offering personalized shopping services to men and women, whereby seasoned sales staff will help customers outfit themselves with entire wardrobes of matching ensembles all at one time. This personalized service saves the shopper the time of traveling around.

There are other areas in which the busy demographic looks for help in getting things done. Specialized services such as lawn care, nannies, house decorating, and custom car-cleaning are becoming more popular as overworked adults look for time relief. When it comes to shopping, the busy demographic wants the retailer to understand his needs. Yes, he wants and needs to shop, and yes, sometimes shopping is essential. When a birthday or anniversary comes up, even the busy professional feels compelled to go on a serious shopping expedition. He or she not only wants to accomplish the task in an efficient manner, but the job should not be so efficient as to seem unemotional or uncaring. They want to fully experience the pleasure of shopping and gift buying. It just shouldn't take too long.

In general, the young professional and middle-aged demographic has both more money for shopping and less time for it. Retailers that can accomplish objectives that save time, for example, online grocery shopping and delivery, will find that there is a willing audience for their efforts. Today's young urban professional does not have time to wander the malls or travel downtown on a leisurely shopping expedition. Neither do they have time to stand in line returning a defective product nor do they have the inclination to drive all over town looking for a particular product. Efficiency and convenience are the watchwords for the retailer, whether it comes to changing oil, selling cars, setting up travel plans, or buying groceries. Busy people want speed and no hassles; they want shopping to be but a small part of their lives so there is more room for the big things, like that Christmas concert at the elementary school. On a busy person's slate of priorities, shopping is far down on the list.

Busy people still shop for price and value. But they want it quickly and efficiently. One of the reasons for the success of stores like Price/Costco is that shoppers know they are getting good quality merchandise at a good price. Price/Costco makes shopping decisions easier. Many other chains have similar reputations for value, and probably they are largely unaware that one of the major reasons why consumers patronize them is because *they take the guesswork out of shopping.*

The busy demographic group is ready to buy, and demand for product is almost insatiable. Young married adults want all of the things they aspired to as teenagers, *plus* the things they should have as adults. They have conflicting desires. They want a huge, high-end audio system and they want baby furniture. They want a sporty car and one that will carry groceries. They want to impress their friends with their cool furnishings and they want the in-laws to be impressed with their sensibility. Young marrieds represent a huge market. They are just setting out in life and so have need of a large number of products. In addition, young marrieds may have often just purchased a first house and so are ready also to furnish that house with all of the necessities of life. In addition to all of the products that young singles want, young marrieds also want the almost endless line of home furnishings that are available.

The things that young couples buy help them to define themselves as a couple, instead of as two separate individuals. Often, for the first time, couples are buying items that are to be shared with another person. Compromise and negotiation become an important part of the buying process, as does the art of sharing the shopping experience on a more-or-less permanent basis. Shopping not only defines the self, it also defines the relationship, and communal items and purchased experiences become part of a couple's shared life.

Food presents a dilemma for the busy demographic. At some times, they will prefer to eat like teens and grab a fast-food meal. At other times they'll want to eat at a classy sit-down restaurant. The market has responded to this demographic by creating trendy establishments that are targeted specifically to a younger audience. Such restaurants are usually less formal in their design, menu, and service than are older restaurants, and typically they also function as bars. Although these bars are more popular with the *single* young adults, they do cater to both sides of the young adult demographic.

THE BABY BOOMER SHOPPERS

The baby boomers are that huge group of people born during the 20-year period between about 1946 and 1964. As of 2005, they will be between 40 and 60 years of age. If one looks at the number of people in each demographic age group, one sees that the baby boomers dominate. This is a huge group of potential shoppers who are at midlife. More importantly, they are currently in the years when they are making the most money of their lives, so they have big spending power as well. How do the baby boomers affect the retail market?

The answer is that they have a huge effect on shopping and spending simply by virtue of their numbers. A case in point would be the large number of sport-utility vehicles (4x4s or SUVs) that one finds on the roads. What is the demographic that is old enough to want these vehicles and that can afford to buy them? The response is that it is the baby boomers that drive trends like this. They are at that stage of life where the psychology of owning a sport-utility vehicle is right for them and they have the disposable income to get what they want. Automakers know who wants these vehicles and they target their advertising to this demographic group. The advertising cachet appeals usually to the concept of off-road adventure, featuring sport-utility vehicles driving through rugged terrain and showing their owners engaged in active sports such as kayaking and hiking. This mentality appeals to the forty-something executive who rarely gets away from her desk. She feels like she deserves the outdoor life of adventure if only she had the time. Buying the SUV is a chance to express her feelings and desires, even though owning the vehicle will be as close as she will ever get to realizing her outdoor dreams.

The baby boomers are sitting in the drivers seat when it comes to mainline shopping trends for big, expensive, and luxury items. Their shopping presence and power is unprecedented. They are the largest, wealthiest demographic of them all.

One needs to consider the major kinds of places where the boomers will spend their money. Houses, cars, cottages, and high-end vacation trips are just a few of the big places where boomers are making their presence felt. The boomers swagger around in the retail market like bulls in a china shop, buying up whatever they want, whenever they want it. They have lots of disposable income and they're at that stage in life where they realize they're not going to live forever. They're willing and anxious to spend their money and to indulge themselves in the best that life has to offer. A new boat? A big-screen TV? A trip to Disney World? A new video camera? A sport-utility vehicle? Boomers will not deprive themselves.

What is the baby boomer to do when it comes to dress? Should he or she even wear jeans? Are they right for this group, or are they too juvenile for such a demographic? The baby boomers are in an extremely difficult position when it comes to shopping for clothing. They have enough disposable income to buy whatever they want but are often at a loss as to what to purchase. In a youth-driven market, it is nearly impossible for the middle-aged baby boomer to shop for clothing. Half of it seems too young and the other half seems too old.

Clothing retailers would be wise to try to make the baby-boom shopper feel comfortable with herself and her age group. Is it possible to find clothes that are in style but that are not teen copycats? This is the secret to dressing the boomers. They want to feel comfortable and in style, but they do not want to try to look like they're 16 years old either. It's a difficult challenge, and retailers and manufacturers do indeed struggle to try to find the pulse of the baby-boom generation when it comes to clothing. For the boomers, clothing has to strike a chord between being grown up but also not being old. In the same way that teens do not want to dress like their parents, the baby boomers do not want to dress like their own mothers and fathers either. They had their own look when they were teens and they still want to maintain that sense of identity. As a result, this is one of the most difficult markets for clothing retailers to target.

When it comes to homes and furnishings, the boomer group is definitely upscale. A big house in the suburbs, tastefully furnished, is the order of the day. Making a good appearance when entertaining friends and neighbors is important. The presence of the baby boomers in the housing market has steadily driven up housing prices since the early 1970s. The boomers born in the years after 1945 were ready to buy houses by the time they were in their mid-twenties, that is, by about 1970. Similarly, the boomers born by 1965 were ready to buy houses by about 1990. Their huge demand for housing drove the market for more than 20 years. And, even though the last of the boomers have bought their houses, demand continues unabated, as the *children* of the boomers continue the market pressure. Boomers born in the 1950s, for example, now have children in their mid-twenties and they too are ready to buy houses. The upward pressure on prices is likely to continue as the children of the boomers continue to grow into the age of buying their first house.

When it comes to shopping for vehicles, the boomers often indulge their teenage fantasies for sporty cars. One need only note the redesign of cars that has occurred over the last few years to appreciate that the market is being driven, in part, by baby boomers. Almost all old-style sedans have been replaced with sportier looking models, as automobile manufacturers try to target an aging audience.

The baby boomers are also the prime age group to be concerned with luxuries such as cottages and family trips to one-stop destinations. This group has made it financially, and so all of the upscale extras are part and parcel of the package. Luxury vacation trips, motor homes, and cottages in the country, with all the toys, are part and parcel of the image.

No discussion of the boomer generation should take place without mentioning that this group also stands to inherit huge sums of money. Many of them have already discovered this sudden source of income, while many more are on the threshold of instant wealth. The boomers are now closing in on the age range between 40 and 60, which suggests that their parents are between the ages of approximately 65 and 85. There is a huge bubble of saved wealth that is about to come into the hands of the baby boomers as their parents die. This group, which is already in a high income bracket, stands to have even more spending power in the years to come.

One place where the current and future wealth of the baby boomers is of huge interest is in the field of finance and investment. Most financial advisers are really in the business of selling investment vehicles such as mutual funds, and so there is a major area of growth in the future of the financial services retail sector. Cash-rich baby boomers will be looking for places to invest their newly acquired, inherited wealth in the years to come, and wise sellers of these products will be prepared to fill this demand. While the boomers are anxious to spend lots of their cash and get all the good things in life, they are also at the age where they are starting to worry about retirement. For them, this means making proper investments for the future so that their opulent lifestyle can continue into their retirement years.

For the remainder of the retail sector, a baby-boom generation flush with inherited cash means a continuing high demand for all of the expensive things that people used to just dream about. The boomers are the wealthiest generation of all time and their shopping needs and desires are unprecedented. If you think they've spent a lot so far, just wait until they inherit their parents' estates. Retailers would be smart to create new areas of demand for the boomers. Many of the members of this generation are literally saturated with all of the goods and services they could possibly want. They have been able to shop for, and acquire, almost every possible thing they can imagine, from the big house and the big trips to the luxury cars and the expensive clothing. They have everything they ever hoped for, and indeed the marketers have run out of ideas for products they can sell the baby boomers. What do you buy for someone who has everything they could possibly want? It's up to the manufacturers, the retailers, and the advertisers to answer that question. There is no doubt that there is pent-up demand out there for shopping of all kinds, if the marketers could create new demand for products and services that have yet to be invented.

There is room to reinvent demand, to re-create demand in traditional areas where it has lagged behind. An excellent example of this is found in the revival of bookstores, which has taken place through the emergence of the giant big-box, superstore bookstores. Although this trend may seem just to have reinvigorated interest in books, the more likely truth is that this phenomenon has simply tapped into the baby boomer market at the right time. As the boomers age, they settle into more sedate leisure-time activities such as reading. The giant bookstores have taken advantage of this resurgence of demand for books among baby boomers and reinvented demand where it had previously been soft. There is a lesson to be learned in this. There is room to re-create demand in other areas of interest to aging boomers. Examples that come to mind include such sedentary activities as gardening, traveling, taking cruises, watching television, sewing, cooking, and so on. There is likely to be growth in demand for any areas that will keep the boomers occupied as they enter their years of greater leisure time.

Boomers shop just like teens. They not only shop to reward themselves, they also shop to emulate their peers. This is a very important time in life, for it is the time when people really start to measure their success in life by the things they own, and by the experiences they purchase.

Middle-aged happiness involves keeping up with the Joneses. The baby boomers aspire to have all of the fine things in life, and at this stage people seem convinced that happiness can only be obtained through purchases. Thus one gauges one's place in the world through the products that one has accumulated, and further satisfaction is acquired largely by additional shopping. The manufacturers and retailers do an admirable job of creating new demand by inventing new products and services that middle-aged consumers will be sure to want. The home theater system represents an excellent example of such a new, highly demanded product that didn't even exist 10 years ago.

The middle-aged shopper rewards himself for the prosperity he has achieved in life and career through his purchases. By buying a large new boat, or taking the family on a cruise, he pays himself for the success he has achieved. *He is celebrating his achievements in life*—and should be treated accordingly.

While baby boomer shoppers might pride themselves on being mature shoppers who can spot a bargain, the truth of the matter is that when it comes to self-reward, the actual dollar costs of purchases may not be that significant. In the same way that the preteen or the teenager will pay exorbitant costs for the correct fashions and labels, adults too will often pay whatever it takes to achieve success in rewarding themselves, and in making a statement. In this context, adults are just as guilty as teens of following the crowd and buying things just for appearances' sake. In fact, the adults are worse than the teens, because the sums they spend to impress their peers can be much greater than those a teen will spend.

Boomers are upgraders. Even though they have most of the things they need in life, when it comes to shopping, they have a tendency to want to upgrade their possessions. Old stereo systems are replaced by new sound systems, old furniture is upgraded to leather, a regular TV is replaced by one with a giant screen, kitchens are remodeled, appliances are replaced, and so on. Just like everyone else, middle-aged people like to shop, and having acquired all of the necessities of life doesn't stop them from pursuing still more purchases. There is always something better, newer, or bigger to buy. Upgraders like to be given the opportunity to upgrade. Taking that old TV to the cottage or giving it away to the children provides the perfect excuse to upgrade.

When it comes to food, the baby boomer demographic presents a stark contrast to the teen and young adult market. While middle-agers occasionally indulge themselves in fast food, by and large this is the demographic that supports the mainstream, sit-down restaurant business. As a consequence, this group sets the standard for high-quality restaurant fare and expects a lot for its money. There are fads in restaurants, just like in other things, but by and large, over the long haul, quality wins out. The importance of the restaurant market is growing. More people are eating out more often. Many restaurants have had to adjust as people's tastes have matured and expanded through time. Restaurant themes and menus have gotten more exotic as the growing wealth of the baby-boom generation has enabled it to indulge itself by eating in better restaurants more often. Quality food and good service are the order of the day, and most people are willing to pay a premium price to get what they want.

THE AGING BABY BOOMER

As the baby boomers approach midlife they will have fewer responsibilities at work. Climbing the career ladder will become less significant to them as they see the years slipping by. It will become more important to them to start to enjoy the simpler things in life, like bird-watching, cooking and gardening. This lifestyle trend will further enhance their shopping interest in activities that fill leisure time. Of course, when *they* begin these pastimes they suddenly take on greater significance than ever before. This is, after all, the self-centered generation. Nevertheless, there should be reinvigorated demand in all sedate areas of leisure activities, especially those based in the home, such as hobbies and crafts. The Internet also comes to mind as a place for shopping and other activities that can take place in the home. Any activities that fill leisure time will take on much greater retail significance.

As the baby boomers age, they will suffer the empty-nest syndrome. Children will grow up and leave, and boomers will be left behind. All of those activities and errands that used to be associated with the children's lives will cease to exist, and this means still more leisure time will become available to aging boomers. One might expect that with more leisure time, boomers would spend more time shopping. The problem is that they have fewer things to buy. With the children gone, expenditures on furnishings, toys, household repairs, hardware, and a lot of recreational equipment go by the wayside. While these elderly boomers will have more time and more money than ever before, they also have fewer things to buy than ever before. If there is anything that will sell to older shoppers, it's nostalgia, and a lot of retailers are tapping into this vein of demand by offering old songs, old movies, old television and even housewares and furnishings that hark back to earlier days. Restoration Hardware, a chain that specializes in selling home furnishings that have an antique look, is a good example of this nostalgia trend in action. As their Web site notes:

> We know how an eggbeater can prompt a whole wave of emotional responses . . . and how a set of salt cellars brings back happy memories. This is more than our way of finding and selling products; it's a way of life we highly recommend.

One area where aging boomers will be very interested in shopping is when it comes to buying things for grandchildren. It is surprising that there does not yet seem to be a chain, such as *Grandparents "R" Us* or *Grandma's* stores to cater to this demographic that will grow in importance. Grandparents need guidance when it comes to buying toys, games, and especially clothing for their grandchildren, and a store that would provide this guidance would probably find itself a success. Undoubtedly, well-off grandparents would be willing to pay a premium price for merchandise that will bring smiles.

As the prices of goods and services continue to escalate, many older shoppers lose touch with price trends and are shocked when they finally do discover newly inflated prices. *Sticker shock* is the well-known phrase that describes this phenomenon and it comes from the auto-retailing world. It refers to the fact that people are sometimes shocked by the list price of new vehicles. This is all the more true if people haven't bought a new car in quite a while and so are unused to the new vehicle prices. For the aging baby boomer, sticker shock becomes an almost daily occurrence as prices of all items creep up steadily.

As people age they buy things less often. A pair of shoes that used to be worn for a year suddenly lasts much longer. A coat that used to go out of style after a year or two now seems to last for many years. Shirts, pants, tops, and sweaters that previously were put in storage after a year or so of use now continue to be used for several years. In the world of the older person, time passes by faster and faster. As it does, shopping takes place less and less. "I thought I just bought that last year," might be the phrase used to describe a dress that is three years old. "That's nearly brand-new," might be used to depict a suit that is five years old. As time passes by more quickly, purchased items have their shelf life extended. This means that as people get older they shop less often, and this will occur for the baby boomers just like it does for everyone else.

The conclusion to be drawn from this scenario is that the shopping impact of the boomers will lessen as they get older. While this huge demographic group is still a shopping force to be reckoned with, it will start to have less and less effect on the retail market as it suffers the common experiences of aging. In spite of their own self-proclaimed importance, the significance of the boomers as a retail phenomenon will begin to diminish. It will fall into the hands of their heirs to spend their huge accumulated wealth.

As an ever widening segment of the shopping community gets older, product mix and selection will reflect these demographic changes. Stores, of course, should be made more accessible to older generations and should be made more user-friendly to seniors. For example, portions of foods in grocery stores are being geared to couples or singles in an attempt to satisfy a growing marketing niche.

As for entertainment, this is a demographic that is largely ignored. Movies, especially, are targeted to younger audiences, and this may be an area where the movie industry may be doing itself a disservice.

Part III

THE CHALLENGE FOR RETAILERS

Chapter 10

THE LEVELS OF RETAIL NEED

Human behavior is complex. It is difficult to describe, let alone understand. Just consider shopping as one supposedly simple manifestation of human behavior. Shopping can be an individual activity, yet it almost always involves more than one person. Shopping is apparently mostly about acquiring needed goods and services, yet shopping is also about defining oneself as a person. Shopping is about defining oneself, yet it is also about defining the self in relation to others. Shopping is about spending money wisely and finding bargains, yet shopping is also about rewarding oneself for a job well done. Shopping is about being penny-wise, practical, and pragmatic, but shopping is also about flair, fashion, and style. Shopping is supposed to be a pleasurable experience, yet shopping involves making sometimes important and difficult decisions. Sometimes shopping is fun, sometimes shopping is hell. Sometimes shopping is pleasing oneself and sometimes shopping is about pleasing others. Shopping is about "Keeping up with the Joneses," yet shopping is also about satisfying one's own desires. No matter how you look at it, there is more to shopping than meets the eye, and even the best psychologists, behaviorists, and economists in the world would have trouble explaining why and how people shop.

It would be useful to have an organizing framework, a guide that would help us to understand what shopping is all about. To find such a framework we can go back in time to the 1940s, when a psychologist named Abraham Maslow developed a very popular idea about how people organize their lives. Maslow was interested in human beings' motivations for behavior. He envisaged that people functioned on a day-to-day basis according to a Hierarchy of Needs. This hierarchy or list of needs is arranged such that people are seen to have lower- and higher-level needs. Furthermore, the lower-level needs must be fulfilled before the higher-level ones can come into play.

The *physical survival needs* at the bottom level of the hierarchy include the basic requirements such as hunger and thirst. Next we find *security needs.* This includes such basic needs as safety against physical danger or having physical health. At the third level, we find *belongingness and identification needs,* such as those for affection or social acceptance. At the fourth level come *esteem needs.* This level includes the desire for self-respect, prestige, and success. Finally, at the fifth and top level comes the *need for self-actualization*—that is, for self-fulfillment, worthwhile accomplishments, personal growth, and so on. Maslow argued that people work their way through such a list of needs, where those needs at the bottom levels must be satisfied before those near the top can be accomplished. Maslow's Hierarchy of Needs is probably one of the best known and most popular ideas in psychology. It is well known and well remembered because it is simple and agrees with our own ideas about our behavior. This helps to explain why the Maslow Hierarchy retains its popularity long after other competing ideas have disappeared.

It is possible to define a similar hierarchy of shopping needs. One need only look at shopping as a particular type of human behavior to make this idea work. Consider a five-level diagram of shopping needs, where the five levels are laid out as in Figure 10.1. At the bottom level of the shopping hierarchy we have *shopping for physical survival needs.* All of the shopping products at this level are at the must have level for subsistence. They ensure that basic physical needs for food, clothing, and shelter are met. At the second level we find *shopping for security needs,* including items that are essential to basic health and safety. This would include items such as those for accommodation, personal health, and hygiene. At the third level there is *shopping for belongingness and social acceptance.* This would include those items people buy in order to fit in with their peers, especially with regard to style and fashion trends. At the fourth level there is *shopping for esteem needs.* This would include the items people buy in order to feel good about themselves. Here we would include things such as nonessential items that are purely for prestige and respect. Finally, at the top of the diagram comes *shopping for self-actualization,* that is, shopping to make oneself feel worthwhile, self-fulfilled, and personally satisfied.

Figure 10.1
The Levels of Shopping

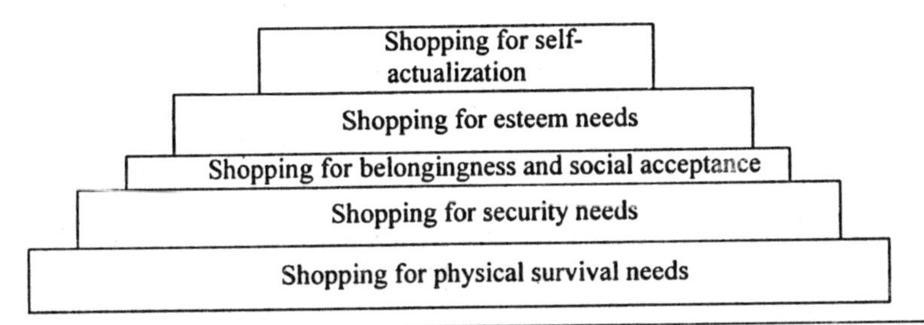

THE FIRST LEVEL OF SHOPPING

It is easy to apply the idea of the hierarchy to everyday shopping. In the first instance, there is shopping for physical survival needs. This would include basic foodstuffs and essential clothing. This is the shopping that people must do to survive. Everyone has a need for bread, milk, and eggs, as well as socks and underwear, and at one time or another, everyone shops for such products. There are certain basic essentials of human existence, and these needs must be shopped for. In most cases such shopping is combined together with the purchase of other products and thus does not stand out as a separate and distinct enterprise. For example, when people buy essential foods, they also buy other nonessential foodstuffs. When people buy basic clothing, they also buy other items. Shopping for physical survival needs is usually dull and routine. There is nothing exciting or glamorous about it, because it is just a matter of getting the job done. It is often a burdensome task. Everyday shopping for groceries is the best example of this level of the shopping hierarchy in action, but other examples, such as shopping for a water heater or a washing machine, also come to mind.

THE SECOND LEVEL OF SHOPPING

In the case of shopping for health and security needs, there is little to distinguish it from the previous level. People have an essential need for health and safety, and shopping for products that ensure these needs is as routine as shopping for survival needs. Everyday health necessities include items as diverse as toilet paper and cough drops, as well as humidifiers, bandages, mouthwash, medicines, and razors. Such items are basic to human health and hygiene, and in most cases, they are routine purchases. Security needs primarily include shopping for basic accommodation that provides a basic level of personal safety and sense of protection. Other types of security needs would include smoke detectors or fire extinguishers. Services relevant to health would include trips to the doctor or dentist, while services related to safety might include security systems. Shopping for health and security needs is straightforward and mundane, unless the shopper has an emergency need, as in the case of a medical pain or a nagging toothache.

THE THIRD LEVEL OF SHOPPING

The third level of the shopping hierarchy is more interesting. It includes shopping to satisfy social needs such as those for belonging and affection. People like to be able to demonstrate that they fit in with their friends or peers, and so shopping to achieve a sense of feeling that one belongs to a group is very important. Teens, for example, like to wear clothes that show they are in tune with the latest styles. Such clothing also demonstrates that they are part of a group and that they belong. Adults are no different. Whether the concern is with the latest clothing styles or the most-popular new vehicles, adults also like to fit in. Demonstrating that one is a part of a group through one's possessions and clothing is one of the most important functions of shopping, and it is through this function that people can achieve a sense of identification. Of course, a feeling of belongingness does not just come from one's possessions, but nevertheless possessions are an important part of creating an identity with others. Whether one is 15 or 55 years old, feeling that you identify with a group of people is a fundamental part of human behavior, and part of that feeling comes from the things one owns and the clothes one wears. As an extreme example, consider the various clubs and organizations to which people belong. Often these are defined by the possessions common to the members, as in the case of automobile clubs or stamp collectors.

In order to demonstrate the significance of shopping in creating feelings of belonging and social acceptance, one need only consider oneself and one's relations to others. All people belong to a social group consisting of friends, acquaintances, colleagues, and family members. Part of the collective consciousness of such a group comes about through possessions. Whether it is the clothing that the members of the group wear, or the physical items that they have in common, the shared identity is created to some extent by purchased possessions. The office workers who dress alike on weekdays and go water-skiing together on the weekend, or the mine workers who wear the same uniform all week long and fish together on weekends, are drawn together, in part, by their shared and common belongings. Shopping becomes a means to an end, a way to become part of a group. This shopping might involve activities as diverse as buying skydiving lessons with friends, or signing up at a fitness center where one's coworkers already belong. It might also involve buying a trip to a destination resort, or purchasing a ticket to a concert. Similarly, *shopping to belong* includes buying things to share, such as beer or food. If it involves a purchase that is intended to create a shared experience with others who are not family members, then it is a purchase that involves the third level of the shopping hierarchy.

This level of the shopping hierarchy is very important to many retailers. Shopping at this level is shopping to create a sense of belonging and identity. Satisfying the self is secondary to satisfying the desire to belong to a group. Advertising could be directed therefore to the consumer's desire to belong, to be part of the group that uses or buys the product. Such an advertising strategy is one that should identify a product as being directed to groups of users, where the individual buyer achieves a sense of belonging by buying the product. Clothing, consumables, and all manner of items qualify for such a designation. Whether it is the latest shoes, the hottest new music, a weekend trip, a brand of beer, a car, or the latest movie, the message should be that the purchaser could become one of the group by buying or consuming the product. Shopping at the third level is shopping to extend the self to others, to make the self a legitimate part of some larger collective consciousness.

THE FOURTH LEVEL OF SHOPPING

The fourth level of the shopping hierarchy presents another new set of possibilities. Here the shopper is shopping to meet esteem needs, those for self-respect, the respect of others, and prestige. Reputation and success also come into play. This is the shopping that makes the person in the eyes of others. For children, teens, and adults alike, shopping to meet needs of self-esteem is important. Owning and buying certain products can make one feel good about oneself and can create feelings of self-esteem. Self-esteem comes from the way we are reflected in the eyes of others, and a large part of that reflection is determined by the things we wear and the things we own. Shopping for self-esteem is not just about having enough money to buy expensive things. Rather, it is about showing off. Some people will demonstrate their worth through the expensive things they purchase, while others will show off by being in style, by owning the right things at the right time.

At the fourth level, shopping is also about defining the self. How one dresses, and the things one uses and buys, are intended to send a message to others about how one defines oneself. As always, clothing plays a crucial role. What shopper does not like to demonstrate an ability to stay on top of trends, to wear the very latest fashions, and thereby show off his or her self-confidence to the rest of the world? Sporting such fashions conveys a strong sense of self-esteem to the wearer, a sense not only of fashion success, but also of awareness of style. It sends a message to others that the person is able to stay abreast, to keep up with the times, and to dress accordingly. When one feels good about the clothes they are wearing, that adds a measure of esteem to the self. Teens love to wear the very latest style, and doing so creates an inner sense of success. Adults are the same. Older people like to show off their awareness of fashion sense and an ability to not be left behind. A 60-year-old golfer wants to wear the correct golf shirt just as much as the 13-year-old wants to wear the correct jeans. In both cases the wearer feels a strong sense of esteem and well-being if he or she is wearing the appropriate clothing. The significance of the link between clothing and self-esteem should not be underestimated.

There is more to shopping for self-esteem than just clothing. Everything we buy at the fourth level of the shopping hierarchy is about creating self-respect. It is shopping for the self, for the ego. It is also buying things in order to convey a message to others that says something about our success. Having the right clothes is just the beginning. Owning the right car, the right house, or the right furniture is also about self-esteem. It is partly through one's purchases that one measures one's success in life. And, as was pointed out earlier, it isn't necessarily the dollar amounts of the purchases that matter. Teens are a case in point. They live on a limited budget, and so are constrained in the amount and nature of things they can buy to bolster their self-esteem. Nevertheless, they are able to do so by buying things that are in style, rather than expensive. To them, it is the degree of fashion sense, rather than dollars spent, that is often the defining measure.

What kinds of purchases are indicative of self-esteem? The focus is on purchases that make the buyer feel good about his or her place in life, that is, those that are used to acknowledge successes. How does one reward oneself for that promotion at work? Or that pay raise? Or that success at school? Frequently this involves *buying something*. More often than not, when we celebrate, we purchase something, and thus success is toasted with shopping. For a child, success is rewarded with something as simple as a chocolate bar. For a teen, a new CD or item of clothing fits the bill. For an adult, something as simple as a nice dinner might suffice, or, alternatively, a major purchase such as a new car might be in order. In any case there is a strong connection between success, identification, and the things we buy and own. The results of shopping provide a forum for the expression of self-esteem for most people.

THE FIFTH LEVEL OF SHOPPING

The fifth level of the shopping hierarchy involves a different form of human behavior. It is the level at which self-actualization takes place. This implies that there is a link between shopping and the human need for self-fulfillment, personal growth, and worthwhile accomplishment. This is the level where shopping plays the most important, but least understood role of all. The ultimate form of shopping is for self-reward. So too, self-actualization is about defining and rewarding the self. Maslow's idea was that people would ultimately reach the level of self-actualization, once all of their other needs had been satisfied. Shopping at the fifth level implies shopping of this higher kind. This is the buyer who goes out and buys himself something just because he feels like it, or just because she feels she has earned it. This is shopping as the ultimate form of *self-reward.*

When we say that someone is shopping at the fifth level, the meaning is that they are shopping just for the self—just to cater to themselves. They are not shopping to be in style or to create a sense of belonging, nor are they are shopping to bolster their self-esteem. Rather, they are shopping simply because they feel like indulging themselves. It is difficult to pinpoint the ultimate feelings of exuberance and pleasure that come from shopping for the pure joy of it, yet just about everyone will have experienced them.

At first, it may seem trivial to associate self-actualization with shopping. After all, self-actualization is supposed to be indicative of the highest forms of human self-expression and self-representation. Yet shopping is just shopping. On the other hand, it is important to point out that shopping is the essence of capitalist society, and as a consequence its prominence in life should not be underestimated. Shopping is the ultimate form of self-reward in the free enterprise system. What is the point of one's efforts in life—what are the fruits of one's labors—if not those represented by rewarding oneself by buying things? Do we not buy things to recognize and acknowledge accomplishments? Do we not reward ourselves with our purchases? Think of the middle-aged adult who puts a pool in his back yard for the kids. Does he really just want the pool, or is the pool a symbol, a representation, of the success and achievement that the person has had in life? Such a middle-aged adult expresses his very self through his purchase. In other words, if success at work is one form of self-actualization, how is that self-actualization *expressed* in the real world, other than through buying things that reinforce the self-message of accomplishment? Presumably, self-actualization has to be given some form of articulation in the real world, and one of the most important of these forms must be that of shopping.

Self-actualization is about accomplishment, and self-actualizing shopping is about *celebrating* accomplishment. It can take many forms and need not be restricted to the purchase of major items. A middle-aged adult might buy a swimming pool to acknowledge achievement, but he or she might also indulge themselves in a new novel. The important thing is that a person is rewarding him- or herself in some way and is thereby creating a feeling of fulfillment. It is a way of recognizing personal growth and worthwhile accomplishment, manifested in a concrete way.

Self-actualizing shopping applies at all age levels. Although we may usually think of Maslow's Hierarchy as being applied to adults, there is no reason why it cannot apply to other age groups. A teen might be seen to proceed through the levels of Maslow's Hierarchy and to ultimately achieve self-actualization, say through accomplishments at school. Thus a teen might carry out tasks at school that lead to feelings of personal reward and self-worth. Such behavior might be further self-rewarded by shopping for items that reinforce the feelings created. Perhaps a new item of clothing or a ticket to a concert is seen as a means of self-acknowledging a worthwhile achievement, a way of recognizing one's own attainment. My own daughter will do this. She may perform well on an exam and then spend the next hour at the mall rewarding herself with a pair of earrings.

What about someone who buys a painting, a poster, or a work of art? What about a good book? A new music CD? Are these about shopping to self-actualize? It depends. Is the art for the self, or to show off to others? Is the person buying the book so they can tell others they read it? Are they buying the CD in order to acquire the bragging rights to it? Or are they buying these items for the pure pleasure of using them themselves? If the latter is the case, then this is shopping for self-actualization. The essence of self-actualized shopping is not in the objects being bought, but in the intended purpose of those objects. If one is shopping for pure inner enjoyment—shopping for the thrill of shopping, or the pleasure that it brings—then one is shopping for self-actualization. Imagine the collector who shops neither for investment purposes nor for show, but simply because she enjoys the act of finding and buying something rare. This behavior represents that ultimate, self-actualizing shopping experience.

SHOPPING THE LEVELS

The idea of shoppers shopping at the different levels of the hierarchy of shopping needs and wants is compelling. One can contemplate shoppers of various ages shopping for a variety of items at various levels. The hierarchy is not restricted by age or by sex, nor is it constrained by the number of levels in effect. One shopper may be shopping at just one of the levels, while another may be shopping simultaneously at more than one level. The members of a group of shoppers may each have different individual needs or desires as they relate to the hierarchy. However we look at it, the existence of the hierarchy implies that there is a series of stages at which shopping takes place, with each stage having its own set of unique features.

Individual shoppers proceed through the stages, with the completion of each level often dependent on the level before it. Before a shopper shops for reasons of self-esteem, for example, he or she needs to first shop through the physical survival and security levels. It may be difficult to go out looking at fashions if one does not have basic food or a decent place to live. Similarly, it is difficult to think of someone shopping for self-actualization needs if they have not first met belóngingness and identification needs by shopping to fit in with their peer group. Stated another way, how likely is one to shop for reasons of self-fulfillment, when one has not yet first acquired the basic items that allow one to have feelings of social acceptance or belonging?

Consider some different levels of the hierarchy of shopping needs in action. Imagine the teenager who shops in the first place for basic clothing needs. Today, of course, even the most basic needs such as underwear are imbued with a sense of style and fashion. Because of this, teens are able to simultaneously satisfy basic physical survival needs (socks and underwear) with the need for belongingness and social acceptance (socks and underwear that are in style). The food-related survival needs are satisfied primarily by parents who feed teens, who seem to be hungry at every waking moment. Similarly, parents also satisfy shopping for security needs. When it comes to shopping at the higher levels, teens focus almost exclusively on clothes, accessories, and hairstyles. At the third level, being in tune with the latest trends is essential to creating a sense of belongingness, and those who do not follow current fashion are ostracized. Social acceptance is highly dependent on how one dresses and looks. Once the need to fit in with peers is satisfied through basic clothing and style, teens will move to the level of shopping for esteem needs. This fourth level implies the purchase of items that create a sense of self-image or self-respect. This will include shopping for clothing, accessories, and other items that give birth to feelings of self-esteem—for example, having the very latest style of shoes or necklace. This is more than about being in style; this is about being able to feel good about oneself and one's purchases. Having tickets to an expensive concert or big new movie is about having the bragging rights to those events, and that is about self-esteem. At the fifth level, although still constrained by their limited budgets, teens will shop to self-actualize. As an example of this, consider the teen who buys something just for the purpose of feeling self-fulfilled or personally satisfied. This might include a decoration for her room, an unusual CD, a hidden tattoo, a new magazine, or something as simple as a special food treat. In any case, it is something that is for the self. An item that indulges the shopper. A self-actualizing purchase may also be about self-reward for having had a worthwhile accomplishment or a personal success. It is a purchase through which one pays oneself for an accomplishment.

Adults will also shop the levels in accordance with the hierarchy of shopping needs. After basic needs for physical survival and security are met, adults will proceed to shop the higher levels. Shopping to fit in with peer groups will involve those purchases that are intended to create feelings of social acceptance and belongingness. The exact types of items purchased will be unique to each family or group of friends. People achieve a sense of belongingness through their shared *experiences,* and very often those experiences are determined and shaped primarily by things that are *purchased.* Retailers should understand that many things that people buy are bought to achieve group membership, even though this fact is not evident at the time of the purchase. Memberships in health clubs are a good example of this, where promotions often encourage a prospective member to sign up friends as members. This kind of logic could be applied far more widely to purchases of all kinds, especially those relating to sports and personal entertainment. For example, it may be easier to get people to buy a Jet Ski, scuba gear, golf clubs, tennis racquets, CDs, or bread makers if they are making the purchase in conjunction with a simultaneous purchase by a friend or relative. The shared experience is crucial.

At the next level, adults will shop for esteem needs. This is a very important level and in fact may be the one that drives the majority of adult purchases. People like to feel good about themselves and their station in life, and nothing says more about oneself than the things one owns. And let's be clear—the things one owns do not have to be expensive or extravagant in order to make statements about the self or to create feelings of self-esteem. The list of potential examples is extensive. Some people like to feel good by the cars they drive. For others it's a big house or a cottage. Others will be happy to create feelings of self-esteem through the clothes, makeup, or hairstyles they wear. Still others will own a collection of CDs or videos. For some people, esteem may come from owning antiques or collectibles. For others it might be a motor home, camper, or other recreational equipment. Some people will feel good about themselves simply because they use the hottest new computer or wear the latest style in sportswear. However you look at it, people can achieve feelings of self-esteem through the things they own and purchase. Shopping this level of the hierarchy is essential to personal well-being and is important for creating a sense of self-respect, prestige, and success.

When adults shop at the fifth level, they shop for themselves. They shop to reward themselves and they shop to create personal feelings of self-fulfillment and personal satisfaction. Why does a person purchase something that is private—that is just for the self? What about that new novel, that knickknack, that painting, that statue, or that video game? When the purpose is self-satisfaction and private stimulation, shopping becomes an event that transcends everyday needs and wants. Shopping becomes a part of the personal experience and an element of the human psyche.

Self-actualizing shopping for adults is also about shopping for self-fulfillment, personal growth, and personal satisfaction. Adults shop to celebrate personal and lifetime accomplishments. After a hard week's work, it is not uncommon for adults to go out on the weekend with an eye to rewarding themselves for their efforts. This is a very important form of shopping, and retailers should be aware of the self-rewarding, self-actualizing shopper. Because she is paying herself for a job well done, there are no limits to which she will not go to acknowledge herself. Decadent, self-indulgent shopping is impulsive and extravagant, and retailers should be prepared to satisfy this significant element of consumer demand.

Shopping at the self-actualization level also involves shopping for experiences. Whether it is a Caribbean cruise or a trip to Hawaii, many people purchase an experience for the pure pleasure of enjoying it. Again this is behavior that goes beyond bragging rights. This is shopping for the pure pleasure of the experience. Other, better examples of shopping for the purpose of buying a self-actualizing experience would include attendance at horror movies, riding thrill rides in an amusement park, or participating in extreme sports such as heli-skiing. These are good examples of high-end retail demand where the ultimate goal is to purchase a self-actualizing experience.

It may be difficult, if not impossible, to distinguish between purchases at the third, fourth, and fifth levels of the hierarchy. Consider a ticket to a concert or a new CD. At one level they may be purchased for reasons of belongingness to a peer group, at another they may be purchased for feelings of self-esteem, and at another level they may represent self-actualizing purchases. The difference between the levels of the shopping hierarchy is not in *what* is purchased, but in the *reasons why* it was bought. Often it will be unclear even to the shopper what the motivation is for the purchase. The distinction between the levels is useful primarily from the point of view of trying to understand that there is almost always more than one reason why people shop. Unraveling the levels is part of the mystery of shopping.

THE EVOLUTION OF THE SHOPPING HIERARCHY

A key element of understanding and applying the hierarchy of shopping is to appreciate that the *significance* of the levels is changing through time. In particular, it should be made clear that the hierarchy of shopping needs is evolving. Most important here is the idea that as people advance economically, they progress upward through the hierarchy. As it becomes easier for most people to satisfy the basic needs at the bottom of the hierarchy, they move onward to the higher-level wants such as self-esteem and belonging. Similarly, as it becomes easier for people to satisfy needs for belonging and self-esteem, they move on toward satisfying needs of self-actualization.

Given the economic progress that has been made over the past couple of decades, it is possible to suggest that most of society is now at the self-actualization level of shopping. The fact that people are seeking out ever more extreme and excessive experiences and activities is testament to this trend. Bungee jumping, white-water rafting, skydiving, virtual reality, and other such extreme activities are being sought after more than ever, as shoppers aspire to higher levels of the shopping hierarchy. The secret to retail success may well lie in understanding that shoppers are moving upward through the hierarchy of shopping and are demanding higher-level products and experiences than ever before. If every middle-income, middle-aged family has acquired all of the basic wants—including the sport-utility vehicle and the trip to Disney World—what else is left of their retail demand? Being able to answer that question, and satisfy that demand, may be the key to success in the emerging retail environment.

As shopping evolves to the top level of the shopping hierarchy, it is obvious that *experience* becomes an ever more important part of the shopping equation. This does not include just extreme experiences, but rather refers to the idea that *all shopping should be experiential.* A good example of this comes from the Ford Motor Company, which announced that they would decorate their SUV showrooms to make them look like camping equipment stores. The concept is to convey the idea that the SUV is more than just a vehicle. The message is that the vehicle is a means to an end, a way to reward yourself for a hard week at the office, or for driving the kids from one activity to another. This is self-actualized shopping, where the idea is conveyed that the sport-utility vehicle provides a means to experience the outdoors *and* thereby a means to provide self-fulfillment, personal growth, and self-reward. The product that is being sold is not anything new or different, but the message and the image being sold reflect the experiential times in which we live. All of this is occurring at the top level of the shopping hierarchy, and this is just one example of an ongoing trend.

The maid services that take care of household cleaning needs are another example of the evolution toward the self-actualizing economy. Busy husbands and wives find themselves short of the time or the willingness to take care of basic household cleaning chores, and so they hire cleaning services to carry out the work. The fact that this happens at all is partly a function of the new levels of wealth in our economy, but it also reflects more than anything a desire on the part of people to devote their precious time to more worthwhile pursuits. Thus the housewife who finds herself with time freed up by maid services might spend that extra time taking tennis lessons or aerobics, while the househusband with extra time might spend it on woodworking classes or racquetball. In either case, a service is being purchased so that another activity at the top level of the shopping hierarchy may be purchased in its stead. The purchase of the maid service is not so much a purchase of a cleaning service as it is a purchase of *time.*

Another illustrative example of self-actualized shopping is found in the explosive growth of Internet services. All members of the family take part in the use of the Internet. School projects, health information, shopping, chatting, movie reviews, and a host of other information sources are available. People purchase access to the Internet as another form of experience, and as a form of self-actualization. Using the Internet is mostly personal; it is not about achieving self-esteem, but it is about personal growth and personal experience. Buying time on the Internet is shopping for self-fulfillment and a sense of personal accomplishment. For those who use the Internet for communicating with others, especially in the form of chatting, it is also about the fourth level of the hierarchy, or belonging. For the first time, individuals can join groups of strangers and become part of a group by participating in chat rooms. This creates a feeling of belongingness and social acceptance for participants.

As shopping at the top of the shopping hierarchy expands, we should expect to see more purchases of items and services that are all about satisfying people's inner needs for self-fulfillment and personal growth. This means an ever increasing emphasis on self-indulgent kinds of shopping. As more customers push the envelope of demand, retailers will respond by increasing the opportunities available at the self-actualizing level of shopping. Many products and advertising campaigns today are all about personal style and lifestyle. The Calvin Klein line of products is one good example of the ambiance a product line can create. Whether it is perfume, underwear, or jeans, there is a certain cachet to the brand that sells the buyer not just a product but also an image about him or herself. This line of thought is pervasive especially in the fashion industry and is another indicator of a trend toward acknowledging that shoppers are becoming more concerned with self-fulfillment and personal satisfaction.

The explosive growth in the movie and entertainment industries is another indicator of the growing significance of the top level of the shopping hierarchy. The number of movies and the number of theaters, especially megaplexes, are growing rapidly. While going to a movie may be all about belonging to a group for teens, for adults it is mostly about buying an experience. Although one does acquire bragging rights to a new release, even the popularity of second-run theaters lends weight to the argument that people are more interested than ever in buying the personal, mental experience that comes with a movie. This is self-actualizing shopping at its ultimate—shopping for one's own inner fulfillment. It is shopping where the buyer purchases nothing but a personal experience.

The amount of wealth and the amount of leisure time are growing in society. Smart retailers are moving to fill the void that these trends create by inventing new products, and new advertising strategies, that target the self-actualizing shopper. People have more disposable income than ever before and more time in which to spend it. Successful manufacturers, designers, and entrepreneurs will do their best to create new products and new demand to fill this void. As people acquire all of the traditional needs and wants of their parents' generation, they start to look for products and services that are unique. More often than not these new products will present the self-actualizing shopper with a new range of experiences that offer personal reward and self-fulfillment.

Consider as an example the range of services and facilities now being offered on major cruise ships as cruise lines strive to entice the maximum number of passengers. Recently, the largest cruise ship in the world was launched. Royal Caribbean's *Voyager of the Seas* will be the biggest and longest on the sea. It will carry 3,100 guests in 1,557 rooms and will have 10 dining rooms and restaurants. To entertain passengers there is an 18-hole golf simulator, a four-story shopping arcade, a jogging track, a fitness center, volleyball and basketball courts, and a 1,350-seat theater. In addition there is a 30-foot rock-climbing wall, a swimming pool, a gaming arcade, nine lounges, a casino, an inline skating track, a Johnny Rockets hamburger joint, and an indoor ice rink. Arline Bleecker, a Florida travel writer, says, "I think there is a point where it doesn't even have to go anywhere. It becomes all about the ship." That's the point exactly. In the self-actualizing world of shopping, buying a cruise becomes more about buying satisfying personal experiences, rather than a trip. The voyage is secondary. The destination is the ship and the experiences that it provides.

Chapter 11

RETAIL STRATEGIES

MENTAL SHOPPING MAPS

Imagine that you are about to head out on a shopping trip to a well-known area where you shop frequently. Some interesting questions to ask concern your mental image of the shopping place. When you go there, how do you know your way? Do you have a map in your mind that shows you the route? Do landmarks play a significant role when you navigate in the city? More interestingly, what is the layout of the stores and shops? Which ones stick in your mind, and which ones fade away? Which stores stand out as favorite destinations, and which ones get lost in the shuffle? What about price and quality of merchandise?

Shoppers carry around in their minds *mental maps of their shopping environments.* Not only are general shopping areas recorded on these maps, but stores and individual businesses are noted as well. The mental map is the shopper's personal guide to shopping, and every retailer should want to place his business on the shopper's mental landscape.

Mental shopping maps create a psychological picture of the city and its shopping opportunities in the mind of the shopper. A veritable wealth of information is stored in the shopper's mental map, and when she goes shopping she relies on this information to guide and direct her to stores and merchandise. The shopping map of the mind is based on years of experience and holds valuable information. Need a new pair of glasses? Shopping for a dress for that dinner party? Looking for a place to rent a tux? What about an outboard motor for your boat? The mental shopping map usually contains a reference to such shopping needs. Assembled over time, the mental shopping map embodies a history of collected experience.

A good example of the significance of the mental shopping map occurs in the case when someone moves to a new city. For a considerable amount of time the new resident finds himself at a loss when it comes to shopping. He has to relearn the shopping map for his unfamiliar new environment. Through exploration, and trial and error, gradually a new shopping map of the new place is put together. But it takes many years for it to become as detailed as those of long-term residents. They will know where to shop for just about everything, including even rare or obscure items that are found in out-of-the-way places. The location of one-way streets, parking lots, and all other kinds of minutiae become a part of the experienced shopper's psychological map.

Shoppers who are new to an area tend to rely on other sources to supplement their sketchy mental shopping maps. A favorite device used to assist the inexperienced shopper is the yellow pages. These provide a guide to shopping and are used to extend the shopper's mental map. Wise retailers should participate in the yellow pages. They not only help to fill in the maps of new residents, but they are also used to fill in voids for experienced shoppers. Actual road maps of the city are another favorite device of the rookie shopper, though these provide limited information on shopping. The inexperienced shopper also relies a great deal on word of mouth when it comes to scouting out new shopping destinations.

Consider just some of the information that you stockpile in your own mental shopping maps. Not only is there store location information—where are the stores located, what are they near—but there is also a memory bank of instructions on how to get to a multitude of particular stores. When you drive to a familiar store, the route you follow becomes second nature, even though the process of getting to that store may be somewhat complicated. The point of this argument is driven home when you try to give directions to someone else to a location that you thought was easy to find. Only then does the urban wayfarer see the real complexity of her everyday travels.

The shopper's mental map expands with age. Teens, for example, will have a more limited shopping map, while older adults will have the benefit of years of experience. Interestingly, mental maps can become outmoded. This is demonstrated frequently by older shoppers who remember where particular stores and businesses used to be.

Mental maps reflect the desires and wishes of shoppers. Studies show, for example, that consumers do not like to drive more than a couple of miles to get groceries. Grocery stores that exceed this range will be eliminated from the mental map. Generally, the less expensive items are, the less the distance that people are willing to travel for them. Geography plays other tricks on the mind. For example, well-liked stores are perceived by consumers as being closer than they really are. The geography of the mental map may bear little resemblance to the real world.

Shoppers also carry around a general image of the stores they frequent. Ask yourself if you can picture some of the stores you often patronize. Certainly you can imagine the stores and perhaps even visualize some of the merchandise. A question that can be asked is whether retailers are effective in creating a positive image of a store, or at least one that contains information that a customer will find attractive.

Another significant part of the mental shopping map is specific information on merchandise. Price is the predominant variable that most shoppers focus on, and so pricing information is well ingrained into the mental map. Likewise, of course, there is information on quality, selection, brand names, sizes, and all the other details on which shoppers focus. Furthermore, in addition to information on inventory, shoppers also keep a mental register of things like the quality of the staff, ease of shopping, convenience of parking, business hours, store quality and cleanliness, and so on. Overall, there exists a broad, general image of just about every store with which the shopper is familiar, and this image plays a central role in determining where shoppers will shop. The mental shopping map directs the shopper unconsciously to his or her favorite stores and locations.

It is hard to believe that shoppers carry all of this mental baggage around with them on a daily basis. Most people go about the business of shopping without giving a moment's thought to the details of their travels or the locations of stores. Yet a large amount of information is filed away and stockpiled for future use. Consider a product like a wedding dress that is only purchased once (hopefully). Even though many people may buy only one wedding dress in a lifetime, most shoppers will know where to go to buy a wedding dress. This sort of *mental inventory* of shopping opportunities is common among shoppers and demonstrates the extent to which people carry a mental stock of their shopping environments.

Retailers should attempt to grab a piece of the mindscape of shoppers. If a store becomes part of a shopper's mental map it tends to stay in place for a long time. Most shoppers, for example, will be familiar with the locations of stores where they may have bought a once-in-a-lifetime item. That unusual part for a refrigerator, for example, may be something that is found at an out-of-the-way store that a shopper may visit only once. But such a location and its products tend to stay lodged in the shopper's mind for many years. Memories linger a long time, and the idea that first impressions are important is as true of retail environments as it is of people. Mental maps of retail opportunities are deeply ingrained in the psyches of shoppers. If a retailer can establish his place in the mind of a shopper, he will hold a part of that mental real estate for the long term.

THE GLOBAL CITIZEN

When it comes to geography, it is safe to say that shoppers are worldlier than ever before. Consumers are aware of products and trends from around the globe and are able to keep pace with new developments anywhere they happen to be. The Internet plays a big role in creating the new global citizen, as does the existence of instantaneous, global communications systems that are made possible by satellite technology. A hundred years ago it literally took days,· weeks, or even months for news to travel the globe. Now any event anywhere, anytime, is reported worldwide in just seconds. The same laws of instantaneous communication apply to products and fashions, as well as to news. Current fads and fashion trends sweep the earth in a matter of hours. A musical group can host a live concert on the Internet and make available for downloading to the whole world a free copy of its latest song. A pop diva can wear a new style of clothing or makeup and touch off an international fashion trend just by the impact of international news coverage. The world has become a much smaller place, and in the years to come it will only get smaller.

As a good example of the new globalism, just consider the selection of products that is now available in the typical grocery store. In the 1950s, '60s, and '70s, most products in the local grocery store were from local or national markets. There were few products imported from the outside world. Products like bananas and coffee were the few staples that came from exotic locations. Today's grocery stores are loaded with products from all over the world. People *expect* more from stores. Shoppers' tastes have become more sophisticated and more global as they have come to experience products from the world over. Years ago, if a shopper wanted lettuce, the choice was almost always limited to plain leaf lettuce.

Period. Now shoppers look for, and expect to find, as many as a dozen types of lettuce from all over the world, and they expect it to be crisp and fresh. Nothing less will do. The grocer has to tap into the global marketplace to keep the modern shopper satisfied, and there is no longer any geographical limit to the products that shoppers expect to find.

Cheap, imported clothing comes from all over the world and has for some time. There is nothing new about the idea that it comes from foreign destinations. What is new is that *fashion and style now circle the globe as fast as news does*. The best example of this new globalization is found with teenagers. Teens literally feel more at one with other teens elsewhere in the world than they do with adults in their own house. Teen fashion trends and styles are global. The kids in Beijing wear the same clothes as the kids in New York. News coverage brings home the truth of the closeness of the global community of teens. When news reports showed people escaping from oppression in Kosovo, the teen girls who were fleeing wore flared jeans and platform shoes. They looked like they belonged on a street in Boise, Idaho, not on a refugee truck in a war-torn battlefield. Even in the midst of war, teen fashion prevails. The same teens not only share fashion and clothing styles, they share the same heroes, celebrities, rock groups, music, and movie stars. They are global citizens.

The new internationalism sweeps the globe and it starts at a young age. Barbie is sold in 150 countries worldwide. Coke is being sold in Tibet and Mongolia. The international corporations are reaching into every corner of the world. What does this mean for the retailer? Several things. First of all, shoppers will be more geographically demanding than they ever have before. Products from the four corners of the earth will be in demand, as consumers become worldlier. Second, product turnover will be faster. As global communication via the Internet becomes commonplace, trends and fashions will sweep by faster and faster. As the earth gets smaller, things happen more quickly. Third, trends will emerge on a more global level than they used to be, and thus it becomes necessary for the retailer to keep up with them at a larger scale. The same products that are hot sellers in London and Paris will also be big sellers in New York, Boise, and Fargo. Shoppers will be more aware of global and international trends, and retailers will be hard-pressed to keep up with the times. When your customers are in chat rooms with fellow shoppers from around the country, and the world, it does not take long for fashion news to spread. Retailers are dealing with consumers who have a global perspective.

PRODUCT TURNOVER

Patterns in the retail world suggest that waves of product innovation are coming along quicker than ever. Indeed, retailers are attempting to rotate their product lines faster than ever before, in a quest to keep newer products on the shelves. It is almost like retailers have become green grocers keeping fresh products on display. Today's product lines must be green and crisp, unblemished and farm-fresh. When consumers make a return visit to a store, a month after their last trip, they want to see new products. Shoppers are coming to expect change and novelty as a regular part of retail enterprise. Staid and static is out, and dynamic and versatile is in. Consumers want innovation, invention, and ideas. Why do shoppers shop? What are the reasons for shopping? Clearly a retailer who gives the shopper innovation creates a motivated shopper.

Retailers are becoming ever more obligated to make stock rotation an almost constant process, and stock is seen to expire at an ever quickening pace. This is good for sales, as it spurs consumer demand, and it is also good for shoppers, as there is an endless supply of innovative products for them to sample. Fashion trends, especially, seem to go by faster than ever as retailers have come to realize that higher turnover is good for sales. New clothes and shoes no longer reflect the changes of season as they used to. Instead, beachwear and cruise wear must be available year-round, so as to satisfy customers with travel plans at any time of year. But even then stock needs to rotate. Shoppers do not want to see the same swimsuits they saw in October again in November. Change is the watchword, and innovative retailers are at the cutting edge, always bringing their customers innovative and fresh products.

A useful analogy is to consider the grocery store of the present compared to the grocery store of the past. In olden days, grocery stores carried the bare necessities of what the shopper needed. Basic staples and traditional merchandise were the order of the day. Today, grocery stores are filled with innovative products from all over the world. Deli sections, ethnic foods, and nontraditional items fill the shopper's basket. Grocery stores set a standard of innovation that many other retailers could follow.

The objective of product freshness applies to all products, not just clothes. Retailers should be looking to expand their range of offerings to consumers. Just like shoppers for clothing, those looking for electronics, sporting goods, makeup, jewelry, and so on do not want to see the same products on the shelf month after month. Most retailers think of their product mix as represented by the products that are currently on the floor. Most of them should think of it as the mix of products that is available over time as well. The thinking should go like this: "What do you have on the floor today that wasn't there last week?"

Consumers will make repeat visits to stores that are known for having a high turnover rate of products. This is good for sales and good for repeat business. Similarly, all consumers will be aware of stores that have the same old items on display, month after long month. Such stores are ineffective in drawing consumers back for repeat visits. The typical consumer might be shopping for a new audio system, a new computer, or a new suit, and might be comparison-shopping over a long period of time. During this period of time some stores will add new and innovative products to their mix and will hold the consumer's interest, while others will offer the same old, tired product line no matter how many times the consumer goes back. Even in such stores, changes of display and arrangement in the store would offer the repeat consumer a new perspective on an old product line.

All shoppers will be aware of stores that seem to be caught in a time warp, where the product displays seem to be frozen forever in the same state in which they were first set up, sometimes even apparently *years* earlier. Everybody is familiar with such stores, where the management and staff cannot be bothered to clean the dust from the displays. Consumers tire quickly of these stores and quickly turn their attention elsewhere. Retailers who want to compete successfully in the new economy will do well to avoid these common problems and to follow the *Greengrocer Principle*—to keep product displays farm-fresh and spotlessly clean. The goal is to make the product look *appetizing* to the shopper, whether it is new shoes or a new appliance.

A good example is found in the show rooms of automobile dealerships. Cars never look better or more appealing than when they are in the showroom, spotlessly clean, and under the glare of hundreds of lights. Many clothing stores follow the same rule by placing perfectly arranged articles under spotlights. Unfortunately, there are just as many stores where little or no thought or effort seems to go into product display, and as a result, consumers are turned off before they ever start. The wise greengrocer puts his fruits and vegetables under display lights and keeps them looking fresh and desirable. Every retailer should strive for the same effect.

LOCATION, LOCATION, LOCATION

A well-known mantra in the retailing business is that location is everything. This only stands to reason. A business can always compete with adversaries by lowering prices, improving services, duplicating products, increasing advertising, and so on. But if that business's *location* with respect to competitors is inappropriate, there is little that can be done about it except to move. An appropriately thought-out location strategy is imperative for the success of retail businesses. The locational decision is perhaps one of the most important ones that a business will make. Good location means ready and easy access to one's customer base, and even small differences in location can have a significant effect on the success of a business. Think of the difference between the retail business that is strategically located at a major arterial intersection as compared to another one that is one block away from that key intersection. Just a single city block might make all the difference in the world to the success of those businesses. Location can be the ultimate key to retail prosperity.

From the shopper's point of view, location is usually but one part of the customer's overall subconscious judgment of a store. Shoppers are not generally aware of the locational advantage of one store over another; rather they simply prefer or patronize one over the other. Location is mostly a *subliminal* element to the shopping consumer. It is taken into account only as one small piece of the shopper's overall impression of a store. Shoppers do not patronize a store *because* it has a good location. They patronize it because they like it, even though the location may represent an important reason why they like it. For the retailer, this means that a great location is a central element of the store's general appeal to customers. For a customer, it is just part of the background of their general impression of the store.

Shoppers are creatures of habit. A retail outlet with a good location will be visible, will be easily accessible, and will feature convenient pedestrian access or parking. Shoppers will often first patronize a store with a good location because they are more likely to encounter it. But shoppers will continue to patronize such a store only if the store itself attracts them on its own merits. A good location for a business can be irrelevant if the store does not stand alone as an equal competitor with others. Thus many businesses will succeed in destroying the otherwise potential benefits of an excellent location. This only goes to prove that *location is not everything*—a lesson that has probably been lost on many a failed enterprise. As an analogy to this, just think of the numerous businesses in out-of-the-way locations that have managed to make successes of themselves in spite of their poor locations. Location is important, but it is only one small piece of the retail puzzle.

Good location implies a high volume of walk-in traffic. A store on the central aisle of a mall, near a major anchor store, for example, will generate far more walk-in traffic than the same store located on a side aisle of the mall. Similarly, a store on a busy street corner, near a large department store, will create a greater influx of shoppers than one on an out-of-the-way side street. Locations with greater accessibility are worth more to the retailer, and this is reflected in their higher rents or locational costs. To the retailer there has to be a balance. The higher rent costs associated with a better location need to be offset by the higher amount of traffic that is generated. As a consequence, it may be more important for businesses that rely heavily on impulse buying to have better locations. More traffic may translate into more spontaneous purchases. Clothing, cosmetics, and jewelry are all items for which a highly visible location helps to spur sales. On the other hand, when the product line is one where plenty of forethought goes into the purchase, a central location is probably a less important consideration. Automobiles and other such major purchases are probably less influenced by vendors having conspicuous locations.

How much does distance act as a deterrent to the walking shopper? Probably a lot, although shopping mall designers do their best to ensure that shoppers will maximize the amount of walking that they do. As you may have noticed, malls are always designed with two, three, four, or more big stores in them. Usually these big stores are the big chain department stores, big-box retailers, major grocery stores, and so on. These big stores are known in the mall design business as anchor stores because they are supposed to be the major magnets of attraction for the malls they represent. The idea is that the anchors are the major drawing cards of the mall and that they attract a large number of customers because of their size. In between the anchor stores you will find the other smaller retailers of the mall. These smaller businesses depend in part for their success on the walk-in traffic that the big anchor stores generate. You will notice, in fact, that many of the kinds of businesses that thrive in malls are the ones where walk-in traffic and impulse buying are important.

But what is so interesting about mall design is the fact that the anchor stores are always spread far apart. In fact, if it always seems to you that you are being forced to walk from one end of the mall to the other, you are exactly right, because that is just the way the mall designers planned it. They want you to walk from end to end in the mall because they want you to walk past all of the other stores in which they are hoping you will browse and, perhaps, buy something from on impulse. The pedestrian traffic generated by the big anchors in the mall is supposed to help the smaller stores generate business. The great irony of it is that even though mall designers do the utmost to make their malls pleasant and pleasing for the customer, they also try to make the customer walk as far as possible. They know that on most of your trips to the mall you will just want to patronize the big anchor stores, but they make it as difficult as possible for you to do that. Many tired and frustrated customers go back to their cars to *drive from one end of the mall to the other* to avoid the lengthy walk that the mall designers have intentionally built in.

Another interesting feature of mall layouts that you will notice is that *competing* stores tend to be located close to one another. This pattern seems at odds with intuition. Wouldn't you think that if someone were going to open a shoe store, for instance, they would want to be as far away as possible from their competitors? In other words, wouldn't a store sell more shoes if it didn't have to compete with other, nearby shoe stores? In fact, what you will see in malls is exactly opposite to this idea. Many stores, and in particular shoe and clothing stores, will tend to be located *near* one another, in clusters. Believe it or not, the stores do this for competitive reasons. If there is going to be a cluster of shoe stores, then every shoe storeowner wants to be near the cluster, because the group of stores will draw a large number of comparison-shopping shoppers. Thus there is more in it for everyone, even if they are all competing with one another.

Shopping on foot in other areas, particularly downtown shopping districts, is not altogether different from mall walking. The collection of stores in traditional urban shopping areas usually arises without any deliberate plan (unlike the malls) and ends up being a rather eclectic collection of assorted shops. However, there is usually a collection of major department-style stores that serve the same function as the anchor stores in a mall. Similarly, many cities also have particular shopping districts where a collection of similar stores—typically clothing or footwear stores—will congregate. By and large, then, the pattern of stores in downtown shopping areas is similar to that of malls even though it is not planned that way. For the walking shopper this means that patterns of travel are similar to those in malls, with foot traffic often going up one side of the street and then down the other. Small stores and businesses are interspersed with major chains and are the beneficiaries of the traffic generated by them.

THE PYRAMID OF RETAIL SHOPPING

One way to think about the issue of location is to think about the role of driving when it comes to shopping. Unlike the circumscribed area of the mall, the area where the city shopper shops in his car is almost limitless. Distance traveled becomes much less important, and instead the *time* expended on travel becomes a real issue of concern. When people shop for major items, they go beyond the bounds of walking around in the mall or in the downtown area and instead usually find it necessary to travel greater distances to get the things they want. What, then, is the role of location from the perspective of the driving shopper?

The shopper, for her part, wants to minimize time. Shoppers do not really care where they have to go to get things as long as it does not take too long. Distance, direction, and location are virtually irrelevant to the shopper, who is concerned only with how much time it will take to get somewhere.

Consider the average shopper driving around to buy clothing, food, hardware, and so on. Is there any logic to the pattern of his or her shopping? The answer to this question is that there is a subtle sense to it all. It consists of a *pyramid* of retail shopping that is all but invisible to the average shopper. The pyramid of city shopping forces traveling consumers to travel greater distances for higher-end items. Basically, the higher-end the item, the farther the consumer will have to travel to get it. For example, everyday items such as newspapers and cigarettes tend to be available in nearby, convenient locations, while higher-end items, such as computers or audio systems, tend to be sold at greater distances away from the consumer.

The pyramid of retail centers in an average city is illustrated in Figure 11.1. The essential ingredients of this pyramid are that as we move from top to bottom, there are more shopping opportunities at each level. The average-sized city usually has one major, downtown shopping area, several major malls, dozens of minor shopping centers, and hundreds of convenience stores or neighborhood convenience centers. The question, now, is how this pattern of retail shopping comes into existence. How does the shopping behavior of thousands of individual consumers cause such a retail pyramid to emerge?

Figure 11.1
Retail Centers

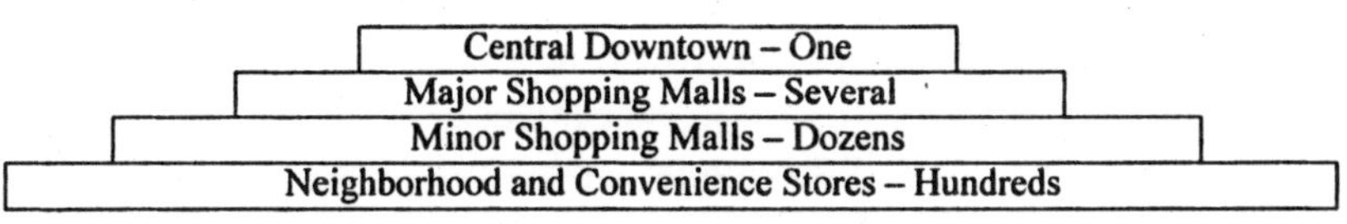

Consider the shopping patterns of a stay-at-home housewife or house-husband during a typical span of a few days. Let's suppose that on day one, our consumer needs milk and bread and so travels to a neighborhood convenience store. Often, such a store is located in a neighborhood convenience center that might also provide gasoline, newspapers, and so on. This is the closest shopping opportunity to the home. Normally the local convenience store is able to charge higher prices in exchange for the convenience that it provides. This convenience not only includes its closer location but also the fact that it has extended hours of operation.

On day two our consumer needs to make a trip for fast food and a visit to a florist. Along the way he or she visits the bank. This might involve driving to a minor shopping mall that is not too far from the home. The minor mall is likely not enclosed and offers other essential services such as a small drugstore, a dry cleaner, movie rental store, or similar businesses.

On day three the consumer desires to go shopping for groceries and children's clothing. Typically this might suggest travel to a major shopping mall and visiting two of the big anchor stores in the mall. In all likelihood the consumer will find it necessary to travel further on Day Three than on the previous two days. There are fewer major malls, and they tend to be spread farther apart.

On day four our shopper decides to travel to the downtown shopping district to shop for adult clothing, in particular, evening or formal wear. This trip covers a still larger distance in order to have access to some of the specialty shops in the downtown area.

In any retail market, storeowners strive for an edge—any edge that will give them a leg up on their competitors. Location can sometimes provide such an edge. It is clear in the example above that consumers expect certain goods and services to be available at certain convenient distances. If an entrepreneur can satisfy that demand, he or she can be successful. Finding a business opportunity in a mall or plaza location requires the identification of a marketing niche that has yet to be filled in that location. It is necessary only to look at other successful entrepreneurs, in other locations, in order to identify market niches that have been profitable elsewhere.

What is interesting about consumer behavior in the pyramid of shopping is that at each stage, not only does the consumer travel farther, but also he or she invests more time and money in traveling. The time and travel costs expended to shop for formal wear downtown are far greater than those involved in going to the convenience store.

Recognizing that there is a citywide market for some goods is another way for a potential entrepreneur to identify market niches that have not been filled. In other words, it is necessary to ask what kinds of new businesses could survive if they were the only one, or one of a few, in the city. This is how really specialized stores come into existence. A good example is a store that sells only costumes for special occasions such as Halloween. Only a few such specialized businesses usually can survive in a city. The number will depend upon the size of the city.

A further and important component of the life of the driving consumer is found in what is known in the retailing industry as the multipurpose shopping trip. This describes the situation in which a consumer goes shopping for more than one item at once. Thus if a shopper goes to the bank, and then the mall, and then the gas station, she is considered to be making a multipurpose trip. From the retailer's point of view this suggests that it can sometimes be important to be located near to other retailers, regardless of what they are selling, simply because they become a part of the shopper's daily travels.

A further idea is that of a retailer locating near to what we might call a sister business, that is, one that sells closely related products. For instance, a paint store might be interested in locating near a decorating store, or a drapery shop near to a furniture shop. Many businesses can be successful merely by associating themselves, by location and product mix, with other already successful enterprises. This success by association will work in malls as well as in other retail environments. Pairs or groups of stores can have a symbiotic retail relationship that mutually benefits one another.

Chapter 12

INTERNET RETAILING

Internet retailing, or *e-tailing,* as it has come to be known, is heralded to be the new messiah. There is not a news source that does not tout the new era of Internet shopping. This new form of shopping is said to be unprecedented in its sudden surge in popularity and is reported to be challenging the dominance of traditional shopping as a source of revenue for retailers. Those who study the topic suggest that business over the Internet is rising at least three times the rate of traditional sales in stores. Year to year, Internet sales are doubling.

The bottom line, however, is that *shopping is shopping,* and so there are certain inevitable truths that will apply to shopping on the Internet. What are the differences between regular shopping and Internet shopping? What can we learn, and what ideas can we apply from regular shopping that will help us to understand Internet shopping? Are there things about Internet shopping that are unique? What works and what does not work? What makes for an effective shopping Web site?

WHAT ARE THE BENEFITS OF WEB SHOPPING?

For the uninitiated, shopping on the Internet means shopping for products with the use of a desktop computer or television. People connect their computer to the Internet or Web (the names are used interchangeably) by using telephone lines or cable television lines. By doing so they are able to link to (or *visit*) sites made available by retailers. Such places on the Web have electronic addresses, and computer users are able to find a store by its address. For example, if you wanted to visit the Sears Web site you would use the electronic address www.sears.com. If this address is entered into a software program known as a Web browser—for example, Microsoft Internet Explorer—the computer user is able to connect to the Sears retail site and is able to do shopping through the computer. Electronic pages similar to the pages of a catalog appear on the user's computer screen. The shopping is equivalent to mail-order shopping only we could call it *e-mail order shopping*. The computer shopper orders goods online and the company ships them, usually by courier, to the home of the shopper. Payment for items is usually made by credit card.

All sites on the Internet can basically be divided into three categories. First, there are shopping sites such as those described here. These are sites where the first order of business is selling products to visitors to the site. Often such sites are set up so that purchases can be made by credit card. Second, there are sites that just provide information. These would include places such as educational institutions, governments, libraries, medical organizations, mutual funds, stock markets, consumer watchdogs, and so on. In most cases these sites provide their information for free and there is little or nothing for the Web-surfing consumer to buy. Well-known Internet search engines such as Yahoo or Excite are within this category, as are places for Internet auctions such as ebay.com. The third group of Web sites can be classified as those that are for entertainment purposes. Here users will find games to play, contests to enter, and so on, usually at no charge. The primary uses of the Internet reflect these three types of use, but more and more, shopping is becoming a significant part of it, as more companies establish a retail presence on the Web.

On the surface, online shopping does not really seem to do anything different from mail-order shopping or catalog shopping. In fact, the best way to think about Web shopping is to think of it as being just like shopping from a catalog. Instead of looking at the pages of a catalog, the shopper looks through the pages of the retailer's Web site. He or she selects the items wanted and places an electronic order for them. A few days later the products are delivered to the door. By and large, this is just catalog shopping done through a computer. What, then, is the huge fascination with Internet shopping? If it is virtually the same thing as catalog shopping, why is everyone, and apparently every company, so interested in getting on the Internet shopping bandwagon? What is the source of the infatuation with this new way of shopping?

The answer is that this new mode of shopping exploits the power of the Internet. Rather than having a traditional catalog to shop from, Web shoppers literally have the world at their doorstep. They can have online catalogs, or Web sites, from virtually every retailer in the world available on their home computers. Moreover, there is a new fascination and interest in Internet shopping that is fueling demand like never before. It is as if there has been a resurgence of interest in catalog shopping and every store in the world is trying to get in on the action and deliver its catalog to your door. This raises the biggest problem of the Internet for retailers, and that is how to compete in this electronic universe where literally every competitor is trying just as hard as you are to establish an Internet presence.

If Internet shopping is just like catalog shopping except that there are more stores, are there any other advantages that the Internet has over the traditional catalog? The answer is that there are several. One is that while a catalog is limited to a set number of pages, a Web site is limitless. It can have as many pages as the retailer wants. It would not be unusual, for example, to see a Web site with thousands of pages if that is what the seller wants. Wal-Mart reports that its Web site has more than 600,000 items, for instance.

A second advantage of the Web over a conventional catalog is that the Web is more up-to-date. While that Sears catalog may be six months old by the time the consumer sees it, a Web site can be updated quite literally minute by minute. This raises the idea of the Greengrocer Principle that says shoppers want farm-fresh and crisp merchandise. They want items to be up-to-date and as timely as possible. The Web provides this edge to the maximum. Of course, those familiar with the Internet will also be familiar with stale Web sites, where there is a message that says, "This site last updated on such and such a date," and where that date has long since expired.

A third advantage of a Web site over a catalog page is found in the amount of information that can be conveyed. A catalog is limited to a picture of the item, a brief verbal description, and ordering information. With a Web site, an unlimited amount of information can be displayed. Although the basic format still copies the catalog and consists of a picture and a verbal description, there is a variety of additional information that can be included. For example, the consumer can be shown a product from several angles, or the picture can be rotated through 360 degrees. It is possible to zoom in for a close-up look at the item. It is also possible to change the colors of a product so that the shopper can actually see the item in the various shades available, as opposed to the color-swatch approach of the catalog. Web sites also use virtual mannequins to demonstrate how clothing will look. In addition, video and/or sound clips can be made available to show the product in action, whether it is an item of clothing or a new car.

Still pictures of products will be passé on the Internet. The technology is changing so rapidly that it is difficult for entrepreneurs to keep up with it. The operative word is bandwidth. As Internet providers continue to offer ever more bandwidth, the very nature of the Internet will change. So-called Webcasting will shortly replace static pictures on the Internet. The shopper's Web connection will look just like a television screen, and indeed the difference between the look of the television screen and the Web screen will disappear. The two devices will be interchangeable, as they already are with Microsoft's Web TV. For the shopper, the electronic catalog of pages will turn into a television, with seamless transitions between live-action perspectives.

A further benefit of the Internet for shoppers is that product status information can be made available directly online. Is the desired product available? Is it available in the right size and color? How soon will it ship? All of these things of interest to the shopper, and more, can be made available.

A fifth area where the Web has an edge over a catalog is the extra product information it can provide. Not only can it provide detailed product specifications, for example, for an audio system; it can also provide reviews of the product that have appeared in other publications. In addition, some companies go so far as to put the actual product owner's manual on their Web site. Furthermore, the Web can present written comments and feedback from other consumers who have bought the product before you. For example, booksellers will provide online reviews of a book from interested readers who have already purchased it.

It is in the category of the provision of information that many people see the real power of the Internet. It brings power in the sense that information about all products can be readily exchanged among shoppers on the Internet. If a shopper has a bad experience with a retailer or a product, he or she can post a description of his or her encounter for other wary shoppers in chat rooms (Web sites for dialogue). Similarly, there are Web sites that devote themselves exclusively to the job of rating Web businesses. Bizrate.com, for example, evaluates online stores for shoppers, billing itself as a place where shoppers can "find the online stores that best serve your needs" and "start shopping with confidence." This democratization of information presents huge new challenges for retailers.

Another advantage of shopping on the Internet is that it is available 24 hours a day. While the same can be said of a catalog, it is also necessary to remember that the information on the Web can be live, while the catalog is essentially last year's information. Moreover, a big plus of the Web for the consumer is that a competitor's products are only a few clicks away. With the Sears home catalog, the shopper's selection is usually limited to the pages he has before him, while on the Internet, every competitor can present products in a head-to-head competition.

Unlike the catalog, the Web is available almost anywhere. Wherever a consumer has access to a computer, she has access to shopping on the Web. Many new vehicles are being made ready for the wireless world of the Web, and it is only a matter of time until people are regularly shopping while they sit in their cars. Of course, this raises the question of just how much shoppers *want* to shop, but in today's time-deprived world it is not difficult to imagine consumers Christmas shopping from their cars while they are stuck in commuter traffic on the way home from work.

Alliances are being formed between car companies and Internet companies. General Motors has formed a partnership with America Online, for example, while Ford has teamed up with Yahoo. General Motors estimates that its new partnership with America Online will bring in over 35 million extra visits per month to its Web site. This is the kind of impressive numbers that the Internet generates.

Television-quality, high-speed connections to the Internet are already available to consumers in some areas for free. The providers of such services make their money through advertising that runs on the consumer's computer screen. What is new and exciting about this approach, however, is that as consumers watch television-quality ads on their computers, they just click on any products they wish to purchase. This brings a whole new dimension to what we mean when we think of television, but it also makes the medium truly interactive for the first time. Clearly, this goes way beyond the capabilities of the old Sears catalog.

The idea of product placement in television and movies is an old one. Advertisers will pay to have their products featured on the latest television show or Hollywood movie. It is not unusual to see stars drinking a favorite soda pop or eating a well-known cereal. As point and click becomes ever more appropriate to popular media, it will be more common to see products of all types become available to the viewer. The idea of making all the products seen in a show or movie interactively available to shoppers was anticipated in the movie *The Truman Show,* starring Jim Carey, where the supposed viewers of the show could purchase almost any of the products seen on the screen. Kitchenware, houses, and even the actors' clothing were portrayed as being available for purchase. Active, online television-quality Internet capabilities will make this futuristic scenario come true for shoppers everywhere. Do you like that shirt that one of the stars of the television show is wearing? Soon you will be able to click on it, and order it. Shopping and television watching will merge into one and the same activity. The time when this sort of shopping will be an everyday occurrence is not just around the corner; it is already a reality.

Imagine the shopping possibilities. Imagine that all of the time that people spend watching television also becomes shopping time. Imagine that viewers can purchase *any* item they see on television at any time. This will change the whole television experience. Formerly passive television watchers will suddenly become active shoppers, when every moment of every scene presents a buying opportunity. Will this change programming? Will there be a conscious effort on the part of the producers to include more products for shoppers? The answer is almost certainly in the affirmative, and this means that the very nature of television programming will change. What if every show becomes a vehicle for sales? Will the programming and story line become secondary to the goal of selling products? In *The Truman Show,* the products being sold were a deliberate distraction that took away from the supposed story line of the show. Will the same thing happen to regular television viewing? Will television transform itself into an altogether different medium than it is right now? There are some difficult issues on the entertainment horizon, and the boundary line between entertainment and shopping is becoming ever more blurred.

There are several other ways in which Web shopping has advantages over catalog shopping. In addition to all of the things discussed above, the Web can also include features online such as giveaways, contests, special offers, links to other sites and related companies or products, recent announcements, company information and history, financing arrangements, online maps of dealer/retailer locations, answers to frequently asked questions, product test results, club membership arrangements, and so on. The list is endless. A recent innovation is bringing virtual salespeople to the Web. These are humanlike characters that greet the shopper online, answer his queries, and provide shopping guidance. Several companies are in the process of developing such virtual, interactive online agents. These are seen as the next wave of the Internet.

Sites that allow parents to establish credit accounts for their kids enhance direct shopping by teens on the Internet. One of the big obstacles to teen shopping on the Web has been that teens do not have credit cards and so have difficulty in paying for merchandise. Sites like rocketcash.com are set up to enable teen shoppers to overcome this limitation. Parents can use a credit card to set up credit for their teens, and then the kids are free to shop as they please.

I's there anything that the catalog does better than the Internet? Are there any lessons to be learned from the catalog? One big advantage of the catalog over the computer is its portability. If a shopper wants to look at the catalog in her favorite chair, at poolside, or while lounging in bed she can do so. Similarly, the catalog offers more privacy. While Web sites can track what the person online is doing and looking at, the catalog browser is entirely on her own. It might also be said that the catalog is a more leisurely method of shopping or browsing than is the Internet. The catalog shopper is not confronted with the hundreds of choices and decisions that face the Web shopper.

While many people might prefer the comfort and privacy afforded by catalog shopping, there is no denying that shopping on the Web presents a large number of advantages and opportunities for shopper and retailer alike. Paying testament to these advantages is the growing number of shoppers who are using the Internet to shop, and the growing number of retailers that are going online. At one point many Web watchers were wondering whether the infatuation with shopping on the Internet was just a passing fad, like so many others. This has not been the case. Many retailers report continually growing sales in the Internet portion of their sales, and indeed many have been pleasantly surprised by their results. Unfortunately, this is not necessarily true for all Web enterprises. There are no doubt a large number of unreported cases of Web shopping failures where large budgets have been spent to get online, only to find that expected sales did not materialize.

HOW DOES THE WEB COMPARE TO TRADITIONAL SHOPPING?

The old-fashioned selling of products in a traditional store has come to be known as *bricks-and-mortar* retailing. This name is to distinguish it from Internet e-tailing where a traditional, physical store is not needed. Proponents of Web shopping argue that it has a number of advantages over traditional shopping. How do shoppers benefit from Web shopping? Why is it growing so in popularity?

A bricks-and-mortar store has a limited geographical range. Customers have to travel to the store and the total number of potential customers is therefore limited by geography. With a virtual, Internet store there are no geographical limits to the customer base. Quite literally the whole world is at the doorstep, with all potential customers being only a few clicks away from ordering products. This is the greatest retailing revolution that the Internet represents. It essentially destroys the old-fashioned geography of bricks-and-mortar stores and puts all retailers, big or small, on an equal footing. A big store chain used to be able to dominate the market by having many outlets in a large number of places. This is, for example, still the strategy used by Wal-Mart as it continues to open more stores in more locations.

In the world of the Internet, however, anyone with a Web site can compete equally with anyone else with a Web site. The number of retail outlets does not matter, and this gives the owner of a single successful Web site a huge advantage. Think of an example. A regular, bricks-and-mortar bookstore like Barnes and Noble needs to build a retail outlet and hire staff in every major market in the country. That costs a lot of money. Compare this to Amazon.com, an online bookstore, which can compete head to head with Barnes and Noble while having to have only *one* location, *one* set of staff, and *one* inventory. The cost savings are enormous for the Web store as compared to the chain of traditional stores. Furthermore, these cost savings can be used to undermine the competition with respect to prices. Price savings can be passed on to customers in the form of lower prices. Internet stores have a huge competitive edge over bricks-and-mortar stores and this is one of the reasons why they are so popular. Basically, anyone with a computer can aspire to set up his or her own Web business with the whole world as his or her potential market.

There are plenty of other reasons why Web shopping is so popular. For one thing, it frees people from having to make an actual trip to a store or the mall. Web shopping can be done from the convenience of home and so saves a lot of time and effort, not to mention the cost of gas or travel. There is no need to get in the car, contend with the traffic, look for a parking spot, walk through the mall, or fight the crowds. No standing in line at checkouts or hauling heavy purchases through the store. Shoppers will not have the frustration of finding the product they want, only to discover that it is out of stock or not available in their size. No more dealing with pushy salespeople or rude customers. Web shopping frees the shopper from a lot of problems and a lot of hassle. Shoppers can find what they want on the Web, order it online, and wait for it to be delivered. Web shopping frees up time to do other things. A three-hour trip to the mall can be replaced by 10 minutes on the Internet.

A lot of people are voting for the convenience and ease of this style of shopping.

For those shoppers who long for the idea of shopping at the mall, the Web has its own equivalent. Web-based virtual malls, or directories of shopping sites, try to make it easier for the online shopper to shop. These virtual shopping centers put a large number of stores together in one online location and make it possible for shoppers to visit multiple stores without having to surf around. Every store is only one click away from every other store. An example can be found at Yahoo.com, where Yahoo! Shopping advertises "Thousands of stores. Millions of products." Another is ShopNow.com, which describes itself as "The Shopping Marketplace."

On the Web, people in northern climates do not have to head out into the cold weather in order to make a shopping trip. If it's 20 degrees below outside, or the driveway is not shoveled, the Web shopper can go about her business from the comfort of her home. The same applies for those people where it is 100 degrees in the shade. In areas where people feel unsafe traveling the streets at night, for example, the Web makes shopping from home a reality. A survey by Supermarket News found that more than 50 percent of shoppers are concerned about personal safety while in store parking lots.

With the Internet, people who live in rural areas can go shopping just like their counterparts in the city. No longer does living in a country or rural setting imply that one must travel into the city to undertake shopping. Rural residents are on an equal footing with city dwellers when it comes to shopping on the Web. In this regard, the Web provides a service for country folks that the catalogs did in the past. The importance of the Internet for noncity shoppers should not go unnoted. It brings them into the realm of mainstream shopping. It puts them on an equal footing with city residents in terms of price, quality, and style. No longer does the teen in a rural area have to make a trip to the big city to find items of fashion, for example. The latest and most up-to-date styles are available right at home.

Web shopping provides access to thousands of shopping sites 24 hours a day, seven days a week. Shopping on the Web is a real boon to working people who do not have time during the day to get to stores. The Web allows them to shop in the evenings or on weekends, without having to travel around from store to store. Elderly people, invalids, women with young children, shift workers, and others will find that the Web brings the world to their doorstep.

In major urban areas, even the prospect of waiting a day or two for the delivery of items ordered online has become a thing of the past. In

New York, for example, there are Internet delivery services that bring products within an hour of their being ordered. The almost instant delivery of snacks, magazines, flowers, books, and video games has become commonplace as Internet delivery businesses spring up to compete with one another. A Web sales and delivery business in New York will even deliver food items like ice-cream bars to workers in offices in a matter of minutes.

Another application of the Web comes from the idea of gift registries. These registries have been in use for generations by department stores. Expectant mothers and prospective married couples create a wish list of the gifts they most want others to buy. This used to be done at a favorite department store. The existence of the Internet allows all businesses to create online registries for their shoppers. Teens, for example, who are always difficult for adults to shop for, can create registries of the things they most want for Christmas, birthdays, or at any time. The Internet brings the idea of the gift registry to a new level of sophistication and widespread use.

Web shopping heightens one's ability to carry out comparison-shopping. Regardless of what product you are shopping for, it is possible to visit dozens of competitors' sites within a matter of minutes in order to comparison-shop. This will often be far easier than traveling from store to store, or mall to mall, in the city. If you are looking at cameras, for instance, you can visit all of the sites of the major, brand-name camera manufacturers by clicking around on your computer. Within a short half-hour you will have been able to look at a dozen different cameras and gotten a good idea of their features and prices. Web shopping empowers the consumer, putting unprecedented amounts of information literally at her fingertips.

A further boon to comparison-shoppers on the Web is found in the use of Web sites that comparison-shop for the shopper automatically. The shopper needs only to identify what she is shopping for, and one of these automated sites will carry out an Internet search for the best deals. An example of such a site is bottomdollar.com, which bills itself as "The Shopping Search Engine."

The Web provides shoppers with extra information for purposes of comparison-shopping. A survey by J. D. Power and Associates, for example, shows that nine percent of new-vehicle buyers use online information services when they shop for cars. "We believe more shoppers will move into 'cyberspace' as they become more familiar and more comfortable with online vehicle services," says Jon Osborn, manager of auto sales research at J. D. Power. He notes also that "Consumers have quickly turned away from shopping only at dealerships as Internet sources have become available."

Interested in accessories when you shop? Many Internet sites monitor the shopper's selections when she shops and then make recommendations about accessories and related items. For example, when the shopper orders a book online, the Web site will suggest other, closely related titles that may be of interest. Order a blouse, and a matching scarf will be suggested. Order a shirt, and the Web site will recommend a tie. Although some would regard this as an invasion of privacy, others would see it as a convenience, letting the software take some of the strain out of shopping.

Shopping on the Internet also brings the whole world to the shopper's doorstep. Consumers who were previously restricted to the products available at local stores now have access to products from the world over. This feature is truly one of the liberating features of shopping on the Internet. Items that were previously available only in segmented market areas can now be made available to consumers anywhere. Internet shopping literally revolutionizes the geography of shopping.

Another edge that goes to Internet stores is that they have the capacity to allow customers to special order products. Nike.com, for example, has a Web site that allows shoppers to special order custom-designed shoes. Reebok and Adidas are believed to be following suit. This represents just the beginning of a host of custom-made products that shoppers will be able to order online. Similarly, the Web allows customers to directly and anonymously order embarrassing products or those with which they want to be discreet.

One of the ways in which shoppers are exploiting the power of the Internet is to use it *in combination* with regular shopping. Suppose a shopper is interested in buying a big-screen television set. Today it is possible to surf the Internet and do some serious comparison-shopping before the shopper heads out to look at the actual product. This informed consumer might save himself a great deal of trouble by being able to narrow down his field of choices before he ever leaves home. He is also in a much better position to deal with salespeople, because in many cases he may know more about the product than the salesman does. Even if the Internet does not replace the bricks-and-mortar store, it empowers the shopper with information in a way that has never been witnessed before.

One of the hottest uses for the Internet has arisen in its use for online auctions. Veteran shoppers argue that patient participants in Internet auctions can find excellent deals. Not only can shoppers buy items, but they can also auction off products that they wish to sell themselves. The site that has established itself as the leading name in online auctions is ebay.com. It is one of the Web pioneers.

What are the disadvantages of Internet shopping? There are many. One is that the shopper does not get the hands-on experience of shopping in the store. Looking at a picture or a video of some products is just not the same as seeing them in person. In buying clothing, for instance, the Internet shopper misses out on the touch and feel of the fabric from which the product is made, even though this can sometimes be a crucial factor in a shopper's decision. The same can be said when it comes to the smell of products or how they look in person or how they sound. It is impossible, for example, to experience a big-screen TV on the Web.

Some products are naturals when it comes to selling on the Web, while others just do not quite work. For example, while it is easy for manufacturers to try to sell shoes on the Internet, there will always be the obvious problem of the shopper not being able to try them on in person. Similarly, while some products like computers may be obvious choices to sell on the Web, others, like sound systems, just do not work out very well. There are innumerable products where first-hand experience is essential to a successful sale.

Having to wait for delivery is an obvious drawback of Internet shopping. When you go to buy a product in person, you get the pleasure of being able to take that product home and experience it immediately. This is an extremely important aspect of the psychology of shopping and is one that the Internet fails on miserably. People often buy things just to please themselves, and with Internet shopping the gratification must be delayed until the delivery truck arrives. This is probably one of the main reasons why Internet shopping will never totally replace the traditional store. Shoppers do not shop just to acquire products. The Internet leaves the whole in-person shopping experience out of the equation. There will always be a need for personal shopping. One approach to the problem of delivery has been to create systems where the Internet shopper orders online, but then goes to the mall to pick up the purchases. The mall becomes an e-depot in this approach, which combines the best of Internet shopping with the convenience of getting what was purchased right away.

Although many Web shopping sites offer free delivery, there are still some sites where the extra cost of delivery plays a role. There is also the inconvenience of delivery. Will someone be home when the package arrives? If not, will it be necessary to go somewhere to pick up the parcel that could not be delivered? And what about returns? What do you do with an Internet purchase that needs to go back to the seller? While some retailers allow customers to return purchases to their bricks-and-mortar stores, this is not always possible. Thus the onus may be on the consumer to repackage the merchandise and mail it back to the sender. This not only presents an extra cost but also represents a major nuisance for the shopper. Once again, it becomes apparent that certain products are more natural to Internet shopping than others. For instance, it would be very uncommon for people to want to return a book to a Web vendor, while people would be very likely to want to return clothing. Vendors that have both traditional shopping sites and an Internet site are sometimes called *clicks-and-mortar* stores.

Web shopping sites are not entirely immune to the problems of traditional retailers. Surveys show that one of the top three complaints that e-shoppers have about Web sites is out-of-stock products. This is not surprising when one realizes that shoppers from all over the world might be shopping at a single Web site. The other two main complaints of e-shoppers are with respect to high shipping costs and slow-performing Web sites. In the latter case, Web retailers should be acutely aware that Web shoppers and surfers of all kinds are extremely intolerant of slow Web sites. Any delay at all will usually cause the shopper to click and look elsewhere.

So what are consumers saying by using e-tail? They are saying that (a) they want to shop at home; (b) they want more and better information; (c) they do not like the hassle of traveling to and shopping in stores; and (d) they do not really care if they get the in-store experience. To get the benefits of Web shopping they are willing to give up (a) first hand experience with products; (b) the ability to immediately take products home; and (c) personal service.

WHY DO SOME WEB SITES SUCCEED WHILE OTHERS FAIL?

The success rate of Web enterprises will reflect that of any other. Web-based businesses will be as diverse as those in the traditional retail sector. There will always be one end of the spectrum of e-tailers where results are not as good as expected. The failing end of the group will be made up of those businesses that have tried their hand at Web retailing and discovered that sales did not go as planned. One can only imagine the large number of idle Web sites out there that receive only a few hits per day. The size of some of the budgets that some companies have spent on establishing Web sites will no doubt have been very large, and yet results will have been disappointing. For instance, in 1999 Disney reported that its Internet effort lost over $1 billion. At the same time, there will be the other end of the spectrum of Web retailers where sales have caught on. Newspapers are filled every day with stories of the latest young entrepreneurs to become millionaires when a big company buys out their fledgling Internet site. Many retailers will have succeeded handsomely with their Web sites, and these are undoubtedly the ones that trumpet the great potential of the Internet in media reports. Many have come to believe that their own success on the Internet has been duplicated by everyone else who has given it a try. In between the two ends of the e-tailing spectrum one will find the huge majority of businesses. These will be the ones that have worked hard at establishing an Internet presence and who have also had a modicum of success with their sites. While they see achievement, they also see room for improvement, and are inspired by the accomplishments of other firms that get reported in the press.

What is it that makes for a successful Web site? Why do some sites become instant hits, while others languish in the doldrums of the Internet? Any person that can provide a definitive and easy answer to that question has the means to become wealthy. Successful Web sites receive hundreds of thousands or even millions of visitors per day. There is a surfing public out there that is looking for places to go on the Internet, and a few lucky Web sites are able to become instant, overnight winners. It is basically the same as any form of entertainment. Why does one rock group become a worldwide success while another, just as talented, languishes? Why does one singer achieve international fame while another never gets beyond her hometown? The answer is that it has a lot to do with luck. Many Web sites achieve celebrity status among the global community of Web surfers. Word spreads quickly about an attractive or interesting Web site and people flock to it. They tell their friends, relatives, and coworkers about it, and before long it seems like the whole world has heard about it. Everyone who surfs the Web will have experienced the phenomenon of being informed by another person of a must-visit Web site. Just like any other human enterprise that depends on word of mouth, a bandwagon effect turns some Web sites into instant overnight success stories.

Luck is just one ingredient of the many successful Web sites that exist, however. There are many other Web sites, in fact the majority, where success has come about through hard work. Having a good Web site is only half the battle. The other half is attracting visitors to a site, and in the highly competitive dot-com world, this is easier said than done. Most of the successful Web enterprises have worked long and hard at promoting and advertising their sites to the public.

What good is a good Web site if no one knows about it? Promotion is the key to success. It could be suggested that at least two-thirds of the budget for a major company Web site should be devoted to advertising and promotion. Give yourself a test. See how many names of Web sites you can remember if you do not go by well-known company names. It is probably not very many. The fact is that people just do not remember dot-com names very well. Right now the race to create memorable Web site names is like a land grab, with companies competing for their share of the customer's Internet mindset.

There are several types of Web site names that are memorable. First of all there are those associated with brand names like TVGuide.com, Ford.com, QuakerOats.com, Kodak.com or Campbellsoup.com. Such names are easy to remember and rely on the strength of well-established brand names for their success. Second, there are those that were first on the scene and established names for themselves long before the big stampede to Web sites started. Amazon.com is probably among the best known of what we could call these Web site pioneers. Third, there are those Web sites that use a common word to describe themselves. Sites like cars.com, toys.com, and cameras.com are intuitive and do not require the shopper to memorize a name. Sometimes these can lead to major Web sites, as in the case of toys.com, which connects to etoys.com, a large Internet toy supplier. Other times, they can lead to small Web sites, such as cameras.com, which links to an independent camera store, E. P. Levine, in Boston. Fourth, there are Web site names that describe an event or feeling. Examples such as IcraveTV.com or iwon.com let the Web surfer know why he is going to a particular site. Fifth, there are Web site addresses that lead the surfer to related sites. For example, a search for freestuff.com takes the Internet surfer to gamesville.com. Sixth, there are also many Web sites where the name of the site does not describe either what you expect to find there or a company name. One example is uproar.com, which is a site for games. Apparently the creators hope that the name is simply memorable on its own merits. Another seventh possibility is to name a Web site after a geographical place; for example, for Canadians there is a site called Canada.com. Eighth, we might identify those companies that were already successful at doing sales by phone when the Internet revolution started. Some of these, like Dell computers, were already successful at online sales and it was easy for shoppers to make the transition to Dell.com. Finally, there are many companies trying to establish an all-in-one identity by having a Web site address that also matches their 1–800 toll-free number and their corporate name.

Even if shoppers do remember the name of a Web site, it is another thing altogether to get them to visit it regularly. A good example of a Web site advertising campaign at work that creates multiple visits is the one by the people at iwon.com. They hype their site by promising cash prizes to surfers who visit. Not only does this provide an incentive for people to visit on a regular basis (the site gives away cash daily), but it is also an easy Web address to remember. The name itself is evocative of an experience the surfer hopes for. It is a stellar example of a strong Web promotion. Another good example of a way in which to promote a Web site comes from Wal-Mart. They have joined forces with America Online to create an Internet service provider (ISP) business of their own. That way, if there are consumers who cannot afford an Internet hookup, Wal-Mart can provide them with its own discount Internet service.

Brand names are a huge reason for the success of many Web sites. It does not take much thought or imagination for consumers to go looking for well-known names like Ford.com or Sears.com. Brand-name success in the traditional retail world leads to success in the online world. When consumers are overwhelmed by too much information and too many dot-com names on the Web, they will quite naturally fall back to well-known and trusted brand names that they know. We might call this the *Disney World* phenomenon. Disney World represents a brand name that has three important characteristics: it is a name that everyone knows, it is a place just about everyone wants to visit, and it is easy to remember. These should be the criteria for every Web site. Companies that have a recognized brand name but are not using it on the Web are missing a big opportunity to exploit the status of that consumer recognition. Most of them satisfy the three Disney World criteria without even being aware of it.

Internet shoppers prefer to shop what they are familiar with. This fact is confirmed by research from Jupiter Communications, Inc., a worldwide authority on Internet shopping. Recent surveys show that site recognition and trust are significant determinants when shoppers select a Web site. In addition, Jupiter research shows that 39 percent of shoppers indicated that they would shop with online merchants with whom they had previously shopped through stores or catalogs.

Even with a well-known brand name, it is difficult to get surfers to visit a Web site on a regular basis. Promotional efforts are necessary even if a company has a recognized and well-known name. A further consideration is whether a Web site is intended to be a point of shopping and sales, or whether it is just set up as a method of customer relations and information. For example, Campbellsoup.com does not sell soup. It just provides information, recipes, contests, and so on, for its customers. Compare this to a site like CircuitCity.com, which is all about sales. Many such successful retail sites use shopping-cart and aisle metaphors to make the shopper feel comfortable and to make the shopping experience more familiar.

The actual design of a Web site is an important criterion in Web site success. Internet surfers soon learn to distinguish a good Web site from a poor one. A good site functions smoothly and seamlessly for the shopper, and indeed, the shopper is not even aware of the properties of the site because he is so wrapped up in the product he is looking at. A poor Web site design is awkward and poorly organized, and the shopper using it finds it to be a distraction. There are many firms these days that specialize in Web site design, and their professional sites are usually pretty easy to distinguish from the amateur ones that many people try to create on their own. Big companies with deep pockets have a decided edge when it comes to placing high quality Web sites on the Internet. This suggests that just as is the case with traditional shopping, it is more difficult for the small retailer to compete.

Part of the success of a Web site is to get it linked to other sites where surfers are likely to be browsing. Mergers and acquisitions are becoming ever more important in the Internet world as one big Internet site links to another. Retailers are joining forces with major Internet players in order to increase the strength of both. For example, Kmart, one of the biggest American retail chains, has joined together with America Online to create its own Internet company named Bluelight.com. The site is intended to give consumers *free* Internet access to Kmart online shopping services. As company chief executive Floyd Hall said, "The way we see it, you don't have to pay to get into a Kmart store, why should you have to pay to visit the Kmart Web site?" A similar cooperative deal was also forged between America Online and Circuit City. Under this alliance, Circuit City will promote America Online in over 600 retail stores while America Online will feature Circuit City on its online shopping channels. Yet another big partnership has been formed between Microsoft and RadioShack. Microsoft will invest $100 million in RadioShack's online store, while in exchange RadioShack will promote Microsoft Internet services. In all three of these alliances it is big businesses that are getting bigger, at the expense of smaller market participants.

Some retailers may just not belong on the Internet. While brand names like Coke and Pizza Hut may be well known, they do not generate a lot of Web traffic. Basically products that are frequently purchased and low in price, such as pop and pizza, do not sell well on the Web. A survey by Forrester Research shows that the most popular businesses on the Web are technology firms, online retailers, travel, financial services, and automakers. There are, no doubt, many businesses that believe they should have an Internet presence but where Web shoppers will be largely indifferent.

WEB SITES—GOLD RUSH FEVER?

So what do you do if you are a company that does not have a well-known brand name and you want to set up a successful Web business? How do you distinguish yourself? How do you stand out from the crowd? The answer is that just having a good Web site is not enough anymore. There is too much competition these days, given that virtually anybody can create a Web site. In the highly competitive, modern dot-com world, a firm is going to have to continually and repeatedly advertise itself and its Web site if it wants to attract Internet business. It is going to need deep pockets to do so. There is just too much competition to make it possible for a small, stand-alone Web site to be a big success otherwise. If you do not have a well-established brand name, you are doomed to obscurity in the dot-com world unless you pull out all the stops to promote and advèrtise your site. Consider, for example, a company that wishes to sell mutual funds over the Internet. There are literally thousands of competitors in this business, and no matter how good one company's Web site is, it will not be very successful if it does not draw enough attention to itself and its Web site to make it stand out above the competition. Try a test. Name a mutual fund Web site. If the reader can name one at all it would only be because he is already familiar with it, or because it is very well promoted. By the way, Fidelity.com is the biggest mutual fund company in the world. Did you remember their name?

Advertising has always been important in the success of one enterprise over another, and the same is now becoming true of the Internet. In the infancy of the Web, many retailers could be successful simply because they were there first. The great success of some early innovators, such as Amazon.com, leads others to believe that they can be just as prosperous. Quite literally, a sort of gold-rush fever has taken over the Internet, where everyone believes they can achieve success by simply staking their claim and setting up their own Web site. Just like the real gold rush, the success stories of a few lead the masses to follow, chasing a dream of easy riches. Software to create your own Web site is available in every computer store, and almost everyone thinks they can get rich by setting up their own Internet business, or else by setting up a Web site for an existing business. The truth of the matter is that the market is already saturated with Web site wannabes and there is little room left for amateurs. The gold rush is over. A few got rich, but many more will be disappointed by their efforts.

Just take a look at some of the junk that exists on the Internet already. A search for almost any subject brings up lists of amateurs sites created by would-be entrepreneurs. Assisting in this effort has been the creation of enterprises like geocities.com that assist individuals in setting up their own Web sites for free. Such efforts have only added to the already huge mass of amateurish and nonprofessional Web sites that clutter the Internet. Sure, there are always a few success stories, but by and large the Internet is being overwhelmed by sites that are almost always dead ends. This is the price one pays for democracy, but at the same time when it comes to shopping on the Web, one has to be very wary of dealing with incompetent businesses that got on the Web for the price of $40 worth of software.

THE NEW WEB

The Web world has become a highly competitive business and there is no longer any room in it for the faint of heart. If Disney can afford to lose $1 billion a year on its Web site, how can the little guy compete? Big business will come to dominate the Web because it has the resources to engage in head-to-head competition with all comers and will ultimately succeed in drawing attention to its Web sites over others. Although the Web started out as a democratizing phenomenon in its infancy, it is quickly falling prey to the forces of capitalism, where deep pockets ultimately prove to be the bottom line. Surfers will continue to keep the Web democratic through their dialogue and free expression, but ultimately, *shopping* on the Internet will be under the control of those big businesses that can afford to promote their Web sites to the exclusion of the competition. The pattern is already evident if you watch television or read magazines. It is the big guys, the big corporations, that are heavily pushing their Web addresses and, as they continue to do so, small business will get lost in the shuffle. The titans of industry and commerce will come to rule the shopping world of the Web. Big retailers like Sears and Wal-Mart dominate the existing retail market and they will come to dominate e-tailing. Small retailers will serve niche markets on the Internet, just like they do in the bricks-and-mortar world.

Virtually every major retailer is finding it essential to set up a Web site and get online. There are few if any of the traditional big retail players that have not set up sites for Internet shopping. Simultaneously, many of the big, pioneering Internet businesses are setting up traditional retail stores. A good example of an Internet retailer setting up bricks-and-mortar stores is found with the Gateway Company, one of the pioneers in Internet computer sales, which has now opened nearly two hundred traditional stores. Gateway is the third-largest seller of personal computers in the United States.

The New Web is virtually beyond the reach of the small entrepreneur. No matter how good the Web site, or how attractive the products, there is almost no room left for the small Internet business. The big retailers have the power to advertise and the budgets to be able to keep their name front and center. American Internet companies spend more than $15 billion a year on television promotion alone. Advertising is the key to success with the modern Internet, and smaller businesses just will not be able to compete with the big guys. It is only the big dot-com companies that can afford to spend the $3 million it takes to buy a 30-second spot during the Super Bowl.

It is interesting to compare the Web to television. Think of all of the years when there were just the three big television networks. Even at that stage of the game, the networks had to compete fiercely with each other for market share. Ultimately, other networks started to emerge, and everyone's piece of the pie got a little smaller. Networks had to compete even harder for market share. But still consumers only had to choose between twenty or so channels. Now we are in the two-hundred-channel universe, and as a consequence the television market has become very fragmented. Yet, if we look at the numbers of people watching television, it is still just three or four major networks that dominate the airwaves. Consumers stick with what they know and they do not like their lives to be too complicated. Compare this scenario to the situation with the Internet, where there are literally thousands and thousands of Web sites for consumers to choose from. Who will rise to the top? Which sites will consumers remember? Which sites will they visit repeatedly? If television is any guide to go by, the answer is that consumers will stick with the largest, best-known retailers on the Web because those are the ones with which they are most familiar and most comfortable.

Favorites are an essential component of Internet e-commerce. Shoppers will quickly develop lists of their favorite sites for shopping and it will often be the most prominent, well-known, and long-established retailers that make the list. Consider as a similar example the set of favorite radio stations that you have in your car. There are dozens and dozens of choices available on the car radio at any given moment, yet some bright automotive engineer at some point realized that car owners would prefer to keep a set of favorites in memory. The ingenious invention of the push-button car radio accomplished this task. Most drivers prefer the convenience and ease of using the preset stations, and this limits their listening experience to those stations that were *first chosen* when the buttons were set. The question is, where do consumers set the buttons in the first place? The answer is that they overwhelmingly prefer those stations they already know. Familiarity, reputation, and history play a big role in deciding what stations they will choose. The same principle is at work with the Internet. When consumers choose their lists of favorites they go with tried-and-true sites where there exists a certain comfort level.

Just like the big radio stations in a city, the big Internet entrepreneurs can make themselves known to consumers. Large-scale advertising on billboards, buses, television, radio, and in other media can draw attention to a Web site and make it a leader. When there are thousands of possible Web addresses from which to choose, only a few leaders will emerge in the minds of consumers. For Internet start-ups, either go big, or do not go at all. This is one business where it pays to be a leader rather than a follower.

This is the New Web. In the early days, when the Web was a novelty, consumers were willing to explore all kinds of obscure and irrelevant Web sites. Surfers spent hours exploring this new medium and just the newness of it was enough to keep them occupied. Not any more. The days where consumers are willing to spend valuable time doing essentially random surfing are fast disappearing. The Web is quickly becoming an efficient tool to get things done. Shoppers on the Web do not want to fool around looking at inconsequential or dead-end sites. They want to get the job accomplished and they want to do it quickly and efficiently. The best way to do that is to shop among a reliable set of favorites. This behavior is no different from the everyday pattern of shoppers shopping in traditional stores. Most people develop a set of favorite stores where they shop most of the time. This saves the time and inconvenience of shopping at new stores where there is a level of unfamiliarity. The same principle applies to shopping on the Web. As was pointed out earlier, ultimately shopping is shopping, and consumers want to get the job done on the Internet just like they do in a traditional store—that is, with a minimum of hassle.

At the present time the Internet is still going through the pangs of birth. Retailers and other Web site originators are jockeying for position. For e-tailing, there is a process at work as suppliers attempt to adjust to the demand that exists. Businesses are still sorting through the process of discovering how much demand there is for sites and products of different types. As the Internet matures we will settle into a period where the major success stories of the Web will flourish while those who have failed will wither and die. Promotion is everything on the New Web and only those who manage to rise above the crowd will succeed.

Retailers would do well to remember that they have impatient, time-deprived shoppers out there. As more people become comfortable with shopping on the Web, the level of competition for loyal consumers will elevate. Sophisticated Web shoppers will soon learn the ropes and will quickly develop personal preferences for Internet shopping. They will be intolerant of inventory shortages, shipping delays, slow Web sites, and shipping costs. They will be intolerant of anything that makes shopping more difficult. The slightest distraction or provocation easily turns off consumers in traditional stores. The same is true of Web shoppers, who are always only a simple click away from moving on to another retailer. It is essential to remember that it is the convenience of Internet shopping that got the consumer online in the first place. Anything less than perfection will not be tolerated.

What are the demographics of shopping on the Internet? Studies show that about forty percent of the U.S. population is online. Of those, men and women use the Web for shopping in about equal numbers. These shopping trends are quite different from those in the bricks-and-mortar world described above. Men use the Internet to shop just as much as women, although forecasts suggest that women shoppers will soon dominate. And why not? If women are going to be responsible for doing 75 percent of household shopping, why wouldn't they avail themselves of the convenience of the Internet as much as possible? As the number of women surfers exceeds that of men, Internet retailers can expect to be selling more items along the lines of apparel, health, beauty, and toys, according to Jupiter Communications.

Studies also show that the majority of those who shop on the Web are high-income earners. This is not surprising, given that it takes a higher income to be able to afford a computer and acquire Internet access in the first place. Internet retailers are aware of the high-income potential of their shoppers, and many entrepreneurs have accordingly opened Web sites that specialize in high-end goods. Studies show that American consumers now spend about fifteen percent of their total shopping money on the Internet. Forecasts suggest that this will soon rise to about one-third of all shopping money.

Chapter 13

CONCLUSION

THE SHOPPING REVOLUTION

This book addresses one central question: Why we shop. Answering this question has allowed us to weave a complex tapestry of the form of modern shopping. This tapestry has proven to be a rich one, full of ideas, contradictions, and seemingly irrational behavior that often proves to be logical after all. It gives us insights into the minds of consumers and allows us better to understand the mindset of the contemporary shopper. We have seen that shopping is not always what it appears to be, and that the present-day shopper sometimes shops for a multitude of reasons that, on the surface, are not all that clear. Understanding modern shopping involves the appreciation of a psychologically complex process that exists at a number of different mental levels for the shopper. Pretending that shopping is just about acquiring goods and products is tantamount to denying that people live rich and psychologically deep lives, and that they have profoundly compelling reasons for the shopping behaviors they exhibit.

This book identifies many trends and scenarios for the immediate future of shopping. We looked at several ideas, principal among them that sometimes shoppers wear their hearts on their sleeves. They shop for emotional reasons, and not for the practical reasons that we assume. But there is more to it than that. They also shop for subtle psychological reasons that are not always apparent to the objective observer. If nothing else, we have learned that it is extremely difficult to pinpoint just what it is that the modern shopper is after. Sometimes it's about self-esteem or feeling confident, but other times it is just about feeling good.

Shopping is taking place *outside the box,* and the new shopping is all about understanding the aspirations of the new shopper. These aspirations are complex and intriguing, and exploring them takes us down many new avenues of shopping behavior. Shopping has become so important in our society that wants have become needs. The things we used to strive to buy on a whim have now become the most fundamental purchases of all. Shoppers are operating at a new level where even something simple, like a new watch, becomes an important status symbol that the buyer sees as a must-have item. Such an item is so important to him that he does not just *want* it anymore; instead he *needs* it as much as he needs food and water. In this new era of shopping, price becomes no object and the traditional economic rules of supply and demand go out the window.

What are the motivations for shopping? Bargain hunters were likened to modern day warriors who are on the hunt for brand-name merchandise at bargain-basement prices. The point was made that even for bargains, the point is not to save money but to shop to satisfy emotional reasons. This is also part of why we shop. Finding a bargain results in feelings of inner well-being and a sense of accomplishment. It is all part of the psychology of shopping. People shop vicariously. So desperate are people to shop that when they run out of things to buy for themselves they shop for others. Shopping is more about the thrill of the chase than anything else, and people will go to great lengths to avail themselves of the excitement of shopping. People also shop their dreams. Shopping provides everyone with a way to live their fantasies by shopping for, and looking at, extravagant items even if there is no intention to buy them. Shopping is competition. When people shop they compete with family and friends over bragging rights to the products they buy. We all gauge our success and our accomplishments in life by how they stack up against those of other people, and serious shopping is a way to make our dreams come true. Advertising also provides one of the motivations for shopping, and its power should not be underestimated. Ads turn wants into needs in an economy where consumers never have enough and where demand is *created.* Advertising is powerful.

Consider the emotions of shopping. Shoppers have ulterior motivations when it comes to shopping, and gift giving is as much about the giver as it is about the recipient. A gift is an emotional statement and so the onus is on the shopper to provide a gift that makes a personal statement. We get emotionally involved when we shop for gifts. Shopping is also about socializing. This is one of the most important functions of shopping and people will use shopping as an excuse to socialize with family and friends. Counterfeit shopping is not shopping at all; it is socializing in the form of shopping. And often, shoppers just need moral support. One of the emotions of shopping is impulse shopping. We have all done it and it is an integral part of the shopping experience. Impulse shopping is about the psychology of rewarding the self; it's a way to reward oneself for one's accomplishments in life. The fact that the impulse buy is unplanned only adds to the pleasure of the experience. Shopping is also a form of entertainment, and nothing could provide better evidence of this than the age-old practice of window-shopping. Window-shopping is purely for the enjoyment of the shopper, and is a pleasing event even when no purchase is anticipated. It is an excellent illustration of the emotional reasons for shopping.

The passionate shopper enjoys the thrill of the chase. People get emotionally involved with their purchases and can become completely absorbed in tracking down and buying a product. A good example of this behavior in the extreme is when people try to buy that much sought-after and elusive Christmas toy that is all the rage. People will go to almost any lengths to find such products and once the hunt is complete there is a sense of accomplishment that is difficult to describe. People get on the bandwagon. They imitate the behavior of others and they envy the things that other people have purchased.

People shop for the mind. People shop for the psyche and for the soul. Shopping is empowering. Everybody is equal when it comes to shopping. Part of the illogical nature of shopping is illustrated by the fact that often the most expensive items are the most attractive because they come with bragging rights. This illustrates once again that there is more to shopping than appears on the surface and that it is a complex process that is difficult to fathom.

Perhaps most important of all, we have seen that people attempt to define themselves as human beings through their shopping. It was said that self-definition is one of the most pivotal functions of modern shopping. People define themselves through their clothing and accessories, through their houses, through their vehicles, and through everything else they own and shop for. Shopping is a form of self-expression and people express their inner self—their personalities—through their shopping. Shopping is also about rewarding the self. People work hard, and sometimes the only reward they get for their efforts is in the act of buying themselves something. We work for money, and how else is one to express one's inner emotions about the act of work than buying things to satisfy one's ego?

There are a multitude of levels to the shopping experience and shoppers shop the levels according to a definite pattern. Shoppers fulfill needs at one level, only to find themselves ascending to yet another higher level of the shopping hierarchy. There is logic to it all. One needs to satisfy basic needs before one can expect to try to satisfy higher emotional states. Shoppers seem to progress unconsciously through the levels, shopping to satisfy first one level of needs, then another. At the higher levels there are needs for self-esteem (the third level), for belongingness (the fourth level) and for self-actualization (the fifth level). As shoppers progress through the ranks they aspire to satisfy ever higher emotional requirements through the items and services they acquire. Never to be completely satisfied, they search endlessly in the quest for emotional fulfillment through ever more shopping. They will buy a sport utility vehicle only to find that it satisfies their psyche for a very short time. Soon thereafter they start the quest anew, perhaps buying an in-ground pool to complete their sense of themselves. Such a purchase may then be followed by the acquisition of a major trip to Disney World to further complete the sense of personal success. But even that will not be enough. Soon the emotionally deprived shopper will be back in the hunt looking for still more shopping acquisitions—new clothing perhaps—in the never-ending search for emotional reward. Shopping continues throughout the lifetime, always traversing the levels, as people strive to achieve feelings of self-esteem, belongingness and self-actualization.

We have seen that a revolution is ongoing in the way people shop. Sometimes it almost seems invisible. Shoppers go about their business like they always have, oblivious even themselves to the fundamental changes ongoing in their shopping psyche. In a multitude of ways we have seen that the new shopping is an emotional enterprise that scales the levels of the shopping hierarchy. What is the revolution in shopping? It is the one that takes the hierarchy of needs and turns it upside down. It says that shopping at the top levels of the pyramid is becoming far more important than shopping the lower levels. It says that consumers are *mostly* concerned with satisfying those psychological needs that are found at the top of the pyramid. No longer does it suffice to think that shoppers are overly concerned with shopping for the basic necessities of life. Shopping for such items has become a trivial matter, and the modern-day shopper sets her sights higher when it comes to acquiring goods and services. The future of shopping is about scaling the top levels of the hierarchy and about the consumer satisfying his or her emotional needs more than anything else.

Figure 13.1 illustrates the new era of shopping, and here it can be seen that the shopping hierarchy has been turned on its head. The diagram illustrates how the revolution in shopping looks and how the priorities of modern shoppers will change in the future. This is what shopping is all about, and this is how the shopper of the future will shop.

THE FUTURE OF SHOPPING

What else can be said about the shopping of the future? It is possible to identify several trends that are currently in their birth stages but that may lead to significant paradigm shifts in the way we shop, why we shop, and how we shop.

Teen shoppers are more important than we think, partly because they are the first truly global citizens. Teen fads literally sweep the globe—what's popular in New York is also popular in Beijing—and teens have become an international marketing phenomenon. Teens are remarkably similar around the world. They have the same tastes and the same desires. When a new trend or fad hits the teen world it is unlike any other. While adults may share a taste for the same products, when it comes to teens it is a global phenomenon. This means that shopping trends among teens are international ones and that product demand from teens is worldwide.

Figure 13.1
The New Shopping Hierarchy

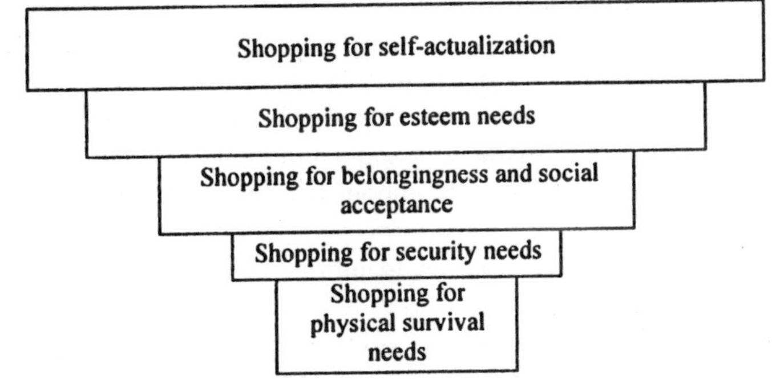

Teens represent a surprisingly large demographic. Not only do they set trends and establish fashion, but they are important to most households when it comes to the purchase of electronics and many other items. According to researchers, teens are important when it comes to making many household product choices, including vehicles, and it comes as no surprise that they also hold sway over clothing and other such purchases. Their shopping power belies their numbers. They are too important to ignore.

Radio risks losing the teen market altogether. As the popularity of the Internet grows, so too does the popularity of Internet radio. While traditional radio has been a staple of teen advertising, the ongoing trends make it clear that advertisers may have to readjust their sights to gain access to the teen market. In the same way that television came to be dominated by advertising, so too will the Internet be funded more and more by advertisers. According to Arbitron and Edison Media Research, the 12-to-24-year-old demographic is tuning in big time to Internet radio, and local radio stations risk losing this valuable age group. Those advertisers who wish to reach this group of shoppers need to tap into the Internet radio market to be successful. It is becoming easier to reach this demographic if advertisers look in the right places. Businesses need to approach the teen demographic at a higher level in the shopping hierarchy, and the best way to do this is through the new medium of the Internet.

The stock market is a place where shopping takes place. Baby boomers are in love with stocks and mutual funds, and these should be big areas of growth for years to come. Being successful in the stock market validates the shopper's self-esteem and so shopping for stocks becomes very much like shopping for other products. The baby boomers have learned to be comfortable with the stock market—they are able to ride out market downturns like seasoned pros and so have become fairly sophisticated investors. There is a strong future in stock markets and those who sell these products should be aware that they are selling a product like any other. Buying stocks not only provides self-esteem but also creates a sense of personal self-satisfaction and emotional well-being. There is more to it than just the money. It's about taking control of one's destiny and about self-actualizing.

Together with the stock market, gambling is a popular new pursuit among the baby boomers, and it, too, represents a higher form of shopping. Casinos, lottery tickets, and video lottery terminals are big business these days and the reason for this is that it plays to the boomer's sense of self-esteem and adventure seeking. What better way is there to self-actualize than to hit the numbers while gambling? Occasional success is almost guaranteed, and each time the player hits the jackpot there results a profound sense of personal accomplishment and victory. Gambling is an important part of shopping at the higher levels and its popularity is likely to continue to expand at an accelerating rate in the future.

The trend toward spending money to save time is one that is likely to continue to accelerate in the future. As time and work pressures continue to mount, more and more consumers will find themselves willing to spend money to buy time. It is also important to remember that working women still spend as much as five hours a day on household chores. As the pay gap closes, women will be more willing to part with some of the household income to make significant cuts into the time they spend on the household. Particularly of interest here is the idea of making the buying and preparation of food easier. Since much of the household cooking continues to fall into the woman's domain of chores, we can look to see ever more ways in which this task is simplified. Grocery stores have vegetable sections and meat departments. They have pre-cooked meal departments where it is possible to pick up a hot nutritious meal on the way home from work. The woman who hires a cleaning service may use the extra time created to go to an aerobics class. The man who hires someone to do the yard work may then go out to play golf. The point is that a higher-level activity is *substituted* for a lower-level one by buying time.

Another example of buying time with money is found in a start-up business called Women's Consumer Network. This is a company based in Washington, D.C., that provides information services for women who do not have the time to do things themselves. The company provides information on things like credit cards; birth control pills, long-distance services, and financial management. The idea is to provide women with information about such products and to save them the time of shopping for such products and services on their own.

Wal-Mart is setting a new trend all by itself. The company has opened Supercenters that, in addition to the usual fare, sell grocery, food, and beverage products. What is this trend all about? It's about one-stop shopping and making it more convenient for consumers to get everything they need at a single location. This sets the bar higher for competitors, who will be hard-pressed to equal the price discount and convenience of the Wal-Mart Supercenter. More importantly, such bundling of goods and services allows consumers to shop all of the levels in a single location.

Another important area of shopping to belong is found in the use of communication on the Internet. The big hit among teens is a product called ICQ ("I seek you") that allows whole groups of teens to chat online. ICQ is the most popular Internet messaging system. It's a huge hit. Estimates put the number of teen users at 80 million worldwide. ICQ allows teens to chat with their friends. There is no limit to the number of people that can join in. Everyone types dialogue that everyone else can read. It's like a conference call on the phone except that everyone is typing. New people can join in at any time and other users can drop out when they've had enough.

Those in the business of television and radio should be worried about the Internet and about programs like ICQ. Studies show that more teens than ever are spending more time online. How does it work? How does the Internet pay for itself? It's just like television and radio. Broadcasters put out a television or radio signal for free in the hope that viewers or listeners will partake of the advertisements that accompany the content. In effect, the advertisers pay for the medium. The Internet now works in the same way. Programs like ICQ are accompanied by advertising. This not only helps to defray the costs of providing the program but also provides the producers with a profit. It is just as important these days to advertise on the Internet as it used to be on television and radio. Eighty million ICQ users, for example, represent a big audience.

The wireless revolution represents another big step forward for shoppers. Companies are providing software that allow customers to compare the prices of items they are shopping for in stores to the prices available on the Internet. In other words, consumers are able to comparison-shop competitors' prices right on the store floor using their mobile phones. This puts the power in the hands of the consumer, who can use this information to negotiate with retailers to get the best deal possible.

How aggressive do retailers need to be? A strong ongoing trend among fashion consumers is to put themselves on waiting lists for the hottest new products. They spot clothing or accessories they want in fashion catalogs, fashion magazines, or at fashion shows and then register with upscale retailers to be the first to get the new products when they arrive. Retailers report that such hot products never even hit the floors because they are bought up as soon as they come in. In the *National Post,* Serena French related a Toronto retailer's report of a trip to New York:

> I was in Bergdorf's and I overheard these two girls . . . [one girl] was wearing the Celine ski sweater, the cashmere one with "Celine" down the arms ($1,200), and the Fendi napa leather baguette bag ($1,900), and she ran into her girlfriend. The girl said, "Oh my God, you got *that sweater.*" And she said, "Yeah, and waited two months." "And the bag?" And she said, "I just got it yesterday. It just came in." These girls, all they did all

> day was put their names on waiting lists. That's their life: waiting for those key items that they have to have.

Waiting lists are so long for such products that global demand outstrips supply. There is intense competition among consumers to be the first to get the latest, high-level products, and waiting lists continue to grow.

Branding is likely to continue to grow in importance. Clothing, accessories, sporting gear, and so on become integral parts of the higher levels of the shopping hierarchy by virtue of their branding. Products that were largely indistinguishable a few years ago are now carefully pigeonholed by consumers by virtue of the labels they carry. A Chanel watch is not just a watch—it is a statement about its owner. The same is true of all branded products. Designer labels propel products themselves into higher levels of the shopping experience, and their importance is only likely to increase in the future.

Size zero? What is that? Size zero is a part of the relentless trend to *downsizing* in men's and women's clothing. In the early 1980s manufacturers were given the wherewithal to set their own sizing in clothing. Since that time they have been steadily downsizing their products so that people can feel good about themselves. Almost all women like to believe that they can fit into a smaller size, and so manufacturers have accommodated them by taking clothing of a given size and labeling it as smaller. The same goes for men's clothes because, after all, who wants to feel like they are gaining weight? The ultimate result for women has been the invention of size-zero clothing, which takes the trend to its ultimate limit. There is even a fixation on celebrities and the sizes they wear. It is well known, for example, that Calista Flockhart, star of *Ally McBeal,* is a size zero, and this just adds to the fascination with such impossible sizing. Downsizing is a trend that is likely to continue because it is part of the psychology of shopping for clothes. People want to feel good about the things they buy, and downsizing helps to make that possible.

Gender separation is another phenomenon that is likely to grow in importance. Stores are steadily coming to the realization that girls and boys are different kinds of shoppers and so they are attempting to accommodate this trend. According to the *New York Times,* Toys "R" Us had plans to go to almost total separation by creating a Girl's World and a Boy's World within each store, where each area would be stocked with items that appeal to kids by gender. Girl's World would feature Barbies while Boy's World would have trucks. This is a strong trend in merchandising that should not be ignored. But for Toys "R" Us, the public outcry was such that it canceled its plans. The message to be driven home is that even the parents of young children are shopping the levels when they buy products. There is more at stake than just buying toys; there is gender definition to be accomplished.

Finally, an area that cannot be overlooked in shopping is the important role that demographics plays in determining who is buying what. Demographic targeting is an important area of research that identifies what consumers will buy according to their demographic membership. Demographic targeting enables us to predict not only what people will want but at what stage of life they will want it. Shopping the levels is different for every demographic group, and so it is crucial to appreciate the differences between the groups. For example, single women living alone have come to represent a major segment of the buying public, but scant attention has been paid to them as the focus of marketing. They have enormous spending power, a sense of independence, and a psychological profile that says they are fairly intense shoppers. They have a lot of time on their hands to shop and they have the disposable income to go with it. Do they shop the levels? Of course they do, and this should be an important consideration when it comes time to market products to them.

There are constantly new developments in the shopping world that are directed to the top levels of the shopping hierarchy. The significance of the top level is likely to continue to expand as shoppers fulfill their needs for emotional gratification.

INDEX

About the Author

JIM POOLER is Professor of Urban and Population Geography at the University of Saskatchewan in Saskatoon, Saskatchewan, Canada. An urban geographer and retail demographer, he views shopping as a multidisciplinary subject that incorporates elements from psychology, marketing, business, economics, geography, sociology, and anthropology.